EVANGELICAL AND METHODIST

EVANGELICAL
AND
METHODIST

A POPULAR HISTORY

RILEY B. CASE

Abingdon Press

Nashville

EVANGELICAL AND METHODIST
A POPULAR HISTORY

Copyright © 2004 by Abingdon Press

This book is printed on acid-free paper.

Library of Congress Cataloging-in-Publication Data

Case, Riley B.
  Evangelical and Methodist : a popular history / Riley Case.
    p. cm.
  ISBN 0-687-04444-8 (adhesive binding : alk. paper)
    1. Methodist Church—United States—History. 2. Evangelical Revival—United States—History. 3. United States—Church history. 4. Methodism—History. I. Title.

BX8235.C37 2004
287'.673—dc22

2003024005

All scripture quotations, unless noted otherwise, are taken from the *New Revised Standard Version of the Bible,* copyright 1989, by the Division of Christian Education of the National Council of the Churches of Christ in the United States of America. Used by permission. All rights reserved.

Excerpts from "Warring Over Where Donations Go" © 1983 TIME Inc. reprinted by permission.

Excerpts from "United Methodists: The View from Portland" by Ed Plowman. Used by permission, *Christianity Today,* 1976.

Excerpts on pages 31 and 40 from *Texas Methodist* editorial by Spurgeon Dunnam. Copyright 2003 UMR Communications, Dallas, TX.

04 05 06 07 08 09 10 11 12 13—10 9 8 7 6 5 4 3 2 1

MANUFACTURED IN THE UNITED STATES OF AMERICA

CONTENTS

CHAPTER ONE

METHODISM'S POPULIST WING, PART I

The blood-washed banner of holiness." That was just one in a tumbling cascade of phrases in Brother Lamoin's gospel message. It was spoken with face flushed and arms upraised and moving, as if the banner were really there, heralding the unconquerable cause of Christ against the onslaughts of Satan. We were there to do battle, against principalities, against powers, against the rulers of the darkness of this present age. It was proclaimed in a voice loud enough that all in Hartford Township must surely know, if they did not know already, that revival was underway at Union Chapel Methodist Church.

I believed in revivals. I believed in Billy Graham and altar calls and "praying through." I knew most verses of "Just As I Am." I thought I was revival-trained.

I wasn't. What I knew about were Preaching Missions and Spiritual Emphasis Weeks and Evangelistic Crusades. This was different. This was revival. This was old-fashioned, devil-fighting, sin-killing, hanky-waving, amen-shouting, foot-stomping Methodist Holy Ghost revival.

The revival was scheduled for fifteen days. That was not fifteen days as opposed to one week, but fifteen days as opposed to six weeks. I was reminded several times that in former days it took fifteen days just to warm up. But times had changed. The revival would be only fifteen days—unless, of course, the Holy Ghost moved in power. Brother Lamoin and Sister Gay, the evangelists, had blocked out days ahead in case the revival needed to be extended.

The district superintendent was uneasy about the revival. Indeed, that is why he had hurried my appointment to the church. Four weeks earlier I had been sweeping floors in a factory. My call came like an SOS. "I need somebody out there immediately," he told me, "to keep an eye on the revival. Don't let it get out of hand."

This was a fearful assignment for a twenty-two-year-old one week into seminary. How did one go about not letting a revival get out of hand?

I spoke to Brother O. P. Van Y. O. P. was my predecessor. Three months earlier he had had a heart attack. The church was without a pastor while they waited for him to recover. Finally the doctor decreed, "No more preaching." That's when I was appointed to the church. O. P. Van Y's visit back to "the Chapel" was his first since the heart attack. He came back because he wanted to be present for the opening of the revival.

The conversation took place in Forest Shoemaker's living room, where we had both been invited for Sunday dinner following the morning service. November 4, 1956, was no ordinary day for either of us. With a month of seminary and two weeks into my first appointment, I was full of questions about the ministry, "the Chapel," the other churches on the circuit, and about revivals. Whatever the old circuit rider had to offer I was willing to soak up. I was Elisha waiting for Elijah's mantle.

O. P. had a mantle to give. Ten years ago, they had given him a retirement dinner, but he would have preached until he died, and nearly did. He came back that day, nearly fifty years after he had been called to preach and three months after his attack, to make one last stand, to tell his story, and to make a witness. I was his only audience.

"I wanted to come back today . . . for the opening of the revival. . . . The doctor said I wasn't ready . . . doctors don't know everything. . . . We used to have real revivals . . . six, sometimes eight weeks . . . morning preaching as well as evening. . . . I was converted in a revival . . . Muncie. . . . Friend wanted me to go . . . under conviction . . . Holy Ghost broke through. . . . People praying at the church all day . . . 1908 . . . God got ahold of me . . . filled me with the Holy Ghost and called me to preach all at once."

The old man slapped his knees and laughed. "I told God no . . . I couldn't preach . . . twenty-eight years old . . . good job as a glassblower . . .

presiding elder heard and told me he'd like for me to go to Deerfield next Sunday . . . wouldn't take no for an answer. . . . So I was up early Sunday . . . twenty miles by buggy. . . . A young man got converted that day . . . the people wanted me back . . . that was my first appointment."

The story continued. From Deerfield on, we traveled the years across the Indiana countryside through circuits and small towns with stops to dwell on annual conferences and bishops and life in the parsonages. But mostly we dwelt on revivals—ten-week revivals, one-week revivals, book burnings, saloon closings, evangelists, families converted. O. P. told the story of the North Indiana Conference through the story of its revivals.

Then we were back to where we had started, with the revival at the Chapel. "No need to worry . . . these people are used to revivals . . . the church has had a revival a year. They used to have two, for as long as anyone could remember." He went family by family and entrusted them to my care. He laid down the mantle of Elijah.

I went to the church early that night. I intended to greet the people, but I was still so new I was the one greeted. I was introduced to evangelists Lamoin and Gay—she preached when he didn't—to friends and neighbors visiting, and to parishioners I had not yet met. There was a different feeling in the air. The normally joking and easygoing country people had become deadly serious. This was God's hour.

The church was nearly full. The Sunday morning attendance, which ran about forty, was more than doubled to nearly one hundred. This was revival country. Fringe members who could scarcely make it to church on Christmas and Easter would show up a night or two. Delegations from neighboring churches and the other churches on the circuit were present.

The service began. With long involved sentences featuring a syntax wondrous to behold, the song leader, Glen Dale, expressed appreciation for O. P. Van Y, for other friends who were there, for the evangelists, for the good weather, and for the new pastor who had arrived just in time for the revival, except he was in seminary and would be leaving after the service to attend school but would be back the coming weekend when he would be a part of the service, and everyone was glad for that.

The song service began:

> Over the hilltops, down from the skies,
> Coming from glory—lift up your eyes.
> While we are watching and while we pray,
> A mighty revival is sweeping this way.

It was enthusiastic, emotional, and uninhibited. Union Chapel did not know Methodists were supposed to be mannered, tempered, and restrained. There were no businessmen staring into space and thinking of Saturday sales, no elderly ladies who moved their lips while their teeth were clamped firmly in place. Lorene played the piano evangelistic style country.

It is unfortunate that that song service came so early in my ministry. Enthusiastic singing would have been a greater encouragement fifteen years later when I was sometimes tempted to believe all Methodist congregations had been smitten by the disease of somberness.

Gay and Lamoin sang, pleasantries were expressed, and the sermon began. The theme was revival. God's people were to get on their knees and weep and pray. By God's mercy, sinners would be converted, backsliders reclaimed, and nominal Christians blessed and sanctified. Besides lifting the blood-washed banner of holiness, we drew the sword against principalities and powers and called out for Holy Ghost fire. When no one responded to the altar call, Christians gathered around the altar to pray, and we were dismissed.

I was 240 miles away the next day, on Chicago's north shore, back in seminary, in a totally different world in which we discussed books and movies and spoke in four-syllable words. The religious education professor lectured in pastoral care and counseling on the response of the whole organism. In the commons, a student waved a cigarette and told of passing a "fundamentalist church" in which ladies in fur coats carried Bibles. There was laughter. I thought it the better wisdom that my little band of believers at Union Chapel should not know what seminary was really like.

Most of the talk in seminary, however, was about the national election. To the seminary community on Tuesday, November 6, 1956, America was at a crossroads: Adlai Stevenson, for justice and righteousness, or Dwight Eisenhower, for capitalist repression. A straw poll indicated that 88 percent of the faculty favored Stevenson. Someone commented that since there was a Socialist alternative, it should not be assumed the other 12 percent favored Eisenhower. This was the seminary view of diversity.

On Tuesday night, we gathered around the television set to watch the returns. For a number of students already caught up in the seminary's view of the world, there was gloom and despair. Eisenhower won.

Wednesday, we analyzed the election and the future of America—in every class. In Philosophical Approach to Theology, we spent two days hearing about the troubling, disturbing conservative trend in the nation. The voters had returned the war man, the general, to Washington. The election was a sure sign that the nation was backing away from social justice and a desire to care for the poor. There were comments about the journal *Christianity Today*, volume 1, issue 1, left in stacks on a table only a few days before. The magazines were free, a sure sign of big money promoting fundamentalism and right-wing politics. The view was expressed that the magazines should not have been allowed in the seminary.

It was a usual week of seminary fare. Religious talk turned frequently to politics. A few professors were declaring for neo-orthodoxy, with disciples in tow. Predictable cynical remarks were made about Billy Graham and Norman Vincent Peale and about "fundamentalism," a dying and irrelevant but still troublesome vestige of the past. The comment was made that fundamentalism would be gone in one more generation. Thinking people would never stand for it. There was not too much talk about Jesus that week.

I was back at Union Chapel the next weekend and the weekend after that for the closing of the revival. There were evaluations of the revival, not with questionnaires or checklists, but with comments: "The woman could preach as well as the man. . . . People had been blessed. . . . Seekers came to the altar . . . " But then a pause, and the pause represented the real evaluation: The revival was not extended. This would not be remembered as one of the great revivals of the past. I dutifully reported to the district superintendent that the revival had gone well and had not gotten out of hand.

Several months later, I had my first meeting with the district Board of Ministerial Training (in my part of the country, we assigned pastors as needed and credentialed in due time). They were supportive. They wondered how I was getting along at the Geneva Circuit, and, especially, how I was balancing the contrasts of seminary and parish. They were concerned, lest I be in some kind of trouble at the churches. Then came the telling comment: "They are not really Methodist churches, you know."

I did not respond, but I was bemused. Union Chapel people believed strongly that they were a Methodist church. They could discuss old-time Methodist issues such as entire sanctification and sin in believers. They still held a class meeting. They followed the old Methodist custom of kneeling to pray and praying all at once. Following their Methodist forebears, they believed that those who did not support Prohibition would probably not go to heaven. They were regulars at the area Holiness camp meetings. Their yearly revival was in direct lineage with the revivals of twenty years and fifty years and one hundred years before. They sang the gospel songs of Phoebe Palmer and Fanny Crosby and James Black, Methodists all.

But, of course, I knew what was behind the comment. Union Chapel had not been indoctrinated in the new ways of the denomination. It drew its preachers from the ranks of the Conference Course of Study pastors, all of whom had escaped seminary. The congregation was not reasonable, formal, or prestigious. It did not use the denominational Sunday school material.

Several months later, I had my first meeting with the conference Board of Ministerial Training in preparation for deacon's orders. They asked no doctrinal questions, evidently assuming that enrollment in a Methodist seminary qualified me acceptably in theology. Rather, they asked three institutional questions: What did I think of Methodist Sunday school material, what did I think of the Methodist hymnal, and did I smoke. I gave a definite answer on smoking and a sufficiently ambiguous answer on literature and the hymnal.

This particular experience with the contrasting worlds of the rural church and the denominational seminary, though not typical, even for that time, still serves as a mirror into one of the largely unexplored realities of Methodist doctrine and ethos: There is not one Methodist identity, but several. The charge that evangelical United Methodists associated with the Good News movement are "not really United Methodist" can only be based on a very narrow definition of what "Methodism" is.

It is the thesis of this book that the commonly expressed observations about the Good News movement—especially the observation that Good News was primarily a conservative reaction to the social and political unrest of the 1960s and 1970s—do not capture the essence of Good News. Good News is better understood as a movement authentically Methodist, authentically Wesleyan, in direct lineage with the doctrines and ethos of the Church's past, but with an eye to renewal in the Church's future. I have labeled that authentic part of Methodism, representing the driving force behind the Good News movement, as "populist evangelicalism."

To understand populist evangelicalism, it is helpful to trace the development of Methodism in America, especially with the inclusion of Methodism's populist wing. If it is possible to speak of populist evangelicalism, where did it come from, how did it develop, and what is its status today?

Methodism in America grew from fewer than 5,000 members in 1776 to more than 130,000 members in 1806. Unlike the Congregationalists, Episcopalians, and Presbyterians, who relied on educated clergy and the position of privilege to advance their causes, Methodists conducted spiritual warfare without benefit of colleges, educated clergy, book concerns, or general boards and agencies. They commonly railed against "formalists" and "aristocraticists." Methodism from the beginning developed a distinct New World flavor. Despite its respect for the Wesleys, it disdained the Wesleys' enthusiasm for turned-around collars, the Sunday service, and the Anglican view of the church.

Methodist bishops served as generals deploying troops and then rode with those troops as they crossed rivers and mountains, fought the elements, and preached in log cabins and in the open air. Methodist preachers formed class meetings conducted by laypersons and fought the devil in taverns, in dance halls, and wherever people gathered.

Their message of salvation for all appealed to the rough frontierspeople, to the poor, and to blacks both slave and free. From 1776 to 1850, the percentage of religious adherents in America who called themselves Methodist increased from 2.5 percent of the population to 34.2 percent. Such spectacular religious growth was unprecedented in modern church history.

But along the way, part of Methodism began to change. Methodist-converted settlers in areas west of the Appalachians turned their interests from tavern life, with its alcohol, dancing girls, and gambling, to farming and family life and small businesses. Some Methodists vaulted into the middle class and began to talk about book concerns, colleges, and brick churches with steeples. Sons and daughters of Methodists became doctors and lawyers and ran for public office. Along the way, this new breed of Methodists began to express discomfort at the unbridled enthusiasm and the excesses and uncouth manners of their country cousins. Methodists were becoming respectable.

Not all Methodists were happy with the changes. Peter Cartwright wrote in 1856: "The Presbyterians, and other Calvinistic branches of the protestant Church, used to contend for an educated ministry, for pews, for instrumental music, for a congregational or stated salaried ministry. The Methodists universally opposed these ideas; and the illiterate Methodist preachers actually set the world on fire."[1]

Slowly there began to develop two forms of Methodism. One strand might be called establishment Methodism. This is the Methodism usually described in denominational histories. It was the Methodism of tall steeples, rented pews, robed choirs, General Conferences, denominational journals, colleges, and bishops. It was Methodism becoming institutionalized, with authority focusing more and more in bishops, presiding elders, conferences, and (later) committees and agencies. This focused authority—later identified simply as "the hierarchy," a "mediated" faith—one best filtered and controlled by those with education and experience.

The other strand of Methodism might be called populist Methodism. It was, for the most part, "unofficial" Methodism. It was the Methodism of log cabins, moral crusades, circuit preachers, revivals, camp meetings, prayer bands, and indigenous Methodist gospel music, including Negro spirituals. It was an "unmediated" Christianity, one not needing to be filtered by educated clergy or annual conferences. It was democracy in religion. Its authority derived not from the *Book of Discipline* or the blessing of bishops, but from the anointing of the Spirit and appeal to the power of primitive Methodism, or "old-time religion." It is often referred to as "grass roots" Methodism. It was Methodism not as an institution, but as a movement.

The 1878 "official" hymnal of The Methodist Episcopal Church serves as a window on these two expressions of Methodism. The General Conference that authorized the hymnal was conducted without benefit of women delegates and with only a few black Methodists. The token presence of laity at the conference was still a novelty. Almost none of the delegates were circuit preachers or evangelists. Typical of General Conferences, the clergy elected to offices were the kind described in Matthew Simpson's 1878 *Cyclopædia of Methodism* as "distinguished," "eminent," and "prominent." *Methodist Quarterly Review* described the committee selected to compile the new hymnal as men of "local distinction as poets, and even national reputation as composers . . . college presidents, professors, presiding elders, a pastor, and one lawyer, (who) were representatives of distinct classes of culture, position, and experience."[2]

Of 307 authors in the new hymnal, 66 were Episcopalian, 22 Congregationalist, 20 Presbyterian, 14 Unitarian, 13 Lutheran, and 13 Roman Catholic. Only 10 were part of The Methodist Episcopal Church, none of whom were from its revival or holiness wing. Only 7 percent of the hymns were of American origin. Out of 1,117 hymns, only 3 were identified with anyone west of Rochester, New York, or south of Washington, D.C. Only three hymns in the entire hymnal carried a refrain or chorus. The hymnal was so unusable that within ten years, the church was clamoring for another revision.

The 1878 "official" Methodist Episcopal hymnal appeared at the height of what might be called America's golden age of gospel music. Largely Methodist-inspired, gospel hymns and Sunday school songs and spirituals flooded the countryside, permeated home parlors, and were the fare of choice for revivals and camp meetings. The Methodist Sunday school superintendent, Sankey, published *Gospel Hymns* volumes 1 to 6, the total sales of which reached fifty million.

The origins of these gospel songs can be traced to the earliest days of the Methodist revival. As one writer observed:

> At the commencement of the revival these familiar hymns (Wesley's), known in all our orthodox congregations, were used; but it was soon felt that they gave but imperfect expression to the ardent feelings of the worshippers. The deficiency was principally supplied by the preachers. Hymns, or "spiritual songs," as they were more frequently called, to the cultured ear rude and bold in expression, rugged in meter, and imperfect in rhyme, often improvised in the preaching stand, were at once accepted as more suited to their wants. These were quickly committed to memory, and to a considerable extent usurped the place of the older and more worthy hymns.[3]

Spirituals, both black and white, were the mainstay of the early camp meetings.[4] The camp meeting was one of the first—perhaps the first— social institutions in America in which blacks and whites gathered more or less on equal terms. The Methodist message of free grace was readily received by slaves as well as by others who were devalued by society. The message emphasized that Christ died for all; therefore any person—rich or poor, male or female, black or white—could be saved. This bestowed essential worth on all people. Furthermore the Methodists proclaimed that religion could (and should) be experienced, that is, felt. The essence of Christianity was not in theological training, liturgical correctness, or dressing up on Sunday mornings, but in the new birth.

This populist message resonated with black Americans, slave and free. In 1800, only about 4 to 5 percent of all African Americans were listed as church members. As the Methodist revival spread, that percentage doubled and tripled. Within the first few decades of the 1800s approximately 16 percent of all Methodists were black, and this even after the split of the African Methodist Episcopal Church (AME) in 1816 and the African Methodist Episcopal Zion Church (AMEZ) in 1820.

During the period of remarkable growth in the early 1800s, there was a tremendous sense of unity in Methodism around matters of doctrine and the understanding of mission. Inasmuch as there was tension, it tended to center around issues that might be considered populist in nature. Methodist populism wanted a gospel republican in nature that did not have to be mediated either by bishops or by trained clergy or conferences. In 1828, the Methodist Protestants split over issues of episcopal authority and lay leadership. Were the conferences to be run by only an elite few clergy, or could the church be inclusive enough to include common, ordinary laity?

The issue with Orange Scott and the formation of the Wesleyan Connection in 1843 was how the Church should respond to slavery. For Scott and his followers, it was not enough that conferences should pass resolutions against slavery if the Church would not discipline members, including bishops, who were slaveholders. An established Methodism had become so concerned about institutional unity that it had compromised the primitive Methodist prophetic voice against slavery and injustice.[5]

The Free Methodist split of 1859 can be cast even more clearly in populist terms. Methodism's climb up the social scale brought with it more formal worship, emphasis on intellectual faith, rented pews, instrumental music, and a willingness generally to make peace with the world. This led to compromises in the witness against alcohol, fashionable dress, worldly amusements, and secret societies. The camp meeting, the revival, the class meeting, and plainness and holiness in personal life were becoming less and less the distinguishing marks of a Methodist. When B. T. Roberts and several others in the Genesee Conference in New York were expelled for being troublemakers, the Free Methodist Church was formed in 1859.

The United Brethren in Christ Church, though it also dealt with the same issues that divided The Methodist Episcopal Church,[6] had avoided open division throughout most of the twentieth century. This changed in 1885 when the General Conference in a controversial move approved an interpretation of the *Discipline* that would allow a change in the Constitution so that the prohibition against secret societies could be eliminated. Those who argued for the change—the "liberals"—argued that the Church needed to adapt to the realities of the modern world, a world in which prohibition against secret societies was keeping many good people from becoming church members. Under the surface was the tension between rural Brethren and city Brethren, and between populist Brethren and those who argued that openness to secret societies would make the church available to persons of prestige. Writing in the *Telescope*, February 1885, Bishop Jonathan Weaver wrote:

> In some of our large towns and cities we are tugging along with little mission churches until our people in the rural districts are getting tired of paying money to support them. If it were not for our sweeping law against all secret orders, we could to-day have large, self-sustaining congregations in towns and cities where now we have nothing at all, or at least only little mission congregations.[7]

In 1889, the United Brethren in Christ (Old Constitution) was formed by those who resisted the idea that church growth was related to respectability and conformity to the culture around the church.

Few Methodists were affected by these early church divisions. Methodism continued to thrive even as it was becoming more pluralistic. While primitive and populist Methodism provided spirit and fervor, establishment and institutional Methodism provided stability and respectability. Overall, Methodists were not only moving into America's cultural mainstream, but also determining what that mainstream looked like. Methodism was both at the same time unlettered and cultured, enthusiastic and restrained.

All the same, the momentum was with the growing respectability. By the mid-1800s even as revivalism continued to flourish, the founding of church colleges had almost become an obsession. In almost every new village established in the expanding West, the Methodists erected their imposing church edifices in town center and were designated as leading community citizens. Such Methodists were not necessarily convinced that true religion was enhanced by the rejection of fashion, education, culture, and wealth.

Bishop Matthew Simpson reflected this new face of Methodism as well as anyone. Born in Ohio in 1811, he became a college vice president (Alleghany College) at age twenty-six, a college president (Indiana Asbury, now DePauw University) at age twenty-seven, editor of *Western Christian Advocate* at age thirty-five, and a bishop at age forty. Like a number of others, Simpson basically skipped the local church in his climb up the institutional scale.

Simpson was totally committed to the cause of Methodism. He saw Methodism as God's agent for reform in the new world to be accomplished, on the one hand, by revivals and camp meetings (he studied with Phoebe Palmer and was a regular speaker at camp meetings) but, on the other hand and more important, by influencing the political, educational, and cultural life of the nation. He was a friend of Abraham Lincoln, preached Lincoln's funeral message, and lobbied in government directly with four presidents on behalf of Methodists. He supported lay representation at the General Conference in large part because he believed people of wealth and influence were needed in the church councils. By the 1860s, Simpson was acclaimed as "the most influential man in the denomination."[8]

In 1878 Simpson edited the *Cyclopædia of Methodism*, a massive compendium detailing Methodist growth and presence throughout the world. It is an impressive piece of work, representing extensive research. But reading Simpson's *Cyclopædia* gives one the impression that Methodism was composed primarily of bishops, colleges, professors, book editors, General Conferences, historic churches, and a few prominent and eminent laymen.

Not clearly pictured in Simpson's *Cyclopædia* was the other side of Methodism. That side was the Methodism of African Americans and women and evangelists and lay pastors. Its life was in Sunday schools and camp meetings and gospel hymns and prayer bands and reform movement revivals. And by Simpson's time, Methodism's rallying point became more and more the doctrine of Holiness.

Holiness—the conviction that the believer could be sanctified and made perfect in love through a second work of grace—had been a part of Methodist preaching from the days of the Wesleys. It was not, however, the dominant theme in early American revivals and camp meetings. This changed with leaders such as Phoebe Palmer, the National Camp Meeting Association, a proliferation of traveling holiness evangelists, and other developments after the Civil War.

It can be argued that Phoebe Palmer (1807–1874) had as great an influence on American Methodism as any other person in the nineteenth century, even though she was a laywoman who never attended a General Conference. Palmer held Tuesday home meetings in the front parlor of her New York home. She taught that by placing "all on the altar," one could instantly be sanctified through the baptism of the Holy Ghost. Throughout the 1840s, 1850s, and 1860s, Methodists and non-Methodists from all over the country streamed to New York to sit under her teaching. Phoebe Palmer wrote books, hymns, and edited an influential periodical, *The Guide to Holiness.*

The new emphasis on Holiness and the experience of the "second blessing" created a whole new subculture in Methodism. In 1867, the National Camp Meeting Association for the Promotion of Christian Holiness was organized. From 1867 to 1883, a total of fifty-two National Camp Meetings were held, most on Methodist campgrounds. The meeting at Round Lake, New York, in 1874 attracted twenty thousand worshipers, including seven bishops. Holiness associations were formed by states, then by counties. Holiness evangelists traveled the country preaching Holiness doctrine and experience.

The Holiness movement does not generate a lot of space in denominational histories, because it never was "official," that is, it was not initiated or controlled by bishops or legislated by General Conferences. It also was not strictly denominational since numbers of non-Methodists were caught up in Holiness fervor. But for many ordinary Protestant Christians in the last half of the nineteenth century, "Holiness" was synonymous with Methodism. Holiness fervor dispatched missionaries, inspired music, and led to the publishing of tracts, periodicals, and books. By 1888, four publishing houses were committed exclusively to the dissemination of Holiness literature. In 1892, forty-one Holiness periodicals were being published throughout the country, all independent of church control. Hundreds of thousands claimed the experience of the Holiness movement's "second blessing."

At first, the institutional church reacted to the Holiness movement with support, then caution, and then charges of disloyalty. D. D. Whedon wrote in *Methodist Quarterly Review* in 1878, "The holiness association, the holiness periodical, the holiness prayer-meeting, the holiness preacher, are all modern novelties. They are not Wesleyan. We believe that a living Wesley would never admit them into the Methodist system."[9] An observer commented in 1885: "They have changed the name of our meetings, substituting Holiness for Methodist. They preach a different doctrine . . . , they sing different songs, they patronize and circulate a different literature; they have adopted radically different words of worship."[10]

There was legitimate cause for alarm. Without denominational oversight, the Holiness movement spun into extremism. Some Holiness evangelists preached "sinless perfection." Others added a third work of grace, then a fourth and a fifth. The movement seemed obsessed with matters of dress and "worldly amusements." The focus of their discontent was with a "cold and formal" Methodism. Those who were most adamant about the Church's spiritual decline urged people to leave the denomination and became known as "come-outers." Others left the denomination but insisted the problem was not "come-outism," but "push-outism" or "crush-outism." They had not wanted to leave, but persons in authority had "pushed them out."[11]

About the turmoil in the Church in the 1880s and 1890s, John Leland Peters comments in his study, *Christian Perfection and American Methodism:* "The Methodist Church was coming into a period when diverging estimates of the nature of the Christian faith were giving rise to separate camps whose theological positions would be mutually incomprehensible."[12]

The same tensions existed in both the United Brethren and the Evangelical Association and were one of the major reasons for the Evangelical Association split in 1891. The 1887 Evangelical Association General Conference was torn by charges and countercharges around doctrinal matters resulting in two separate General Conferences held in 1891. (The factions reunited in 1922.)

Though popular at the grassroots level, Holiness forces in the Methodist Episcopal churches were effectively controlled and then suppressed by church hierarchies. In 1894, the General Conference of the M.E. Church, South, took a strong anti-Holiness stand, starting what some later called the "war of extermination." In both the northern and southern churches, efforts began to bring music, literature, mission work, revival meetings, and camp meetings under denominational control. The appointment system was used to penalize those preachers who kept insisting on their Holiness ways. The uneasy alliance between establishment Methodism and populist Methodism was fracturing.

As a result, a splintering began to take place that, in some cases, felt like a mass exodus from the Church. Scores, perhaps hundreds, of sects, groups, and new denominations sprang up and were filled with the exiles from Methodism. The Church of the Nazarene and the Church of God (Anderson, Indiana) were organized from several of these groups. Some groups used the name "Holiness," others "Pentecostal." The preferred name for many was some form of "the Church of God." Within a few years, many of these groups were caught up in the famous Azusa Street revival, tongues-speaking, and the launching of the modern Pentecostal movement.

The populist revolt in Methodism corresponds in many ways in time (1895–1900) and place (the rural South and Midwest) to the agrarian revolt that culminated in the national rise of populism and William Jennings Bryan candidacy for the presidency in 1896. The tensions within Methodism reflected the tensions within the larger society. At the same time that some of Methodism was rejoicing that they had so moved up the American respectability scale that one of their own, William McKinley—Republican, imperialist, and friend of the wealthy and powerful—had been elected president, another part of Methodism was crowding the cultural and social fringes.

In 1900, James Lee, Naphtali Luccock, and James Dixon concluded their monumental *Illustrated History of Methodism* with a chapter entitled "The Methodist Outlook of To-Day," which rejoiced in the transformation of Methodism-as-reproach to Methodism-whose-value-was-recognized-by-the-cultured-and-learned.[13] In discussing the glories of Methodism, the authors offered 101 sketches of illustrious Methodists. Of these, 45 were related to colleges and seminaries, 22 were editors, and 25 were former Methodists now well known in other denominations. Others were writers, politicians, agency heads, and benefactors. Fewer than ten were pastors, only two were women, and none was African-American. There were no evangelists.

The work of Lee, Luccock, and Dixon should be seen in contrast to the observation of Nathan O. Hatch and John H. Wigger in their excellent study on early Methodism, *Methodism and the Shaping of American Culture*:

> Although early Methodism was a complex phenomenon and incapable of reduction to any single economic or political orientation, the movement eroded patterns of deference to established authority and tradition, and dignified the convictions of ordinary people on important matters—whether religious, political, or economic. It elicited choice and participation by people long ignored, and bound them together in disciplined and supportive groups . . . . Religious leaders from the rank and file were phenomenally successful in reaching out to marginal people, in promoting self-education and sheltering participants from the indoctrination of elite orthodoxies, in binding people together in supportive community, and in identifying the aspiration of common people with the will of God.[14]

It was precisely in these areas—deference to established authority and traditions, the dignifying of the convictions of ordinary people on important matters, choice and participation by people long ignored, the reaching of marginalized people, and the sheltering of participants from the indoctrination of elite orthodoxies—that official Methodism had reversed field. Creativity and unrestrained enthusiasm and ragged edges sooner or later had to be "organized" and directed, if not manipulated. And so over a period of time, Methodist leaders developed an authority system in which a chosen few saw themselves as guardians of the many.

The resulting "gap" between "official" mediated Methodism and Methodism's own populist wing would grow even wider as the Church progressed through the twentieth century. A growing and evermore powerful group of mediating elite would seek to deconstruct doctrine, replace evangelism with education, advance liberal social action as the mission of the Church, and then claim that their "progressive" ways represented the true ethos of Methodism. The populists would increasingly be labeled as "reactionary" or "fundamentalist" or "persons fearful of change."

By whatever label, and despite all the predictions, populist Methodism did not die. The revival meeting and the gospel hymn were still the distinguishing marks of grass roots Methodism well into the 1920s. Sunday schools thrived under lay leadership. The great majority of pastors were not seminary trained, and many were not even college trained. Methodist membership through most of the twentieth century was clustered in small churches and in rural areas. These Methodists continued to take their stand against alcohol, tobacco, dancing, and movies and dressed plainly. At the time of World War I, despite the forming of at least three main African American denominations out of Methodism, black people still made up 9 percent of The Methodist Episcopal Church.[15] Methodists could still shout and jump over pews and claim the second blessing and wave white handkerchiefs and invade the saloons on behalf of Prohibition.

The 1930s, 1940s, 1950s, and 1960s were difficult days for Methodism's populist evangelicals. As much of the church leadership became increasingly liberal and controlling, populist Methodism became less and less visible. Still—and this in part is the argument of this study—there was a remnant that was faithful to Methodism's original vision, and the remnant was larger than was usually recognized. Many local churches had never bought into what the institutional church called "the Methodist

Way." Some churches and individuals were influenced by fundamentalism and, after World War II, the neo-evangelical world of Billy Graham;
journals such as *Christianity Today, Eternity,* and *Christian Life;* and parachurch groups such as Youth for Christ and Campus Crusade.

It is out of this background that the thinking of Charles Keysor must
be understood. Converted in a Billy Graham meeting, profoundly influenced by John Wesley and the stories of early Methodism, educated at a
Methodist seminary, politically trained by his years at *Together*—
Methodism's family magazine—immersed in populist Christianity
through his experiences at David C. Cook, Keysor surveyed the religious
landscape of the 1960s with a great deal of insight.

Keysor's article "Methodism's Silent Minority," intentionally or unin-
tentionally, rang the populist bell. It was not an intellectual assault on the
theological liberalism of the day (that would come later), or a diatribe
against liberal politics, but an appeal to the church at large to recognize
the faithful, orthodox, long-suffering, disenfranchised, but still loyal
believers of Methodism who would like to influence the future of the
Church.

CHAPTER TWO

METHODISM'S SILENT MINORITY

Within The Methodist Church in the United States is a silent minority group. It is not represented in the higher councils of the church. Its members seem to have little influence in Nashville, Evanston, or on Riverside Drive. Its concepts are often abhorrent to Methodist official-dom at annual conference and national levels.

. . . I speak of those Methodists who are variously called "evangeli-cals" or "conservatives" or "fundamentalists." A more accurate descrip-tion is "orthodox," for these brethren hold a traditional understanding of the Christian faith. (Charles Keysor, "Methodism's Silent Minority," The Christian Advocate [14 July 1966]: 10)

These were the opening words in the article "Methodism's Silent Minority" by the Reverend Charles Keysor, which appeared in the July 14, 1966, issue of *Christian Advocate*. Keysor, pastor of Grace Methodist Church in Elgin, Illinois, made a plea for sensitivity and tol-erance. He went on in the article to assert that orthodox Methodists are often overlooked and misunderstood and frequently accused of being nar-row-minded, naive, contentious, and potentially schismatic. That was unfortunate, for they loved the Church and had been faithful Methodists all of their lives. They were characterized by a commitment to the historic fundamentals of the faith: the inspiration of Scripture, the virgin birth of Christ, the substitutionary atonement, the physical resurrection, and the return of Christ.

Did the listing of essentials of the faith make Keysor a fundamentalist? Keysor, at least at first, reacted against the use of labels. What he stood for was simply historic Christianity, or "orthodox" Christianity. By whatever name, this form of Christianity still existed within The Methodist Church. As evidence Keysor pointed to the continued popularity of gospel music in Methodist churches and the fact that ten thousand Methodist churches had defected from the use of Methodist Christian education materials, preferring materials based on orthodox theology.

Was there a future for this orthodox Christianity within Methodism? Keysor quoted a church official who had declared, "We are going to stamp out the last vestiges of fundamentalism from the Methodist Church." He also quoted Dr. Paul Hessert, his own professor at Garrett Biblical Institute, who foresaw a continued eclipse of orthodox influence within the seminary-trained Methodist ministry, but who believed orthodoxy could continue among Methodism's supply pastors and in pockets of laypeople.

Hessert's assessment reflected the prevailing sentiments of the mainline seminaries. "Fundamentalism" and its twin sister "literalism" (referring to the view that the Bible was to be interpreted literally) had no future among reasonable, thinking people, according to this viewpoint. It could be understood sociologically as a longing for a rural, simpler past, psychologically as fear of change, and theologically as prescientific. Despite the numbers attracted to Billy Graham crusades, the religion of those crusades—fundamentalism—could never attract the upcoming generation. According to these observers, this outdated form of religion might linger in isolated, rural areas or among people who thought like those who lived in isolated, rural areas, but its days were numbered. It was bad theology and an embarrassment to thinking Christians. For many church leaders of the 1950s and 1960s, the sooner "fundamentalist" and "literalist" thinking could be purged, the better the Church would be.

These church "leaders" were out of touch. Wishing that fundamentalism would go away and predicting its demise was not making it happen. As early as 1926, *Christian Century* had written fundamentalism's obituary.[1] Fundamentalism had suffered public humiliation during the Scopes trial. It held no respect among the nation's elite. It controlled no major seminaries.[2] It claimed no major publishing houses. But the loss of intellectual respect did not necessarily mean the loss of popular support. The throngs were there and loyal. Liberal church commentators simply did not see them or, if they did see them, admit that their presence was in any way significant.

Nor did liberal commentators seem aware of the wide diversity within what they branded "fundamentalism." There were dispensationalists and Pentecostals and Baptists and neo-evangelicals and Reformed traditionalists and Holiness Methodists and—perhaps mostly—common ordinary believers who wore no label but who held and sought to live the ancient truths. Among these groups, all committed to historic Christianity, tremendous changes were taking place.

As early as the 1940s, careful observers of the American church scene were making distinctions between "fundamentalism"—an approach to faith linked with the influences of dispensationalism—and "evangelicalism"—a word that often included fundamentalism but that also covered a much broader range of theologies and Protestant church cultures.

In addition, new ministries and parachurch groups were springing into life with growing vitality. In 1938, Young Life launched a ministry to teenagers. In 1941, Inter-Varsity Christian Fellowship began work with college students. The same year, the American Scientific Affiliation organized a scholarly society for evangelical scientists. The National Association of Evangelicals formed in 1942 around the issue of religious radio and the Federal Council of Churches. The Federal Council had attempted to monopolize all religious radio programming by informing the Federal Communications Commission that they alone represented Protestants, Catholics, and Jews and all not approved by them should be excluded. In 1944, evangelical broadcasters began an organization known as the National Religious Broadcasters. In 1949, Billy Graham jumped into prominence in his Los Angeles crusade. In 1956, *Christianity Today* published volume 1, issue 1.

By the 1960s, schools such as Fuller Theological Seminary, Gordon-Conwell Seminary, Trinity Evangelical Divinity School, and Asbury Theological Seminary were attracting numbers of highly qualified students even though their graduates had difficulty being accepted by credentialing agencies of mainline denominations. Independent mission agencies were opening new fields and were sending more missionaries even as the traditional mainline agencies were pulling back.[3]

Methodists in a number of places were being caught up in this evangelical enthusiasm. At the same time, many Methodists were sensing that their denominational leaders were going in a different direction. The focus at many denominational meetings was on the importance of involvement in the political and social matters of the day. Under the slogan "Let the world set the agenda," the Church was encouraged to shift its concern from pietistic and individualist concerns of Bible study, prayer, doctrine, and conversion to interaction with secular culture, involvement in politics (always liberal politics), and commitment to freedom movements wherever they might be found: Alabama or Rhodesia or Latin America or the grape farms of California.

By the time of Keysor's article, even neo-orthodoxy—a more conservative reaction to the liberal theologies of the 1920s and 1930s—was in retreat. Theological discussion concentrated on Death of God theology, a chief exponent of which was Thomas Altizer, a professor at Methodist-related Emory University. The secularizing of theology was symbolized by the highly acclaimed and frequently quoted book *The Secular City* by Harvey Cox. For Cox, the future of the church was not with supernaturalism, but in reinterpreting the gospel to the culture of the day. Theater, films, and the arts were the vehicle in which the content of religion could be found, according to Cox.

The subjects of interest that appeared in Methodist's *Christian Advocate* the same year that Keysor's article was printed included film criticism, Death of God, Consultation on Church Union (COCU), the EUB merger, Vietnam, and Marshall McLuhan. The larger American scene had already seen Woodstock, Angela Davis, the John F. Kennedy assassination, and increasing student unrest. Within months, newspapers would report on the increased national division over Vietnam, the assassination of Martin Luther King Jr., and Watergate.

Liberal seminaries, reflecting the secular culture of the period, were committed to "relevance," academic freedom, and social change. Traditional studies, and the traditional professors who taught them, were to give way to training in political action. Disruption, sit-ins, and demonstrations became the strategy to bring about this just, new social order.

For many ordinary and populist Methodists, these fast-moving cultural and ideological shifts brought bewilderment on the one hand, but renewed faith on the other. Believers continued to tithe and confess the historic creeds and pray for their church leaders as they always had. Their Sunday school classes reacted negatively to Death of God talk and student demonstrations and seminarians with long hair, grungy clothing, and strange politics; but their commitments were not that easily shaken. The liberal agenda never did penetrate completely into Methodist ethos. Methodists made up a considerable percentage of those who flocked to Billy Graham crusades and Youth for Christ rallies and read journals such as *Christianity Today, Eternity,* and *Moody Monthly.*

These were the people who responded to Chuck Keysor's "Silent Minority." What Keysor spoke was true. Evangelicals did exist. They liked gospel songs; they experienced conversion; they mistrusted Methodist Sunday school material. At the same time, they were loyal Methodists, and they were often silent. For some, the only point in the article worth arguing about was whether this group was a minority or actually represented the majority of Methodists. Their understanding of Methodism was quite different from the perception of the seminaries and of many church leaders.

But these ordinary folk were also aware that they were being increasingly marginalized in their own denomination. More letters poured into *Christian Advocate* as the result of the Keysor article than from any other single article in the history of the magazine. Many persons wrote Keysor directly or phoned: "We didn't know there was someone else who felt as we do." "You have expressed our own feelings perfectly." "What can we do?"

By training and experience, Chuck Keysor was the man who could figure out something to do. He was a second career forty-three-year-old pastor with training and experience in journalism and publishing. A recent graduate of Garrett Biblical Institute and a former managing editor of *Together,* Methodism's family magazine, Keysor knew the denomination. A convert of Billy Graham and a former editor for David C. Cook Publishing Company, he also knew the evangelical ethos. Chuck Keysor's vision? A magazine. A magazine for Methodists that would exalt Jesus Christ and be a forum for the discussion of church issues and a rallying point for people of like-minded convictions. Keysor tested his magazine idea with newfound friends who had responded to his "Silent Minority." They urged him to proceed.

He also shared his vision with one bishop, Bishop Gerald Kennedy of the Los Angeles Area. Though Kennedy made no claim to be in the evangelical camp, he was still a hero of sorts to evangelicals. He had served as co-chair of the Billy Graham Crusade in Los Angeles in 1963. He was one church leader who had been able to sort out the difference among fundamentalists, evangelicals, and liberals and was able to speak with some appreciation for evangelicals. Kennedy was also one of Methodism's most respected bishops. When *Time* magazine did a feature on Methodism in its May 8, 1964, issue, it was Bishop Gerald Kennedy whose face appeared on the cover. *Time* referred to Kennedy as the "unofficial spokesman for Methodism."

Keysor sought some time with Kennedy when Kennedy came to Chicago on a speaking engagement. The bishop responded positively to Keysor's plan and volunteered to help if he could. Keysor was soon to accept the offer.

But words of encouragement do not themselves launch a magazine. Keysor asked his supporters if they would meet him in Elgin. Those who came would have to pay their own expenses. They would be housed in the homes of Keysor's church members. Could they be organized into a legal entity? For purposes of incorporation, twelve persons were needed. The first meeting drew only eight persons, but those who came found an instant sense of unity. Was the magazine idea feasible? Where would the money come from? The support staff? A mailing list? What would it be called? What purpose would be behind it? Was it of God?

Almost single-handed, Keysor made it work. There were no marketing surveys, no foundation grants, no supply of writers, no support staff. But there was a lot of prayer, a strong sense of God's leading, and a willingness to commit energy and labor.

Volume 1, number 1 of *Good News* magazine appeared in the spring of 1967, just one year after the *Christian Advocate* article. Keysor's opening editorial shared the vision:

> We invite you to share a dream.
> We have dared to dream that evangelical Methodists might be united in fellowship across the Church.
> We have dared to dream that this fellowship might have a publication, knitting us closer to each other, and to Jesus Christ our Lord.
> We have dared to dream that such a *koinonia* will strengthen the Church we love and serve.
> We have dared, even, to dream that our voices may be heard as we seek to articulate historic Methodism: forever relevant, forever vital.[4]

Bishop Kennedy delivered on his promise and prepared an exclusive five-page article entitled "The Place of Evangelicals in the Methodist Church Today." He spoke with respect for classical evangelical doctrine, including belief in the verbal inspiration of Scripture, and suggested that narrow-mindedness was not limited to one theological camp. More important, he expressed his conviction that The Methodist Church could not afford to lose the evangelicals in its midst. For a publication conceived and edited in a pastor's study, the first issue was surprisingly well done. Keysor's journalistic experience had paid off. This was no glorified church newsletter. Keysor always insisted on journalistic and publishing quality. From somewhere or other, nearly six thousand addresses had been accumulated for the first issue. Keysor family members stuffed all six thousand magazines into envelopes, and the family station wagon delivered them to the Elgin post office.

Reaction to volume 1, number 1 was overwhelmingly positive. There was indeed a silent minority that ought not to be silent any longer. Some responded to the first issue by saying that though they did not espouse the theology Good News advocated, it was a voice that needed to be heard. Others gave cautious endorsement but (in true institutional style) warned against divisiveness and stridency. Still others expressed eagerness to "sign on," even if—and this was mentioned by no small number—it meant "paying a price." There was an instinctive feeling that controversy would be in the Good News future.

Official Church response was muted and, in the case of the official Church press, practically nonexistent. Spurgeon Dunnam of *Texas Methodist* however, realized the significance of the journal and wrote a perceptive editorial:

> While affirming our publication's openness to a variety of opinions, we recognize at the same time the value of and need for responsible journals of opinion which reflect a particular theological point of view. Within our own tradition, *The Christian Advocate, Concern,* and to some extent, *Together* have served as Methodists journals of opinion. However, there is in our judgment some justification for the conservative complaint that each of these Methodist periodicals represents a basically "liberal" point of view. There really has been no responsible publication representing the "conservative" viewpoint within the Methodist Church. Hence, many "conservatives" have joined other denominations or subscribed to independent publications of varying quality from "conservative" sect-groups.
>
> The *Texas Methodist* is pleased to make known to its readers that within the past year a responsible "conservative" journal of opinion has been born within the United Methodist Church. It is called simply *Good News,* and we think it is just that.[5]

A look at the early leaders of Good News reveals that this was truly a grassroots, populist, bottom-up movement. No aspiring episcopal candidates affixed their name to the Good News masthead. There were no large-church pastors vulnerable to the appointment system or seminary professors. Few were active in general church politics. There were no wealthy laymen with a conservative agenda. Those who risked being identified with Good News were risking little, for they had little to lose. They tended to be young evangelicals, fundamentalists in established churches, revivalists, Sunday school teachers, mavericks, naive reformers, and populists of several varieties.

Philip Worth, first board president, and probably more than any other early leader a true fundamentalist, was pastor of the Methodist Church in Collingswood, New Jersey, a congregation that had sent more than one hundred men and women into full-time Christian service. Despite its commitment to historic Methodism, the Collingswood church had a reputation for being an "outsider" church even in its own conference. Larry Sounder, a lay member of the first board, also from the Collingswood church, was a dispensationalist.

Dale Bittinger, second board chairman, was an Asbury Holiness preacher. Jim McCallie was a circuit preacher soon to become a full-time evangelist. Mike Walker was a recent seminary graduate and an associate pastor. What they shared in common was a commitment to historic Methodist doctrine and practice and a belief that they might make a difference in a denomination that seemed to be losing its way.

Holding this group together by the force of his personality and convictions was Chuck Keysor. By phone, letter, and personal appearance, he counseled, cajoled, and defended. Phone bills were astronomical. Correspondence was voluminous. Many of the contacts were from hurting evangelicals who were finding themselves increasingly disenfranchised and unwelcome in their own churches and were wondering if there was any hope for Methodism.

Letters to the editor in response to the first issues told the story:

> After reading my first issue of "Good News," I felt like Elijah must have when the Lord told him there were still 7,000 who had not bowed the knee to Baal. Ours is a small rural church, former E.U.B. We have been so unhappy about the new literature. . . . We are praying that the Lord will raise up enough good, Bible-believing Christians to influence the church.

Thank God for your courageous voice in a time of apostasy and liberal thought.

We need all the help we can get to keep us from literally "throwing in the towel" and going elsewhere where they still believe in the truths of the Bible and its application to everyday living.

God has raised up "Good News" for such a time as this.[6]

For the most part, Keysor was pastoral and encouraging to those who contacted him: "There is hope. . . . God will honor your faithfulness. . . . It is with people like you that the denomination can be renewed. . . . Don't give up on Methodism." On other occasions, Keysor was forceful and blunt: "That is not our issue" was a frequent response to racists and political right-wingers who would have taken the young movement in a different direction. From the very beginning, Good News had to careful about allowing itself to be used as a front for other causes, some good, some not so good.[7] Keysor never wavered from his conviction that the need for renewal was primarily spiritual and theological. Good News for him was about the good news, the truth that Jesus Christ was the divine Son of God who died for our sins on the cross, making possible our salvation that comes by grace through faith.

But if Good News was to have a future, it needed more than a board and a magazine. The twentieth-century Methodist landscape was strewn with renewal efforts that flourished for a while and then faded. H. C. Morrison and others formed the American Methodist League in 1915. Morrison also published the journal *The Pentecostal Herald*, which championed the cause of Holiness and evangelical theology. In 1916 Leander Munhall, widely traveled lay evangelist, began publishing *Eastern Methodist*.[8] In The Methodist Episcopal Church, South, *Southern Methodist* was published by R. A. Meek, a former editor of a denominational paper. In 1925, Harold Paul Sloan organized the Methodist League for Faith and Life and began publishing *The Essentialist*.

The Methodist League for Faith and Life is the best known of all of the early renewal efforts. Within a year of its founding, it claimed a membership of 2,000 drawn from 62 annual conferences of The Methodist Episcopal Church. At the 1928 General Conference of The Methodist Episcopal Church, Sloan brought memorials (petitions) signed by nearly 10,000 persons from 41 states and 540 communities. Most of the memorials had to do with the Course of Study (the recommended books pastors in training were to read) and Sunday school literature. Sloan felt that his perspective was shared by 95 percent of the clergy and by almost all of the laypeople. That may or may not have been true. What was true was that it was not shared by the delegates of General Conference, a powerful minority of whom were committed to "modernism," and a greater number committed to avoiding controversy at any cost.

If the League had hoped to save Methodism for evangelical Christianity it was probably twenty years too late. By 1928, the modernist tide could not be stemmed. By the early 1930s, the Methodist League for Faith and Life had slipped into oblivion.

In the 1930s and 1940s, the best-known renewal effort was centered around the person of Robert Shuler of Los Angeles, or "Fighting Bob" as he was known. Shuler pastored Trinity Church Los Angeles, a Methodist Episcopal Church, South congregation, from 1920 to 1953. Trinity became one of the largest churches in the denomination. Through his pulpit, a radio station that was estimated to have as many as 100,000 listeners, and a periodical, *Bob Shuler's Magazine*, he fought corruption in California and became known as a political powermaker. He was a strong candidate for bishop in 1938. After merger, Schuler took on a new cause: evangelicalism in The Methodist Church. In 1943 he launched *The Methodist Challenge* a magazine that soon reached 20,000 subscribers. Shuler claimed that three-fourths of the laity and a majority of the clergy were theologically conservative, and they, like the Methodist reformers before, and not the liberal leaders, were the true Methodists. After Schuler retired from Trinity Church, he continued to publish *The Methodist Challenge* until he reached the age of eighty in 1960.

One of the problems with these and other renewal efforts was that though they claimed to represent grassroots Methodism, none of them ever put together an effective network of grassroots support. In almost every case, the reformers were also pastors (never college presidents or seminary professors or church bureaucrats or bishops) who were trying to balance pastoral duties with reform efforts.

Good News was to take a different approach. Chuck Keysor believed strongly in the importance of networking, of sharing stories, and of face-to-face fellowship. Renewal groups were organized in a number of conferences.

But some on the board wanted more than just renewal groups or even regional conferences. They spoke of a "calling out" of evangelicals, a gathering of like-minded people in a gathering. From this came the dream and then plans for the first Good News convocation.

The obstacles were formidable. The Church had sponsored successful convocations before, but these, like the successful Congress on Evangelism, were subsidized by church funds, planned by paid staff, publicized through the Church press, and supported by church leaders. Good News had no funds, no paid staff, no channels for publicity, and no backing by church leaders or people of stature.

Furthermore, no one on the board had had experience in organizing convocations. Still, the group was convinced they were being led by God to plan a convocation. Mike Walker, a twenty-seven-year-old associate pastor from Texas, was willing to head a task force that would put together the first convocation.[9] But who would serve on the task force? The board was convinced that a national convocation needed people of national recognition, and time was spent brainstorming who those persons might be. Two names surfaced immediately—Claude Thompson and Frank Stanger—and these two were approached.

Thompson was a bright light on a Methodist seminary scene that was becoming more and more infatuated with the radicalism of the 1960s. He had become professor of Systematic Theology at Chandler School of Theology at Emory University in Atlanta after being released from Asbury Seminary several years before under a cloud of controversy.[10] He had expressed interest in Good News and had authored an article for the magazine on the doctrinal standards. Thompson agreed to serve.

Frank Stanger was president of Asbury Seminary. He had come to the seminary at a time when the school was without accreditation and needed to gain respectability within the denomination. It was obvious that Good News needed an Asbury connection. Asbury was the rallying point for the same kind of populist constituency that characterized Good News. Good News's basic mailing list and subscription drive had developed after Frank Stanger gave Dale Bittinger, Asbury grad and chair of the Good News board, an opportunity to present the Good News cause at Asbury Pastors' School in 1968. But Stanger was also very much aware that the cause of the seminary could be jeopardized if it became identified with any movement that appeared "divisive," a label already pinned on Good News.

Stanger was cautious about serving on the task force. He believed in the cause but also believed there was too much of a "shoot-from-the-hip" mentality in the Good News leadership. He agreed to be a part of the convocation planning team after hearing that Claude Thompson was involved. Stanger saw an opportunity to build some bridges with Thompson.

The first planning meeting was held September 26, 1969, at Asbury. Unfortunately, Thompson could not be present. Stanger began to pull back. The convocation idea was much too grandiose, and the planning team Good News put together was not, in his opinion, of the quality to match the vision. He feared a disaster in the making.

Then Stanger had an inspiration and a sudden change of heart: Robert Mayfield! Robert Mayfield could make it work. Mayfield was the new Director of Development for the seminary. Prior to that, he had served for sixteen years as the general secretary of the General Board of the Lay Activities. He had been a General Conference delegate and was on a first-name basis with many of the bishops.

Mayfield agreed to be general chairman for the convocation. The task before him and the committee was formidable. The idea was untried. Committee members would serve at their own expense. There would be no honoraria for speakers. Still, many were becoming convinced that the time was right. Robert Lundy, former bishop in Asia and Secretary for Furloughed Personnel with the Board of Missions, consented to be vice chairman.[11] Harry Denman, well-known lay evangelist, agreed to serve on the committee. The place and date for the convocation were set: Adolphus Hotel, Dallas, Texas, August 26-29, 1970.

Speakers and workshop leaders were approached, including some of the best-known names in Methodism who were either identified as evangelical or open to evangelicals in the church. K. Morgan Edwards, of Claremont School of Theology, agreed to give a keynote address. Dennis Kinlaw, president of Asbury College; Ira Gallaway, Board of Evangelism; Howard Ball of Campus Crusade; Bishop Gerald Kennedy; Tom Skinner; Claude Thompson; Frank Stanger; Oral Roberts[12]; Harry Denman; and E. Stanley Jones—all were asked to be part of the program, and all accepted. The Junaluska Singers agreed to furnish the music. Chuck Keysor, Phil Hinerman of Park Avenue Church in Minneapolis, and Les Woodson of Elizabethtown, Kentucky—Good News insiders—completed the program.

The planning committee began to dream. They spoke of as many as seven hundred persons who would attend the convocation. They then enlarged their dream to one thousand and then to twelve hundred. Robert Mayfield was always the guiding light. Publicity made it plain that this was not a "Good News Convocation," but rather a "Convocation of United Methodists for Evangelical Christianity" sponsored by Good News. This supposedly made the convocation more palatable for those who were uneasy about the Good News label. Mayfield wrote personal letters to every bishop in the Church, to every general secretary of the various Church agencies, and to every annual conference council direc-tor. Many of the letters were addressed to persons by their first names. Mayfield used all of the goodwill accumulated from his years as head of the Board of Lay Activities to make the case for understanding for the convocation.

A few of the responses to Mayfield were negative:

> You have occupied such a high position in the former Methodist Church. . . . It is a bit difficult for me to see you functioning in this kind of capacity. I have read some of the statements of the Good News Group and . . . am fully convinced that this organization is trying to turn the clock back. It consists of 19th and early 20th century thinking. It is unwilling to face the realities of the contemporary world.[13]

By far the majority of the responses, however, were positive and affirm-ing. Seventeen different bishops replied to Mayfield, and though there were the usual warnings against "divisiveness," there were also remarks about how the Church needs what "these people" have to offer.

Whatever the expectations of the convocation committee or other persons interested in Good News, Chuck Keysor believed the gathering was a *kairos* moment for evangelicals and for church renewal. Never guilty of understatement, Keysor described the Dallas convocation in metaphors of biblical proportion:

> The time is fast approaching for what may well be one of the most decisive gatherings in the history of American Methodism. . . .
>
> In a dramatic way, the four days of meetings mark the end of an Exile which has seen Methodist evangelicals wandering in a wilderness for roughly 40 years. Somewhere back in the 1920s, liberals gained control of the power structure of Methodism. Since then, evangelicals have been squeezed out of influence in denominational affairs. For many years, it has appeared to the world as if evangelicals could not survive in the increasingly humanist, universalistic climate. But a remnant has survived! They have endured spiritual starvation. They have seen col-leges and seminaries bearing the Methodist name totally repudiate what once made that name great. They have been force-fed church school

literature that is repugnant to New Testament faith and experience. They have seen pulpits taken captive by humanism, secularism, politics, institutionalism and psychology. Their money has been used to finance many programs with which they violently disagree. They have heard themselves slandered, ridiculed and castigated by those for whom Biblical faith was "not relevant."

But many have not bowed the knee to Baal. Many have survived the wilderness journey. And many will assemble in Dallas as a living witness to unquenchable faith in a Savior who is the same yesterday, today, and forever.

We are coming out of exile!

As darkness envelops a denomination which has largely turned its back on historic Christianity, it is good news indeed that Christ will be exalted . . . that the authority of Scripture will be properly emphasized . . . that believers will gather in a joy-full fellowship of prayer and Gospel brotherhood.

It is good news that many have survived in the wilderness these 40 years. It is even better news that evangelical strength is burgeoning. It is the best news of all that many United Methodists do seek to make Christ pre-eminent in all things. We'll see you in Dallas![14]

The official Church press was underwhelmed, but Keysor, it can be argued, had a much better feel for the mood of the Church than the Church press did, and, for that matter, than many of his fellow evangelicals did. On August 26, 1970, at the Adolphus Hotel in Dallas, even Keysor was surprised at the response. Over sixteen hundred persons registered for the event, and evening crowds swelled to nearly three thousand. They came. They worshiped. They wept. They prayed. They said "amen" and "praise the Lord" without generating disapproving stares of those around them. For many, "coming out of exile" described their experience perfectly.

The speakers at the first convocation were inspiring, insightful, and prophetic. In what appeared to be a mantra ritual, each speaker made special effort to stress that evangelical faith must be socially involved and must especially address racism.

There was curiosity as to who exactly made up this "silent minority" that suddenly surfaced sixteen hundred strong. An extensive survey indicated that 20 percent of those attending were between the ages of twenty and thirty-five. Forty-five percent were between the ages of thirty-five and fifty, and 25 percent were between ages of fifty and sixty-five. Forty-eight states and four continents were represented at the convocation.

Fifty-eight percent were lay, 42 percent clergy. Eighteen percent of those attending had graduated from an "official" United Methodist seminary; 18 percent had graduated from a non-official school. Only 3 percent of the clergy were not serving local churches.[15]

Only 6 percent of those attending were favorable to Consultation on Church Union (COCU).[16] Forty percent of those attending said they used denominational church school material exclusively. Eighty percent expressed a belief that there was a gap between laypeople and clergy in understandings and interpretations of the faith. Almost 99 percent believed that God performs miracles today.

But the analysis of who attended or what was said was not the real story. The real story of the first convocation was in the realization that evangelicals had found one another. United Methodist evangelicals were not a vanishing breed. The silent minority was no longer silent. Evangelicals no longer had to apologize for who they were. And, in good evangelical style, renewal needed to start in each individual heart.

Keysor described it later in this way:

> On the final day, Dr. Haqq had called us to a time of repentance and new dedication to Christ. First there was silence, then soft weeping, and spontaneous prayer. A man standing next to me put his arm on my shoulder. There were tears in his eyes as he said, "Brother, I have been a Methodist pastor for 15 years and today the Holy Spirit has made me realize I have been serving myself, not Jesus. Today the spirit has brought me pardon, and given me assurance that from now on I shall put Jesus first."[17]

A movement was launched.

Christianity Today reported on the convocation: "At the closing prayer of dedication, men embraced, tears were shed, and there seemed to be a general reluctance to allow the fragile spell of spiritual communion to be broken."[18]

The official Church press gave a mostly positive but guarded response.[19] The official line seemed to be: The movement is good if it can inspire the Church to more fervent evangelism; however, it needs to guard against an individualistic gospel devoid of social action and divisiveness.

One person bemused by the charge of divisiveness was Spurgeon Dunnam of *Texas Methodist*. In an editorial titled "Constructive Divisiveness," Dunnam commented:

The question which remains is: are the evangelicals a divisive force within the church? Yes, they are divisive. Divisive in the same way Jesus was to first century Judaism. Divisive in the same way Martin Luther was to sixteenth century catholicism. Divisive in the same way that John Wesley was to eighteenth century Anglicanism. And, strangely enough, divisive in the same way that many liberal "church renewalists" are to Methodism in our own day.

A survey of Methodism in America today reveals these basic thrusts. One is devoted primarily to the status quo. To these, the institution called Methodism is given first priority. It must be protected at all costs from any threat of major changes in direction. . . .

The other two forces *do* question the theological soundness of institutional loyalty for its own sake. The progressive, renewalist force has properly prodded the Church to take seriously the social implications of the Christian gospel. . . .

Now the more conservative, evangelical force is accepting the social implication of the Gospel, but is also prodding the Church to take with renewed seriousness its commitment to the basic tenets of our faith: our belief in a transcendent God, our faith in Christ as personal Lord, and our mandate to proclaim Him so that all men have the opportunity of Christian discipleship.[20]

Another evaluation was given by Claude Thompson, who, in his own way, had played such an important part in the first convocation. Writing in the November 26, 1970, issue of *Christian Advocate*, Dr. Thompson reiterated the need for the convocation: "The awareness of a departure from our heritage sufficiently serious to move us to reaffirm our biblical, historic, and experience-centered position." He then commented not so much on Good News, but on the evangelical presence in the denomination: "The evangelical point of view is a position within the larger community of faith. It is our conviction that it is not only one of many possible interpretations of the gospel. We believe it *is* the gospel. And to this interpretation we are committed."[21]

Thompson went on to say evangelicals were not moving toward separation. However, there was no intention of capitulating to a subevangelical faith. There would be no compromise, no armistice, no surrender, no defeat. Evangelicals were committed to evangelism, vitality, and the social revolution.

Charles Keysor was ecstatic. He made plans for a one-hundred-page special convocation edition of *Good News* magazine, complete with summaries of most of the presentations. Twenty-five thousand copies of the special would be printed, meaning that fourteen thousand copies would be available at $1.50 each, beyond the regular eleven thousand subscribers.

This ambitious plan presented a problem for the Good News board. Chuck Keysor was swamped with work. He was still pastoring Grace Church, Elgin, and working with limited office help. Good News desperately needed his time. But this presented problems. The United Methodist itinerant system gave pastors a great deal of security: parsonage, expenses, health insurance, pension. To move to special appointment would require funds that Good News simply did not have. Minutes of the early board meetings indicate that despite a budget that was doubling and tripling each year, the resources were not keeping up with the opportunities.

Then in a crucial and, in the Good News mind, providential development, a solution presented itself. In a significant offer that would have a far-reaching effect on the future of Good News, Dr. Dennis Kinlaw of Asbury College approached Keysor about teaching journalism at Asbury College part-time, with the understanding that a portion of his time could be given to Good News.

For Kinlaw, bringing Keysor to Wilmore, Kentucky, was a natural fit. Kinlaw had known Keysor back in the days when Keysor was a cigar-chomping Northwestern University graduate rubbing shoulders with church leaders as he helped make *Together* magazine one of the finest pieces of journalism The Methodist Church had ever produced. He saw Keysor change though conversion and was intrigued with Keysor's commitment to combine his newfound faith with his journalistic experience. Kinlaw was also committed to renewal in The United Methodist Church. By sentiment, ethos, and conviction, he was a revival-preaching Holiness populist. Converted in a camp meeting, not of the right social class in his hometown church, rejected by the Board of Missions unless he would attend a liberal seminary, told when he entered Duke Seminary, "We don't know if we want Asbury grads with Duke degrees," and then president of a Holiness school in an anti-Holiness denomination, Kinlaw knew liberal bias firsthand. The United Methodist Church was in need of renewal, and Charles Keysor was the man to lead it, and Kinlaw could lend a hand to that. Furthermore, Asbury needed a journalism department, and it was difficult to attract qualified journalism teachers to Wilmore, Kentucky.

Kinlaw was also convinced that Keysor and Good News needed Asbury. The Asbury Methodist constituency was, or at least was potentially, the Good News constituency. For all of his knowledge of the larger evangelical scene, Keysor still had some things to learn. For example, he was still not entirely comfortable with Methodist Holiness revivalism.[22]

Keysor and the Good News board considered the Kinlaw proposal an answer to prayer. The only question had to do with fallout from the perceptions of a Good News-Asbury connection. Good News wished to see itself as much more than a front for Asbury, and Asbury obviously wanted to see itself much more than a front for Good News.

This was especially true for the seminary. The seminary response to the idea of Good News coming to Wilmore was by no means overwhelmingly positive. The seminary was not universally loved and accepted by the conferences of The United Methodist Church. Some conferences would not even consider Asbury graduates for ordination. Others required that Asbury graduates "balance" their Asbury training with courses in a liberal seminary.[23] The school had to present itself as committed to evangelical faith on the one hand and loyal and affirming to The United Methodist Church on the other. Good News already had the reputation for being divisive and confrontational, a reputation could spill over on Asbury Theological Seminary.

With or without everyone's blessings, Keysor and the Good News office moved to Wilmore, Kentucky, in summer of 1972. The move was good for Good News in several unexpected ways. Maintaining an office was inexpensive in Wilmore. There was a ready supply of talented students and student spouses to serve as support staff. And, perhaps most important, Keysor was able to recruit some of the brightest and best from his journalism classes to write for the magazine.

In the fall of 1971, Chuck Keysor had an opportunity to write a second article for *Christian Advocate*.[24] It was a response to an earlier article written by Marcius E. Taber, entitled "An Ex-Fundamentalist Looks at the 'Silent Minority.'" Taber had argued that the Charles Keysor and the Good News brand of orthodoxy was a "theological divider for weeding out dissenters from the official theological 'line.'" According to Taber, Good News was not just a conservative movement, but an "ultrafundamentalist" movement with an emphasis on literalism and minute rules, which was opposed to the spirit of Jesus. As to the new birth, Taber commented: "The real test of a new birth is not in emotion or new piety, but in one's responsiveness to the physical, economic, and social needs of our neighbors."[25]

Keysor's reply revealed how the "silent minority" had developed and changed over the five-year period since Keysor's first article. Keysor first addressed the "fundamentalist" charge by saying the theological climate has changed and it was not helpful to dig up old bones and fight battles from the past all over again. It was a different world with different issues. In his original 1966 article, Keysor had quoted liberals who spoke of "fundamentalism" as isolated and dying. The truth is, said Keysor, it is not orthodoxy that is ossified and dying, but old-time liberalism.

> We had better be reading the signs of the times. They are storm warnings! For a hurricane is battering the Church, and the name of the storm is change. And as United Methodism drifts deeper into the tempest, it will be forced to jettison more of the proud "liberal" superstructure. In fact, the winds of change are already tearing it down. This may be what it means to be "a new church for a new world."[26]

Much of this change, according to Keysor was, as with the Jesus Freaks, taking place outside the institutional church. The street Christians—and many others—had evidently not read the latest theologian's article about "modern man" only responding to a "demythologized" Christ. The Secular City had been largely indifferent to the "relevant" approach of radical humanists and institutional churchmen who dominated the power structure of the National Council-oriented denominations. "Once 'liberalism' aggressively displaced the nineteenth-century churchmanship which was often culture-conformity wrapped in a thin veneer of Bible-sounding piety. Now 'liberalism' itself is passé, and God is reforming his Church again. His change agents today may be the Jesus Freaks, the new evangelicals, and the Black Methodists for Church Renewal."[27]

It was typical Keysor, populist and prophetic. In the years ahead, the Church could test whether what Keysor spoke was true.

CHAPTER THREE

CYANIDE IN THE CHURCH SCHOOL

I t was not Good News's finest hour. Chuck Keysor's editorial "Cyanide in the Church School" in the January-March 1970 issue of *Good News* magazine was a frontal attack on United Methodist church school curriculum. According to Keysor, the material was not just weak or inadequate or unbalanced. It was poison.

What was even worse, according to Keysor, was that ordinary Methodists had no choice whether the material should be used: "Why should viewpoints contrary to United Methodist doctrine be forced upon large numbers of people who want only to be 100 percent Methodist in the church school?"[1]

Keysor went on to complain about the lack of responsiveness on the part of the editor of church school materials to evangelical concerns and called for a flood of petitions to General Conference as well as for a possible economic boycott.

The institutional response to Keysor's editorial was immediate, scathing, and predictable.[2] Good News, as was suspected from the beginning, was fundamentalist, irresponsible, divisive, and disloyal. Such inflammatory language that had appeared in the editorial had no place in the life of the Church and should not be tolerated.

Even the friends of Good News ran for cover and sought to dissociate themselves from the language of the editorial. The "cyanide controversy" created discussion within the Good News board and was the first editorial over which board members raised questions about the wisdom of Keysor's confrontational style. The board agreed that Keysor should write a follow-up editorial.

Keysor did but was unrepentant and, if anything, even more strident. In the July-September 1970 issue of *Good News*, in an editorial entitled "Cyanide Revisited," Keysor acknowledged the storm the "cyanide" language had created and the accusations that his editorial was unfair. But, Keysor argued, it was unfair only that he did not tell the whole story of how much unbelief really permeated the material. The truth was the material was even worse than how it had been pictured.

What had triggered the first editorial? Keysor was reacting to a comment made in the spring 1969 issue of United Methodist *Teacher I and II:* "The drama of Jesus would be far stronger and make a far greater appeal to this post-Christian age without all this supernatural claptrap brought in at the end with a dead man suddenly brought back to life again. Wouldn't the story of Jesus of Nazareth be more powerful and truer to itself in being less self-centered, if his life had ended in death?"[3]

What is revealing about the cyanide controversy in retrospect is that institutional Methodism was much more concerned about Keysor's editorial than they were about what was being written in official Church material. A not untypical comment was: "I don't necessarily agree with what was written about the resurrection, but it does make us think, and Keysor was irresponsible in calling it cyanide."

The cyanide article did a lot to cast the image of Good News as a reactionary and confrontational force in the Church.[4] Up to this time, Good News had presented itself as a movement of loyal sons and daughters of the Church, asking mostly that the concerns of Methodism's "silent minority" be heard in the denominational councils. It had urged the Church to be missions minded, evangelistic, prayer focused, appreciative of tradition, and sensitive in curriculum to the needs of evangelicals. Good News adherents sought to be careful to dissociate themselves from any suggestion of extremism. But patience had worn thin. Chuck Keysor's purist, critical, and reformist spirit was beginning to show.

Frustration over church school curriculum, more than over any other concern, basically launched the Good News movement. Populist Methodist evangelicals who had no firsthand knowledge of *Motive* magazine (the radical left-wing magazine for college youth) or liberalism in the seminaries or the Methodist Federation for Social Action or alcohol abuse at church colleges or the philosophies of the Board of Missions or the discussions at General Conference (or whether there even was such a thing as General Conference) were confronted almost weekly by Sunday school literature that seemed at odds with their own understanding of the Christian faith.

Otherwise loyal Sunday school teachers and parents were convinced something was wrong, although they weren't always sure what it was. The material was either too hard to teach or did not have enough Bible stories or left out the plan of salvation. Whatever the stated reason, when *Good News* magazine mentioned that one of the first items in its reformist agenda was curriculum, the response was overwhelming. At last someone understood and was willing to listen. Within the first ten issues of the magazine, twenty pages were given to curriculum matters.

From the Good News perspective the problem was not just weak theology, but weak theology (or worse) forced upon churches. The General Conference had decreed that only "official" curriculum could be used in Methodist churches. Since "official" material was planned, written, and edited by theological liberals, and there were no evangelical alternatives, the whole curriculum atmosphere seemed repressive and stifling. And this in a denomination known for its populist suspicion of a "mediated" gospel, in which truth had to be filtered through properly educated and ordained clergy or through a bureaucratic curia.

Whether Chuck Keysor was inflammatory, divisive, or harsh, he quite correctly understood that the situation was serious enough to be called a "crisis."[5] Families were leaving the denomination, and one reason frequently cited was "the Sunday school." Churches and Sunday school classes, despite pressure from bishops and district superintendents and professional educators, were turning to independent publishers.

Perhaps no line in Chuck Keysor's original article, "Methodism's Silent Minority," provoked more comment than his claim that "ten thousand churches" were using something other than the "official" Methodist curriculum materials. The figure was immediately disputed. How could Keysor, who had no access to official Board of Education figures, make such an inflated claim?

Keysor's "ten thousand churches" was no exaggerated guess. Keysor had worked for David C. Cook, independent publisher and biggest rival of Methodist materials. The "ten thousand churches" was a projection based on Cook's circulation records.

The fledgling Good News board turned to curriculum almost immediately. Perhaps a face-to-face meeting with curriculum people would result in a new appreciation for the evangelical perspective and translate into some kind of reform, or at least relief. With that in mind, a team of Good News leaders asked for, and received, a hearing with Henry Bullock, editor of church school materials, and several other editors. An initial meeting took place at O'Hare International Airport in Chicago in January 1969.

The Good News team based its presentation around paragraph 1134 in the 1968 *Book of Discipline*, which stated: "There shall be one complete co-coordinated system of literature published by The Methodist Publishing House for the entire Methodist Church. This literature is to be of such type and variety as to meet the needs of all groups of our people."[6]

The Good News argument was quite simple: "Evangelicals" were a group in The United Methodist Church and their needs were not being met. Indeed, the delegation pointed out, there was a "wide and unbridgeable gulf" between the theology of the Sunday school literature and their own understanding of the faith.

The Good News presentation was not well received. Dale Bittinger, early chair of the Good News board and member of the team, interprets in retrospect that the Good News team was "a flea taking on an elephant." The Nashville editors questioned the ten thousand churches claim, argued that they and all their writers were really "evangelicals," defended the literature as biblical—supported by an overwhelming number of Methodist leaders and backed by high circulation figures—and indicated they could not be moved by "fundamentalist" reactionism.

Later, in November 1969, Henry Bullock made a statement to the Conference on Educational Ministries in Chicago in which he spoke of those who would belittle the gospel of Jesus Christ, on the one hand, by identifying it solely with actions of social justice and, on the other, by "identifying it with the five so-called fundamentals of twentieth century biblicism."[7] The statement was widely shared in annual conferences and across the Church. Numbers of people considered it the official response to and the discounting of the concerns of Good News and other evangelicals.

Good News was crushed. Their "dialogue" had served as a time not of understanding, but of alienation. Evangelicals were not asking that the entire system of literature reflect the Good News perspective, only that the prevailing liberalism be balanced by an evangelical alternative. But Good News was being branded as antagonistic and divisive. Out of the frustration came the cyanide editorial.

Historically, populist evangelicals had always been among the strongest supporters of the Sunday school. Following the example of Robert Raikes and the Sunday school movement in England, earliest American Methodist Sunday schools were a form of social outreach, directed at teaching poorer children—including children of slaves—to read. These were almost always lay-led and often existed independently from regular church structures. Within a few years, however, as "common" schools or public schools became established, Sunday schools became identified with the religious education of church members. In all instances, Sunday schools were an extension of the revival with one of the best-kept statistics being conversions.

The earliest American Methodist curriculum used was the Bible as interpreted through the catechisms prepared by English Wesleyan Methodists. Methodists made extensive use of these catechisms, and in 1848, a catechism developed by American Daniel Kidder was officially adopted by the General Conference of The Methodist Episcopal Church. The first catechism in the Evangelical Church dates from 1809 when John Dreisbach translated a German catechism into English. This catechism was used extensively even when there was resistance to the idea of Sunday schools.

The task of the Methodist Sunday school was to lead every child to Christ. Sunday schools were so successful that by the mid-1850s, it was estimated that one of every ten American children between the ages of five and fifteen was enrolled in a Methodist Sunday school. Furthermore, 98 percent of the net growth in church membership was derived from the Sunday school.[8] All of this remarkable Sunday school activity was taking place without benefit of professional leaders and independently from denominational control.

But independence is not easily tolerated in a hierarchical system. In the years following the Civil War, church leaders sought more and more to institutionalize the Sunday school movement. The 1864 General

Conference of The Methodist Episcopal Church required that the Sunday school superintendent be a member of the Church and gave the quarterly conference "supervision" over the Sunday school through a Sunday school committee appointed by the charge conference. In 1868, the new Department of Sunday School Instruction was created in The Methodist Episcopal Church, with John H. Vincent the first general superintendent.

Certainly some denominational direction was long overdue. Vincent, later elected bishop, did much to energize the Sunday school, introducing printed helps and magazines and initiating a mass institute movement to increase the effectiveness of Christian education. Vincent is also remembered as one of the founders of the Chautauqua Assembly, which first began as a Sunday school teacher's assembly.

Vincent was also a major force in the coming together of a number of Christian groups to implement the International Lesson System in 1871, in which the same agreed-upon Bible passages would be used in worship, teaching, and devotional life by all age groups in the Church. The Methodists followed this a few years later, with graded lessons in which age-appropriate materials were prepared.

At the turn of the century, Methodist ethos and life was reflected more in the Sunday school than in any other area of church life. Rally days, picnics, mission bands, children's days, children's choirs, Bible classes for men and women, crusades—all were associated with the Sunday school. Sunday schools became a main source of income and inspiration for the missionary enterprise. These schools were still primarily lay-led, conversion-centered, and largely content-based. Even into the twentieth century, The Methodist Episcopal Church had a larger Sunday school enrollment than church membership.

Radical change, however, was on the way. In Europe, higher criticism began to cast doubts on the reliability of Scripture. The social gospel located sin more in the structures of society than in the human heart and worked with the optimistic assumption that education, politics, and a new economic order could and would usher in a new era of peace not only in America, but also around the world. Higher education turned more and more to science and less and less to faith as the means by which this new era of peace would be served.

At the center of the change was a new understanding of the doctrine of man. Methodism, along with the rest of evangelical Christianity, had always taught that because of the Fall, humankind was born in sin, alienated from God, and facing God's judgment except for the intervening grace of God made possible through Christ's death on the cross. Indeed, the defining marks of "evangelical" theology were the themes of sin, atonement, faith, and the new birth. The wider culture was increasingly uncomfortable with these themes, especially the emphasis on sin. As a consequence, evangelical Christians—Methodists in particular—were never really at home in this world. Populist believers were "aliens" and "pilgrims." They tended not to see themselves as "establishment."

A number of Methodists, however, were, more and more, seeing themselves as "establishment" and were quite ready to welcome the new ideas into the church. Weary of the excesses of revivalism and Methodism's obsession with "conversion," these educated elite turned to theories of psychological development and new educational theory to make the Sunday school more modern and effective. They were especially taken with the writings of Horace Bushnell, a Congregational pastor who, even before the Civil War, was teaching that children did not have to be taught they were sinners before they could become Christians. Indeed, some believed, it was possible for a child to grow up and never imagine anything but that he or she had always been a Christian.

This theory, when taken to its logical conclusion, cut the heart out of evangelical theology. In the new approach to education, one could, and should, become a Christian not by conversion, but by nurture. Thus teachings about sin, the cross, the blood of Jesus, and conversion were not only unnecessary, but also a hindrance to the spread of Christianity. The belief that children were sinners ran counter to modern theories of child development and would need to be corrected.

The radical makeover of Christianity in the name of religious education was traced in 1935 by E. B. Chappell, the editor of church school materials in The Methodist Episcopal Church, South, in his book *Recent Development of Religious Education in the Methodist Episcopal Church, South.*[9] The "recent development," according to Chappell, had to do with the basis on which Christian education was conducted: "Until quite recently the attitude of the Church toward and its interpretation of the meaning of Christian education were determined almost entirely by theological presuppositions."[10]

Earlier leaders, according to Chappell, "lacking in the scholarly equipment which might have enabled them to discover the larger meanings of their theological position," though well-intentioned, taught an inherited

Calvinism leading to "erroneous opinions that became a serious hindrance to the development of effective religious education."[11]

Chappell's "erroneous opinions" inherited from Calvinism and Augustinianism included ideas of total depravity, emphasis on blood atonement, the necessity for radical conversion, and the de-emphasis on moral responsibility identified with free will. Revivals and camp meetings were labeled the culprits. Camp meetings, according to Chappell, "resulted in establishing in the minds of large numbers of good and earnest men and women certain erroneous opinions that became a serious hindrance to the development of an effective (Christian) program."[12] Such erroneous opinions, in Chappell's mind, "if carried to their logical conclusions would render any really vital religious education impossible. And that is precisely the kind of theology that, until quite recently, had largely dominated the Church since the time of Augustine."[13]

In the new thinking, Christian education was based on the presuppositions of the psychology of religion and other scientific approaches to human nature. If Chappell had his way, secular theory, not historic faith, would guide the Church's educational enterprise.

There were a number of areas that needed consideration if the "recent development" outlined by Chappell was to be successful.

(1) Wesley would need some reconstruction. Chappell and his friends had discovered a new John Wesley that evidently had been hidden from everybody else in every age except theirs. According to Chappell, even John Wesley carried over some Calvinistic ideas and did not see clearly the implications of his own theology, which were that man was a free agent and was endowed with goodness that could be developed by proper educational process. As a man captive to his age, Wesley sometimes spoke of the need for children to be converted. But, Chappell explained, that was not the only Wesley. As he set up societies and worked with children, Wesley's actions, according to Chappell, revealed that he saw Christian education was the main way children became Christians.

(2) Uniform lessons would be out. The Uniform Sunday School Lesson System (which Methodists had been instrumental in starting in 1872), with its desire to have all of Sunday school focused on the same passages of Scripture, was all right for its time; but by the early 1900s, it was inadequate. The lesson system assumed the purpose of Sunday school was to fill the minds of students with Bible knowledge. Modern educators wanted to stress vital experiences, not dead facts. Furthermore, the International Sunday School Union was in the hands of untrained

laymen who held to Calvinistic and Augustinian views of sin.[14] It was content-centered and not child-centered.

(3) Graded Sunday schools would be in. The grading of materials became an issue for persons trained in the new ways, not only to make the materials "age appropriate" (a phrase that would become a code word for the new educators), but also to sort out which materials should be considered by children at all. Themes of sin and judgment, for example, ought to be avoided by the young. Miracles and ideas of the supernatural should be considered only by the mature.

(4) The new approach would not be accepted by the Church willingly or easily. This was understandable since the Church, according to Chappell, had for a long time been dominated by Calvinistic ideas of sin and was still committed to the idea of evangelism as a way to make Christians. What was needed was trained leaders to help the Church make the transition.

But for Chappell, the Church had already moved into the new era.

> In spite of the lingering influences of Augustinianism, it was inevitable that Methodism's insistence upon the universal fatherhood and love of God, the universality of the atonement, the freedom and moral responsibility of man, and the ultimate worth of personality should gradually modify its attitude toward childhood and its conclusions in regard to the possibilities of Christian nurture and training and to the importance of carrying out the great Commission.[15]

In 1908, Methodists of both The Methodist Episcopal Church and The Methodist Episcopal Church, South were instrumental in founding a new organization, the Sunday School Council of Evangelical Denominations, in competition with and repudiation of the International Sunday School Association. The new council would be run by trained professionals (rather than by common ordinary laypeople), with the goals of introducing and advancing new understandings of religious education. The changing theology was already making itself known. The mediating elite was winning the day.

All of this was taking place at a time when the distinguishing mark of Methodism was still revivalism. Local Sunday schools were still lay-led. The Bible was still studied, children were led to Christ, and conversions were reported to the quarterly conference. A vast majority of Methodists blissfully continued their old ways, evidently unaware that Sunday school as they knew it was being significantly altered.

A few, however, noted the new developments with alarm. William Henry Burns, presiding elder in the Rock River Conference, wrote *Crisis in Methodism* in 1908, expressing alarm at the general state of Methodism and mentioning specifically John T. McFarland's booklet, *Preservation Versus Rescue of the Child*.[16] McFarland, editor of the Sunday school publications of The Methodist Episcopal Church, was teaching, following Bushnell, that children are already in the kingdom. According to McFarland, Sunday schools should "preserve" the good child from sin rather than try to "rescue" a bad child from sin.

A similar cry of alarm was raised by Leander Munhall in his book *Breakers! Methodists Adrift*.[17] Munhall was an ordained local preacher in the Philadelphia Conference and a delegate to the General Conferences of 1904, 1908, and 1912. He outlined the problem with McFarland and the new theology:

> But the teaching that has given most offense and has led to most of the multitude of protests from all parts of the Church is that which in effect makes unnecessary the regenerating work of the Holy Spirit.
>
> I quote Dr. McFarland's own words: . . . "The child begins life as a child of God.". . . "The child does not come into this world corrupt and depraved.". . . "The child is already in the Kingdom.". . . "There are no unchristian children in the world—none in our fair Christian land, none in our churches or in our homes.". . . "Every soul, by the innermost essence of his nature, is a child of God. . . . If we become His children in the higher ethical sense it will be by voluntarily developing the latent capacities for righteousness in our natures into actual righteousness in our lives and characters."[18]

Munhall went on to argue that McFarland's theology was in violation of the article on Original Sin in the Articles of Religion and ran counter to the "Order for Administration of Baptism to Infants." Even worse, it was contrary to the Word of God.

An even more penetrating analysis was done by Harold Paul Sloan. Writing *The Child and the Church* in 1916, Sloan argued that the crisis in the Church was over not only what books shall be read in the Conference Course of Study.[19] Perhaps, he indicated, an even more important issue was what would be taught to the children. He sensed in the new professional educators a denial of the doctrine of Original Sin, which also led to a denial of the cross, the Atonement, and the doctrine of Christ the redeemer. In what was being called "cultural salvation," "preventive sal-vation," or "educational salvation," faith was impersonal; there was no room for conviction of sin, no need for repentance, and no place for the cross.

Sloan, Munhall, and Burns represented classical Methodism more than populist evangelicalism. They were men of some stature—all had served the Church at General Conferences—who sensed trends in the Church that would eventually effect local congregations and eventually all of Methodism. They noted with alarm the desire to brand the doctrine of original sin as Calvinistic, thus creating suspicion that it was unaccept-able for Methodists.

While the Articles of Religion could not be scuttled, elitist educators were aware that other official Methodist documents could be. The 1905 hymnal (the "official" hymnal for both The Methodist Episcopal Church and The Methodist Episcopal Church, South) simply deleted the section entitled "Depravity," which had been in every Methodist hymnal, English and American, up to that point. The revisionists were also behind the vote at the 1910 Methodist Episcopal Church, South General Conference, which changed the ritual for infant baptism. Deleted from the ritual were the words, "For as much as all men are conceived and born in sin, and that our Savior Christ saith, except a man be born of water and of the spirit he cannot enter the Kingdom of God," to be replaced with language that asserted that children were already members of the kingdom. The Methodist Episcopal Church made the same change in 1916.

These actions did not grow out of ordinary life in the churches but were imposed from the top down. A few decreed for the many what was "best" for all. What had always been historic Methodism as well as his-toric Christianity, Protestant, and Catholic for nineteen centuries was simply voted out by General Conference action, making acceptable and "official" the ancient heresy of Pelagianism.[20] The Articles of Religion remained, of course, and could not be altered. Nor did the revivalists (who probably did not even know what was going on) change their preaching. But for the educational professionals, who took it as their call-ing to mediate enlightenment to Methodism, it was, as E. B. Chappell would declare, clear that the Methodist Episcopal churches had moved completely away from the Calvinistic conception concerning the spiri-tual status of the child.[21]

But these leaders were faced with a formidable task. It was one thing to reinterpret the Bible, introduce the theology of modernism, "correct" John Wesley, revise the hymnal and the church liturgy, and talk about how the "thinking of the church" had changed. It was another matter to convince ordinary Methodists who found the Bible and Wesley to be quite believable and acceptable that they were wrong and needed to be enlightened.

The strategy used to bring ordinary Methodists to a state of enlightenment was one based on centralization and control. In 1924, the General Conference of the M.E. Church consolidated all educational work under one board, called the Board of Education of The Methodist Episcopal Church. This meant, among other things, that Epworth League, still evangelical and up until this time responsible for youth education, would come under board (and modernist) control. A new philosophy called for a "comprehensive program of religious education," the purpose of which was to coordinate all educational efforts in one unified whole. As a result, control of all education in the Church on a denominational level would be consolidated into the hands of a few. As a part of the new approach, since education was all-encompassing and included all settings, the term "church school" would replace "Sunday school." In addition, all churches were to be encouraged and expected to use "official" materials.

In both The Methodist Episcopal Church and The Methodist Episcopal Church, South, this was accompanied with successful efforts to include books by liberal educators in the Conference Course of Study, establish chairs of religious education in the seminaries, engage in extensive teacher training in the new methods, and hire more religious education professionals at all levels of church life. In 1911, E. B. Chappell worked with only one assistant. By 1919, he had eight editorial assistants and thirteen administrative assistants.[22]

The 1920s and 1930s saw an increasing consolidation of power and influence in the hands of modernist educators. In 1937, Ethel L. Smither published the textbook *The Use of the Bible with Children*.[23] The book made plain that it was "official" and "approved" by the Board of Education of The Methodist Episcopal Church. It was not just one person's ideas; it was the thinking of "the Church."

Smither began the book with a discussion of "universal reconstruction"—the old ways were not adequate; the new ways must prevail. The learning of facts, doctrine, and Bible stories was no longer acceptable. What was acceptable was having "vital experiences" and associating them with the Bible. The purpose of Christian education was not to impart knowledge about God or the Bible or salvation, but character growth and personality development.[24]

According to Smither, when the Bible was used for this purpose with young children (with the added mention that the Bible was not God's only revelation), the teacher should start with incidents from the life and teaching of Jesus.[25] Other Bible material was unsuitable for children, unless it reflected a spirit of love, unselfishness, and purity. This ruled out the entire Old Testament, especially for children:

> A reason for withholding Old Testament material from younger children is that their picture of God may not be distorted by contact with various pre-Christian ideas. Many adults suffer from confused ideas of God today because of the teaching they received during childhood and have never outgrown. Old Testament conceptions of God should be withheld from children until they are able to place them in an historical setting. This ability does not develop before late childhood.[26]

Even much of the New Testament was of questionable value for nursery-age children. If any stories of Jesus were told, they should be associated with such things as flowers and birds, which were a part of small children's experience. Even the Christmas story should be used carefully. Children had no experience with shepherds and Magi, although the story might have some meaning if it stresses the mother's love and care for the baby, since that is within the children's experience. However a story about Jesus is told, it must always separate Jesus from God: "In speaking of Jesus to nursery children, teachers and parents will never confuse God and Jesus and use the two names interchangeably. Prayers will be addressed to God, not to Jesus. Song prayers addressed to Jesus will be avoided. Adults will . . . remember the immaturity of the child mind and introduce no theological statements."[27]

Most illustrated Bible storybooks, since they were compiled without discrimination, should be kept from children. Indeed most of what the Church and popular culture had used for religious education was now to be seen as unusable. Memory verses before primary age were a waste of time.[28] Although some Bible pictures could be a useful tool, pictures of angels, halos, and light from heaven should be avoided, at least through the primary years. Jesus should not be pictured on the cross. Juniors were old enough to begin to discuss Easter, though children under twelve would not have any understanding through experience of what the crucifixion or resurrection meant:

> Probably the best way to help children to understand the meaning of
> Easter is to give them opportunities of seeing life enriched and made
> more meaningful for others through their own efforts and through the
> heroic sacrificial efforts of Jesus and of the followers of Jesus. They
> should see all Christian service through the ages and today as efforts to
> follow in a limited way the experience of Jesus at Easter.[29]

While Smither made no mention of basic doctrines such as sin, faith, grace, salvation, heaven, and hell, and argued that the Bible was an adult book and much could not be understood by children, she did believe that the problems of society were understandable: "Juniors are now old enough to face directly such economic and social problems as working for peace and against economic and social inequalities and injustices. So units on these specialized subjects will be helpful for them."[30]

The reinterpretation of Christian faith as articulated by Smither and others became the educational orthodoxy in Methodism during the 1930s, 1940s, 1950s, and into the 1960s and was advanced with a rigidity that rivaled reactionary fundamentalism. During this period, the Board of Education not only was untouched by evangelical theology, but also seemed oblivious to neo-orthodoxy and other theological trends. The phrase "Boston mafia" referred to the fact that many of the curriculum leaders were graduates of Boston seminary and that Boston liberalism and personalism was entrenched in religious education.

Some of us who grew up in Methodist Sunday schools during the modernist era remember them well. My own personal impression of early childhood in a Methodist Sunday school centers on cheery robins and friendly postmen. Easter was daffodils and colored eggs. The story of Jesus and the five thousand featured the little boy who shared his fishes and loaves. Memory verses rotated between "God is love" and "Be ye kind to one another." I had periodically to explain to my Mennonite cousins who came to visit why we didn't have Bible stories in my Sunday school.

Meanwhile, my mother, theologically perceptive in many ways, made life miserable for a series of pastors for what was and wasn't being taught in Sunday school. Mother's analysis of the material in two words was "no cross." The pastors, good men all, appeared to agree with mother but indicated that since we were a prominent church in a county seat, it was inappropriate for us to use non-Methodist material. They seemed continually optimistic that better, more biblical material was promised and on the way.

In response, Mother, concerned about her children's Christian education, shipped my sisters and me off to five weeks of our Mennonite
cousins' Bible school each summer. There, with seven hundred other
kids, we violated every principle of enlightened Methodist Christian education. We memorized the Sermon on the Mount, heard Bible stories
galore, sang songs about fountains of blood flowing deep and wide, had
classes on the Westminster Catechism, spoke freely of sin and grace and
salvation, and were rewarded for our efforts with crosses that glowed in
the dark.

My own perception was that the "better, more biblical material" that
was always "on its way" never did arrive. At the same time, the pressures
to use "official" materials were unrelenting. The 1952 *Discipline* specified
that "Methodist connectionalism requires curriculums which contain the
present Methodist traditions, purposes, programs, and movements. Each
church school shall provide instruction in the curriculums approved by
the Curriculum Committee of the General Board of Education of the
Methodist Church."[31]

Despite all efforts to put a positive interpretation on what was behind
the paragraph, the ultimate effect of the legislation was to mandate that
only the teaching of modernism was acceptable in Methodist churches.
The phrase "present Methodist traditions" was in stark contrast to historic Methodist traditions. The mandate to conform was a blatant effort
at thought control. And the mandate included more than just printed
material. In 1956, legislation added to the paragraph that audiovisual
materials must be in harmony with Board of Education standards. And, if
that constriction were not enough, 1960 legislation also added that music
and hymnbooks must be in harmony with the Board of Education standards. In a crushing display of attempted bureaucratic control, the mediating elite had declared everything off-limits for use in Methodist Sunday
schools unless it met Board of Education (modernist) standards.[32] For
many Methodists, the hierarchical institution had created an oppressive
and stifling atmosphere.

Use of the approved material had by this time become the test for loyalty to the denomination. It was the first question asked me by my own
conference Board of Ministerial Training. About the same time I inter-
viewed with the cabinet of another conference to explore a possible relationship, the first question was, again, how did I feel about Methodist
Sunday school material. When I expressed some reservations, they
affirmed they were a conference that used Methodist material 100

percent. This was amazing to me since even as an outsider I knew of churches in their conference that didn't use the material. It was an early realization of the big difference between what was claimed and what was actually practiced in local churches.

Later as pastor, after a number of letters to editors of curriculum materials with the usual complaints, I received a reply that indicated that though the editor did not agree with me, he liked the way I expressed myself and would I be interested in writing some curriculum. And so, after the experience of writers' conferences and working with editors, and then as a part of the Good News Curriculum Task Force in working with various projects involving curriculum personnel, and later as a member-at-large of the Curriculum Resources Committee, I began to see "Nashville" (the word a number of people used to refer to the whole educational establishment) from the inside. With this came some definite impressions.

(1) By the 1970s, the educational enterprise was no longer driving the Church. During the heyday of modernism in the 1920s and 1930s, there was the feeling that those in the Board of Education, along with the seminaries, were the ideological leaders in the matter of the reconstruction of church ethos and theology. Modernism, and particularly modernism working through education, would bring in the kingdom. Education was the means by which the purposes of missions and evangelism and worship and social concerns would be accomplished. In the general church and on the annual conference level, staff positions in education were power positions.

In the 1968–72 quadrennium, the Board of Education was composed of thirty-nine members, thirty-seven of which were white male liberals. Only seven were pastors; thirteen were associated with universities or seminaries. Most of the rest were bishops and bureaucrats. Methodism had not yet discovered diversity, and a small, like-minded group wielded considerable power as the mediating elite.

But the combination of the Evengelical United Brethren-Methodist merger, the ensuing restructuring, and the social upheaval of the early 1970s brought rapid change. The 1972 restructuring ushered in the day of quotas and affirmative action.[33] It also effectively demoted church school education. Power in the church shifted to the new Board of Global Ministries. Higher Education and the Ministry and Church and Society were given status as "boards," while education, worship, evangelism, laity, and stewardship were all subsumed under the Board of Discipleship.

The decline in morale at the Board of Discipleship was noticeable. People in curriculum development—structurally a part of the publishing house—were no longer writing grand-schemed books about Jesus' program for the kingdom as they once had. Editors and writers no longer were setting the direction for the Church, but simply doing a job, namely, providing curriculum for the Church. In their skills, these editors and writers appeared to be journalists first, educators second, and theologians third.

Furthermore, the whole educational system was under attack, not just from evangelicals, but from the radical left. In the days of Vietnam protests and student demonstrations, the institutional church, and especially the Sunday school, was seen more and more as irrelevant. The modernist view that the purpose of the Sunday school was character development and preparing of persons for life's meanings did not inspire the Woodstock generation. The very term "Sunday school," in fact, became a term of derision—playing at niceness while the world burned.

With the new cultural ferment, United Methodism's youth ministry began to self-destruct. A new philosophy of youth ministry was developing in the 1960s, in which youth were to be given not answers, but rather tools so they could find answers for themselves. The new words were "freedom" and "equality." According to this philosophy, youth must be free—free to make mistakes, free to participate or to say no.[34]

In the early 1970s, college-age student radicals sought to seize youth ministry and, more important, the Youth Service Fund and operate it independently from church control. Church leaders, letting the "world set the agenda," actually applauded youth demonstrators after they disrupted the 1970 General Conference. The Methodist Youth Fellowship (MYF), the successor to Epworth League, was simply eliminated in the new 1972 structure. Its handbook, mottoes, banners, and adult-imposed organizational structure were seen as "Mickey Mouse." Those who claimed to represent United Methodist youth[35] demanded access to the decision-making structures of the Church. A new organization, the National Council on Youth Ministry, passed radical resolutions and set policies but did no youth ministry.

One such policy required that conferences could not be represented at jurisdictional or general Council on Youth Ministry meetings unless one-half of the delegates were ethnic minorities. Some conferences that could not or did not comply were refused vote; other conferences simply did not participate.

The National Council on Youth Ministry was voted out of existence at the 1976 General Conference (after a four-year life), but the disintegration of youth ministry continued. In 1967, there were 13 youth staff under the Methodist Board of Education, 15 secretaries, 52 full-time conference directors, and 1,200,000 pieces of curriculum material per quarter. By 1976, the merged church counted one part-time youth staff, one secretary, and 400,000 pieces of curriculum materials per quarter.[36] Giving to Youth Service Fund simply dried up. Church school enrollment declined from nearly seven million in 1966 to less than four million by 1985, and the youth decline was even greater.

At this point, the professional educators—had they been willing to recognize a problem—should have seen evangelicals as their greatest supporters. In a number of conferences, evangelicals organized youth caravans, summer camps, and youth rallies to meet the needs of local churches. Populist evangelicals were the mainstays in many United Methodist Sunday schools. Sunday school attendance was always strongest in the parts of the country where evangelical theology prevailed, and weakest (namely the Northeast and Western Jurisdictions) where liberalism prevailed.

But entrenched bureaucrats do not easily change. Educators simply did not agree with Good News's assessment that numbers of people were leaving The United Methodist Church for more evangelical churches and that children and youth ministry was the main reason. They also challenged the Good News assertion that fifty years of modernist and liberal theology was at the heart of the problem. But, for whatever reason, the church school was no longer at the center of the denomination's program.

(2) The people associated with the educational enterprise were good and honorable people, but they were out of touch with evangelical faith and practice. The liberal theology of the 1920s and 1930s had been in the system for so long that many professional religious educators understood modernism as orthodox Methodism. When Good News or others would talk about "evangelical" doctrine, practice, and ethos, the response was often a blank stare. A common perception on the part of the educators was that all who worked in curriculum development were evangelicals, and those who made further distinctions must surely be fundamentalist troublemakers.

An article entitled "Non-approved Church School Lesson Material Can Be Subversive" by Martin R. Chambers and printed in *The Church School,* is revealing. According to Chambers, the problem with "commercial" (read: "evangelical") publishers was that, among other things, they advanced doctrines in direct opposition to "present Methodist traditions, purposes, programs, and movements" (the point of view expressed in the *Discipline's* prohibition of such material).[37] Methodists, Chambers asserted, believe:

(1) the physical world is operated according to impartial, dependable laws (as opposed to miracles and supernaturalism);

(2) children at birth are neither perfect angels nor blackened sinners (as opposed to the idea of Original Sin); and

(3) there will be a final triumph of righteousness in the kingdom of God (as opposed to any view of the Second Coming).

The article argued that in some places these "heresies" (miracles, Original Sin, and the Second Coming) were standard Christian beliefs "but . . . were discarded years ago by the best of dedicated Bible scholars and are not acceptable today in present-day Methodism."[38] The rule against allowing churches to use non-approved lessons was to "protect the children, youth, and adults from doctrines repugnant to the Word of God and to common reason and to promote the purposes, and ideals of Christianity as understood in the Methodist Church in this generation."[39]

Chambers, and presumably the Christian education establishment he represented, not only claimed to interpret as "official" a form of Methodism at variance with the vast majority of ordinary Methodists, but also set himself and the educational establishment against nineteen hundred years of church tradition and the vast majority of all Christendom. Then he appealed to church law and the power of the institution to disallow all but the views of a select few.

A number of evangelicals had expressed hope that with The Methodist-Evangelical United Brethren (EUB) merger, the influx of more evangelical EUBs would moderate curriculum philosophy of the new denomination. EUBs had never bought into the extreme modernism of the Methodists. Consequently, what was produced as EUB literature through the decades was more acceptable to evangelicals. Furthermore, there was some but never as much pressure to use only "official" material in EUB churches. Could more evangelical EUBs serve to offer balance to Methodism's entrenched liberalism? Unfortunately, the answer seemed to be no. EUBs capitulated quickly and were soon absorbed into the Methodist system.[40]

The 1972 doctrinal statement gave Good News a new argument for inclusion of the evangelical perspective in curriculum matters. The statement introduced the word "pluralism," which, though offensive to evangelicals generally, did lend itself to the idea that evangelicals ought to have a place at the theological table. Whether because of the Good News argument or not, under the direction of the new editor of church school materials, Ewart Watts, the Curriculum Resources Committee appointed several evangelicals to serve on the committee,[41] formed the Task Force on Pluralism, and intentionally recruited several evangelical writers for curriculum. It also authorized a new series for children, Exploring the Bible, which made more use of the Bible with children than any children's curriculum had for fifty years.

But evangelicals wanted more. A token presence did not assure curriculum that could be used regularly and consistently without apology. Thus the argument was advanced for a separate track of material that would be acceptable to evangelicals.[42]

The idea was rejected immediately. The response was that the current system of material served all of United Methodism well. Separate tracks for separate groups would be divisive. The material was prepared in such a way that whether used by liberal or conservative, rural or city, black or white, one size fit all.[43]

The next test for evangelicals came with the confirmation materials of the newly merged denomination. The idea of confirmation, which had not been a part of Methodist practice, had been appropriated for use by the 1964 General Conference. Evangelicals initially tended to be suspicious of the idea since it suggested a high church theology and seemed to minimize the importance of conversion as the basis for church membership. Chuck Keysor, however, argued before the evangelical community that "confirmation" did not imply bad theology and should be associated with more intensive training in Methodism with an opportunity for a decision for Christ.[44]

Confirmation, however, arrived in Nashville at the same time as the EUB-Methodist restructuring and ended up as a kind of stepchild, with no one really responsible for thinking through the theology and the development of resources for the Church. The basic resource finally offered to pastors and congregations in 1972, *Confirming My Faith*—at least from an evangelical point of view—reflected all of the bad theology of the past fifty years. The emphasis was confirmation as responsible decision making with no mention of sin, the cross, redemption, or repentance.

In late 1974, Good News asked for a hearing with the Confirmation Task Force in order to seek resolution to a very serious problem, namely, that the materials did not truly reflect Methodist heritage and theologically could not be used in good conscience by evangelicals. Good News suggested some specific options that might make the confirmation situation tolerable for evangelicals: new resources or alternate resources or supplemental resources.[45]

Good News's suggestions were rejected. The "official" materials had been produced only recently, according to the Task Force, and it was too soon to think of revision. The Task Force further argued that circulation figures were good for the resources and that market research had indicated that the materials were serving the Church well. In addition, the Confirmation Task Force indicated it could not be held captive to special interest groups.

Good News then did its own research. Two thousand questionnaires were sent to pastors on the Good News mailing list. Of those who responded, only one-fourth indicated they were using the official materials. Of that one-fourth, many indicated they were doing so unwillingly and unhappily. Good News then began to prepare materials that could be used by the evangelical constituency. The basic writing was done by Riley Case,[46] with Chuck Keysor doing two lessons and Keysor and Diane Knippers doing the editing. The material, *We Believe*, was available in spring 1975.

Since Good News was still committed to working within the system, and since the *Discipline* made provisions for materials not prepared by regular channels to be approved for use in the Church, the *We Believe* materials were then presented to the Curriculum Resources Committee for review, with the request that they be given approval as supplemental materials.

A special task force read the Good News materials and recommended to the Curriculum Resources Committee that the Good News materials not be approved as "official" supplemental materials. According to the rationale, the issue was not whether the materials were good or whether they served a constituency in the Church. Rather, the committee argued that confirmation was different from church school materials and the *Discipline* was explicit that confirmation resources could be prepared only by the "official" confirmation committee. The Good News materials had not been so prepared.

But the committee then had a problem. It was pointed out that as a part of the "officially" advertised packet of materials for use in confirmation, items included were prepared by the National Council of Churches and even by the Division on Education of the Board of Discipleship. These materials had not been prepared by the "official" confirmation committee. Were these materials also "unofficial"? To be consistent, the committee declared they too were "unofficial." However, at the same meeting the Good News materials were rejected, and just six months after a report that the official materials were well received by the Church, the Curriculum Resources Committee announced that new market research indicated that 81 percent of pastors surveyed requested replacement or revision of *Confirming My Faith*. New materials would be produced, and the need was so urgent that the normal market testing and lengthy development process would be shortened or eliminated. The new materials could be prepared and offered to the Church possibly within the next nine months.[47]

The Good News materials were designed to address a void in the Church, namely, the need for materials faithful to historic Methodism. They were also designed to reflect the practices and ethos of many ordinary congregations. They assumed the pastor would be the teacher-leader and were written with pastors in mind. They were not conceived as a venture that might be financially profitable. However, as an unexpected by-product, *We Believe* materials almost instantly began showing a profit. Though not of publishing house quality and priced higher than the official materials, the materials entered their third printing within a year.[48] Because of the response, an adult version of *We Believe* was soon added.

With the success of *We Believe*, the Good News board began to see possibilities in other publishing projects. The evangelical resurgence in America was bringing a proliferation of Christian bookstores and new publishing ventures. Evangelical books, study guides, and curriculum lines were readily available for all Christians. It was obvious that United Methodist churches and United Methodist families were relying more and more on these offerings and less and less on materials produced by The United Methodist Publishing House. Though some of the new evangelical material was useful, some of it was also extreme in its teaching, reflecting dispensational sensationalism, various forms of Calvinism, or Pentecostalism at variance with historic Methodism. There was a need for literature that avoided the extremes of the theological right and the theological left.[49]

With this in mind, and since the publishing house seemed unable or unwilling to address the needs of United Methodist evangelicals, in 1987, Good News created the division Bristol Books as the publishing arm of Good News. Its first book, *Launching Out into the Deep,* by United Methodist evangelist Mark Rutland, was published in July 1987. By 1991, Bristol had published more than forty books, along with the newsletter *UMFacts* and the bulletin insert *Our Faith Today.* James S. Robb, son of Ed Robb and former editor of *Good News* magazine, served as publisher of Bristol, with Sara Anderson as the managing editor.

The philosophy of the Bristol division was to provide resources for evangelicals in The United Methodist Church—and even beyond the denomination—but not to duplicate efforts of the publishing house in the area of Sunday school literature or church studies. There was the sense that almost anything Bristol did would not be duplicating the publishing house since the publishing house was not seeking to address the needs of evangelicals.

It is interesting that though there was some concern on the part of United Methodist publishing and education people about whether Bristol would cut into market share, a greater concern was expressed by other evangelical publishers. These publishers would be concerned especially if Good News were to enter the Sunday school curriculum market. They— the independent publishers, not publishing house—stood to lose more if United Methodist evangelicals turned to Bristol for materials.[50]

Their fears were unfounded. The Bristol division was really a minor blip in the growing evangelical publishing business. Though Bristol did publish two very successful studies, *Basic Christian Beliefs* and *Living Morally in an Immoral Age,* not all of Bristol's titles sold well. Bristol was operating with limited capitalization and without a marketing director. Suddenly, instead of being a moneymaker for Good News, Bristol was becoming a financial drain.

In addition, Bristol was hampered by its policy of not competing with the publishing house. Though Sunday school material had always been the major complaint of United Methodist evangelicals, Bristol had not allowed itself to consider that market.

In May 1991, Bristol was purchased as an independent entity from Good News by a team of investors headed by John and Helen Rhea Stumbo. The office and staff of ten persons was moved from Wilmore to

Lexington, Kentucky, and then to Anderson, Indiana. Bristol refocused its publishing philosophy to reflect more nearly its original aim: to resource evangelicals in The United Methodist Church in the area of education. And since the biggest need seemed still to be Sunday school curriculum, and since Bristol was no longer officially a part of Good News, Bristol Books began to explore the possibility of producing dated Sunday school material. Sara Anderson was placed in charge of the operation.

A first agreement was made with Scripture Press to publish Scripture Press materials, edited by Bristol teams and reflecting United Methodist theology and ethos, under the Bristol imprint. But now Bristol had a different kind of problem. For years it had had to deal with the theological left; now it had to deal with the theological right. Material influenced by fundamentalism operated with assumptions, style, and theology different from that to which people associated with Good News evangelicals were accustomed. Bristol found itself doing extensive editing to ensure a faithful United Methodist perspective. Editing was addressed most extensively theologically in regard to themes of judgment, hell, and Satan, and in areas of inclusivity in regard to the place of women. An interesting by-product of the Bristol editing was the discussion and consideration within Scripture Press as to whether all Scripture Press material should reflect the kind of sensitivity reflected by Good News editing.

Bristol subsequently worked with the Nazarene Publishing House in 1997 to do an edited version of Word/Action dated material. This was a more satisfactory arrangement, and the Bristol market share expanded to include about five hundred United Methodist churches.

With the spinning off of Bristol Books, Good News became less and less involved in curriculum matters. There were several reasons for this:

(1) There was a growing recognition among United Methodist education leaders that in a church of diversity it was unrealistic to expect one line of curriculum materials to serve effectively all of United Methodism. Evangelicals were not alone in criticizing the "one size fits all" curriculum approach of the denomination. A number of ethnic groups and other special interest groups began to make the same critique. This lack of true diversity had for some time been admitted privately (but never officially) by a number of Nashville staff at the publishing house. It was also admitted by the staff that many independent publishers were producing materials sound in educational principles and more creative than had been true in the past. It became increasingly difficult to condemn all other publishers. District superintendents became less enthusiastic about

being enforcers of the "only official material" law.[51] With greater freedom to make their own curriculum choices, evangelicals had less reason to invest time and energy in trying to effect change that was slow to come.

(2) Unfortunately, some of United Methodism's brightest and best, including many who had been most vocal in their call for curriculum reform, had already opted for other denominations and groups. Families who were choosing new churches bypassed United Methodist churches because of a perceived idea that United Methodist churches disdained sound Bible teaching.[52] In other words, many of the alleged "troublemakers" left.

(3) Good News found its energies directed to other concerns: missions, seminaries, church funding, doctrine, abortion, and homosexuality. Good News eventually phased out its Curriculum Task Force in the late 1980s.

(4) Perhaps in part because of Good News's influence, curriculum materials in the late 1980s and 1990s became more evangelical-friendly. Some of what Good News had requested came to pass.

In 1973, when Dr. Frank Warden of Dallas, Texas, was a member of the Good News board, he shared his vision of an intensive Bible study based on the popular Bethel Bible series, but from a United Methodist perspective. The idea was shared with persons in Nashville but was rejected, with the explanation that United Methodists were not interested in a content-based, intensive Bible study. Warden developed the idea on his own, and the Trinity Bible series became very successful. In the early 1990s, staff at the Board of Discipleship and The United Methodist Publishing House warmed to the intensive Bible study idea and the Disciple Bible study was launched. The series became one of the publishing house's most successful ventures. Good News observers noted that a content-centered, intensive Bible series that sought to be theologically balanced could be successful.

In the late 1990s, an earlier Good News idea began to take shape. Conversations were initiated between Neil Alexander, president and publisher of the publishing house, and John Stumbo, of Bristol Books, exploring the possibility of a line of curriculum materials produced jointly by the publishing house and Bristol Books. The result was *Faith Files* and its accompanying midweek program *Clues Club*.

For a number of evangelicals, this cooperative effort came too late. For others, however, this was a sign of healing in the Church. The Good News reaction was, if this could happen in the area of curriculum, why not in the area of missions or seminary education or social action?

CHAPTER FOUR

DOCTRINE GONE ASTRAY

Evangelical - Of those Protestant churches, as the Methodist and Baptist, that emphasize the salvation by faith that is in Jesus.
(Webster's New Twentieth Century Dictionary Unabridged, *1971*)

Evangelical - Pertaining to or designating any school of Protestants which holds that the essence of the gospel consists mainly in its doctrines of man's sinful condition and need of salvation, the revelation of God's grace in Christ, the necessity of spiritual renovation, and participation in the experience of redemption through faith.
(Webster's New Collegiate Dictionary, *1961*)

Evangelical - Of or having to do with the Protestant churches that emphasize Christ's atonement and salvation by faith as the most important parts of Christianity, as the Methodists and Baptists.
(Thorndike Barnhart Comprehensive Desk Dictionary, *1958*)

I can remember on more than one occasion, in the early days of Good News, discussing with Charles Keysor what descriptive term or label should be used to describe best Methodism's "silent minority." Like many before him, Keysor wondered why what had always been historic Christianity had to be identified by any label. The very word "Christian" should imply evangelical, catholic, and Bible believing. But labels were necessary to clarify and help identify perspectives. Keysor was reluctant to use the word "evangelical," despite the fact that the word was the preferred choice for those Christians who supported Billy Graham and Campus Crusade and altar calls and *Christianity Today*. Keysor's reasoning was that in the United Methodist setting, the word was so misused it carried no special meaning. Seminary professors called themselves evangelicals. Editors of the denomination's curriculum materials called themselves evangelicals. If everyone was evangelical, then no one was evangelical. Furthermore, the criticism was voiced on different occasions that when Good News used the word "evangelical" to refer to itself, the implication was that others were not evangelical and there was a certain arrogance in that kind of thinking.

But the options to the word "evangelical" presented problems just as great. The word "fundamentalist" had become a pejorative term associated with separatism, dispensationalism, and literalism. The word "neo-evangelical" was being used at the time to refer to those persons who had moved beyond fundamentalism to a new spirit of openness; but Keysor believed that if the Methodist world was confused about "evangelical," they would be even more confused about "neo-evangelical." Keysor liked the word "orthodox" because his concern was for orthodox theology, but that word had never been associated with the revivalist branch of Methodism. Early issues of the magazine often spoke of "Bible-believing" Methodists, but that phrase invited criticism that Good News assumed that those who were not Good News supporters were not Bible believing. "Conservative" was not acceptable, because the word was often used to refer to politics and social stances and would invite misunderstanding.

And so we always came back to the word "evangelical." The word historically had been used to identify a form of Christianity that contrasted with sacramentalism (the essence of the faith was in the sacraments), confessionalism (the essence of the faith was in creeds), or liberalism (the essence of the faith needed to be adjusted to the ways of modern thinking). In the American setting, the word suggested the proclamation of the themes of sin, atonement, and grace, and the experience of the new birth. Or to put it another way, in the American setting, the word suggested early Methodism.

This is verified by a survey of earlier dictionaries. These dictionaries link the word "evangelical" with an approach to Christianity that emphasizes certain doctrines: Original sin, the Atonement, justification by faith, and the new birth. Furthermore, the dictionaries sometimes explicitly associate the word with Baptists and Methodists. One could argue that the word was used not only to describe Methodists and Baptists, but also to suggest that what Methodists and Baptists believed and preached helped define the very word itself.

The claim is sometimes made that The Methodist Church (including the various branches that were separated or unseparated by mergers and splits) was never a confessional church. That is true in one sense:

Methodism came into being not by way of doctrinal controversy, but in a revival. Neither Wesley nor the American General Conferences nor the revivalists ever claimed that the essence of Methodism was in a creed such as the Westminster Confession (Presbyterians) or the Augsburg Confession (Lutherans). Methodism was a unique combination of belief and practice, of doctrine and experience and holy living (including social holiness).

But there was never, or at least should not be, any mistaking that Methodism was a confessing church, if not a confessional church. That is to say, Methodism was committed to the historic teaching of the Church. For Wesley, there was a catholic faith once delivered to all the saints, which he understood to be summarized in the early councils, in the creeds of the church, and in the Thirty-nine Articles of the Church of England. Methodism did not seek to add to or subtract from that faith, but rather to make it come alive through preaching, teaching, and living. Dead orthodoxy could not save, but what did save—God's power working in the hearts of humankind—was based on the doctrinal truths of the historic faith.[1]

One of the geniuses of early Methodism was the ability to distinguish between "opinions," "distinctive" Methodist teachings, and "essential" truths. Opinions, according to Wesley in his famous sermon "Catholic Spirit," had to do with such things as mode of worship, matters of church government, mode of baptism, the Lord's Supper, or to what denomination one belonged. Methodists were not to let matters of opinion stand in the way of true fellowship. "Think and let think" was the motto, and "If your heart is as my heart give me your hand" the slogan.

Methodism's "distinctive" teachings grew out of the revival. The Methodists preached the doctrine of unlimited atonement (Christ died for all, so that all could be saved, as opposed to the Calvinistic view that Christ died only for the elect),[2] the doctrine of Assurance (we can know we are saved by the witness of the Spirit), and the doctrine of Holiness (we can be cleansed from inward sin). But even these "distinctive" teachings, as dear to Methodists as they were, were never confused with the "essentials" of the faith.

Essentials were another matter. These were the truths that distinguished Christianity from false religions, whether deism or Socinianism or other religions. Wesley could disagree with Calvinists, Quakers, and Roman Catholics, but he recognized that they shared with him belief in the core of Christianity and thus were to be accepted as brothers and sisters in Christ. When his friend George Whitefield, who had, to Wesley's disappointment, become a Calvinist, died, Wesley spoke these words at his funeral:

> Let us keep close to the grand scriptural doctrines which he everywhere delivered. There are many doctrines of a less essential nature, with regard to which even the sincere children of God . . . are and have been divided for many ages. In these we may think and let think; we may "agree to disagree." But meantime let us hold fast the essentials of "the faith which was once delivered to the saints," and which this champion of God so strongly insisted on at all times and in all places.[3]

Wesley was a preacher, not a systematic theologian, and never in one place articulated a clear list of all that he considered to be "essential doctrines."[4] It should be incontrovertible, however, that no matter how the list is formed, it would include the doctrines of original sin, the Atonement, and salvation by faith, which are the cardinal truths of evangelical preaching.

Of original sin, Wesley wrote:

> All who deny this, call it "original sin," or by any other title, are but heathens still, in the fundamental point which differences Heathenism from Christianity. They may, indeed, allow that men have many vices; . . . But here is the shibboleth: Is man by nature filled with all manner of evil? Is he void of all good? Is he wholly fallen? Is his soul totally corrupted? Or to come back to the text, is "every imagination of the thoughts of his heart only evil continually"? Allow this, and you are so far a Christian. Deny it, and you are but an Heathen still.[5]

> But there is no "good news" in the doctrine of original sin. The importance of emphasizing original sin is to make clear that it is only by God's grace that persons can be saved, and if it is by grace it is only through the Atonement.

> The gospel (that is, good tidings, good news for guilty, helpless sinners), . . . means the whole revelation made to men by Jesus Christ. . . . The substance of all is, "Jesus Christ came into the world to save sinners"; or, "God so loved the world, that He gave His only-begotten Son, to the end we might not perish, but have everlasting life"; or, "He was bruised for our transgressions, He was wounded for our iniquities, the chastisement of our peace was upon Him; and with His stripes we are healed."

> Believe this, and the kingdom of God is thine.[6]

For early Methodists, such truths as original sin, the Atonement, and salvation by grace through faith were not dead doctrines to be believed only with the head, but living truths on which God's work of salvation rested. Wesley was not a systematic theologian who sought to pull together all truth in one grand systematic scheme, but Wesley was a preaching and singing theologian who believed that Christian truth could be understood by all people. Doctrine was never meant to be some esoteric truth to be considered only by professional theologians or the ordained clergy or any kind of mediating elite, but by the whole people of God. The truth informed the heart as well as the head.

And though individual doctrines, such as original sin, could be discussed separately, all of the essential doctrines were part of one whole, sometimes expressed as the "Order of Salvation." This "Order of Salvation" was so crucial that Wesley, and Methodists who followed, organized their hymnbooks to reflect the doctrinal progression.

Provisions and Promises of the Gospel

    The Sinner

        Depravity

        Awakening

        Inviting

        Penitential

    The Christian Life

        Justification by Faith

        Adoption and Assurance

        Sanctification[7]

In American Methodism in the 1800s, there was striking unanimity in the preaching and teaching of these doctrines. Methodists had their differences. They sometimes disagreed over the place and authority of bishops, but they together taught that Christ died for our sins. They argued over slavery and lay representation and the place of women in the church, but they agreed that humankind was fallen and in need of a savior. Methodists fought over cultural matters, over the use of organs and robed choirs and rented pews and plain dress, but they together were of one mind that the blood of Jesus Christ cleanses from all sin. Whether bishops, circuit-riding lay pastors, camp meeting revivalists, Sunday school teachers, or hymnwriters, all followed the essential truths: sin, Atonement, faith, salvation.

These themes were everywhere reflected in Methodist practice and preaching, in Wesley's hymns or camp meeting spirituals, in the catechisms, in books and pamphlets, in protracted meetings, or in college chapels.

Hundreds of thousands of Methodists memorized question one of the Standard Catechism:

> What is Christianity?
> Christianity is the religion of God's redeeming love manifested in the incarnate life, the atoning death, and the glorious resurrection of Jesus Christ, the Founder of the Kingdom of God. [8]

Methodist hymnals always carried "O For a Thousand Tongues to Sing" as the first hymn:

> He breaks the power of canceled sin,
> he sets the prisoner free;
> his blood can make the foulest clean; his blood availed
> for me.[9]

Methodist camp meeting songbooks started with a different hymn:

> There is a fountain filled with blood drawn from
> Emmanuel's veins;
> and sinners plunged beneath that flood lose all their
> guilty stains.[10]

Matthew Simpson, perhaps the most influential bishop of the nineteenth century after Francis Asbury, summarized Methodist doctrine with these words:

> It teaches the natural depravity of the human heart; the atonement made by the Lord Jesus Christ as a sufficient sacrifice for the sins of the whole world; that salvation is offered to every individual on condition of repentance toward God and faith in our Lord Jesus Christ; that a man is justified by faith in our Lord Jesus Christ; that a man is justified by faith alone, but that good works follow and flow from a living faith.[11]

This to Methodists was gospel. It was not uniquely Methodist, for it was also, with variations, Presbyterian, Congregationalist, Lutheran, and Baptist. But in its Methodist and Baptist forms, as it was preached and taught and sung, it defined the word "evangelical."

But this understanding of the gospel would come to be challenged not from outside the Church, but from within the Church. Starting in the 1890s, American Protestantism, or at least a part of it, became enamored with a different gospel, an understanding of religion that would eventually be known as "modernism." It was a time of cultural and intellectual ferment. A number of developments were taking place at the same time in the intellectual world: Darwinism and the acceptance of the theory of evolution, the new field of psychology, a new trust in reason, German enlightenment scholarship that sought to analyze the Bible like any other human book, and a new confidence in science and the scientific method.

This period is also known as "the gilded age," a time of extravagant wealth (at least for a few), ostentatious living, and philanthropy. An expanding colonialism related ideas of progress and democracy to expectations that a Christian civilization could eventually win the world and bring in the kingdom of God. In this new order, the Church was no longer seen as the bride of Christ, separated from the world, to be presented without spot or wrinkle at the return of the Lord. Rather the Church was seen as a change agent, as the moral and spiritual leader in the creation of the new society. Politics, education, business, labor, religion—all would work together to bring about this Christianized society. With this new understanding came the conviction that the Church and the Church's theology must be brought in line with the new understanding of the world.

While this was taking place, there was also a reaction to the excesses of revivalism and the obsession with holiness within Methodism. The phrase "shouting Methodist" was not worn as a badge of honor by all Methodists. The growing cultural and intellectual sophistication of many Methodists, especially in the cities and in church-related colleges and seminaries, led to the discounting and eventual rejection on the part of church leaders to the emotionalism and anti-intellectual tendencies of populist Methodism.[12] Within a few short years, from 1895 to 1920, a part of Methodism would be so swept away and dominated by the new theology that it would not only neglect, but also actually deny, that which it had always proclaimed, namely, the authority of Scripture and the doctrines of original sin, the Atonement, and justification by faith.

The revision started in the seminaries but soon spread to the Board of Education and then to the General Conferences and the Council of Bishops. One of the earliest revisionists was Borden Parker Bowne (1847–1910). Like many modernists of his day, Bowne studied in Europe. He then took a teaching position at Boston in 1876, where he remained until his death in 1910. Bowne published 17 books and over 130 articles, but he was known primarily as the professor who influenced future bishops and philosophers and educators.

Bowne fashioned and then introduced to Methodism a philosophy known as personalism or personal idealism, a unique Methodist version of modernism, in which the self (personality) becomes the ultimate standard that judges other truth claims.

What Bowne and the other modernists did was to associate revelation with the human mind rather than with the Scriptures, define gospel more as the coming kingdom of God (a sort of politicized Christian democracy) rather than the news that Christ died for our sins, emphasize philosophy of religion rather than of theology, understand the human problem more as ignorance than as sin, shift the essence of faith from doctrine to "values," and see the church as a human institution for change rather than as the mystical body of Christ.

Following the German liberalism and rationalism of Friedrich Schleiermacher and Albecht Ritschl, Bowne and other modernists also sought to redirect the "essence" of religion from Scripture and creeds and conceptual truth to religious experience. In this area, it was easier for Wesleyans to make the modernism shift than it was for Calvinists, since Wesleyans had always held experience in high regard, whether the new birth, or assurance, or sanctification.

Heresy charges were brought against Bowne in 1904. Bowne was charged with denying the Atonement, the Trinity, and the existence of miracles, and generally with teaching doctrines contrary to the Articles of Religion and the established standards of doctrine of The Methodist Episcopal Church. Bowne was not convicted. The charges were brought fifteen years too late. By 1904, Bowne was a popular professor who had been at his post at Boston for twenty-eight years. Many of the leading pastors in New England, including those who were called to sit in judgment on him, had been his students, and the Church was already set on its course toward modernism.

At the time, many believed the Church needed to choose between exciting new thought and dead orthodoxy. Whatever the doctrinal standards had been in the past, "standards" ought not now stand in the way of progress. A new ruling class in Methodism had come on the scene and essentially had decreed that the essentials were no longer essential. The core did not hold. Christian truth was at the mercy of modern thought. Heresy, the idea that certain beliefs were outside the bounds of the faith, was ruled obsolete. If Bowne could not be convicted of denying the doctrines of the Church, then no one could be convicted. After Bowne, there was nothing that could be taught or denied by seminary professors that would make them unacceptable as teachers in Methodist seminaries. Heresy trials would cease to exist not because of an absence of heresy, but because of the lack of will to take doctrine seriously.

There were, of course, many who were still supporters of the *Discipline* and the doctrinal standards. Through the 1890s, a number of articles in *The Christian Advocate* warned against evolution, destructive criticism of the Bible, and the seeming disregard for evangelical doctrine. This was accompanied by articles in other journals and by presentations and books by persons such as Bishop Benjamin F. Neely, J. H. Creighton, professor John A. Faulkner, O. J. Moore (a pastor from Denver), James Buckley (editor), Leander W. Munhall (lay evangelist), and H. A. Boaz (college president).[13]

The common perception that there was little resistance in Methodism to the modernist juggernaut is not true. It is true, however, that none of the seminaries or any major seminary professor took up the cause of historic Christianity. Those who did speak were primarily pastors and evangelists. The voices were not organized and were basically ineffective in slowing or even moderating the modernist takeover of the denomination. The Methodist Episcopal Church became the first of the major denominations whose institutions and official leadership committed to the new religion known as modernism. In other denominations, the struggle was longer lasting and more intense. Conservatives, particularly among Presbyterians and Baptists, who sought to defend the fundamentals of the faith became known as fundamentalists. The ensuing religious wars most intense during the 1920s, became known as the "fundamentalist-modernist controversy."

The Methodist Episcopal Church, South was probably a decade behind the northern Church in its willingness to embrace modernism, at least officially. In the southern Church, the one seminary, Vanderbilt, was the counterpart to Boston in the north, and its dean, Wilbur Fisk Tillett, a more cautious version of Borden Parker Bowne.

The episcopal address at the 1906 General Conference of The Methodist Episcopal Church, South included this statement: "We deeply deplore the hasty, callow, dogmatic declaration of destructive critics which have rudely jostled the faith of many believers in that one book 'in which we find the only infallible rule of faith and practice.'"[14] However, the same General Conference called for a new statement of faith with these words: "While affirming our absolute faith in the Twenty-five Articles of Religion, we do not believe that in their present form they meet the existing needs of the Church as a statement of the doctrinal system of evangelical Arminianism."[15]

Wilbur Fisk Tillett of Vanderbilt understood this action as meaning that a commission with representatives of worldwide Methodism would gather together to write a new creed.[16] In expressing need for the creed, he referred to Francis J. McConnell of the northern Church. According to Tillett, McConnell, a popular speaker on college campuses and a leader of liberal forces, had indicated "not less than a thousand individual students . . . [have] asked him for some brief and authoritative statement of our faith, and he had to his regret to tell them that there was nothing of the kind in existence to which he could refer them."[17] It is evident that, for McConnell, neither the catechism nor the Articles of Religion nor the sermons of Wesley could function among thinking people as the basis for Methodist belief.

McConnell (later Bishop McConnell), it seems, was everywhere across the Church both north and south, proclaiming the new theology. When the southern Church, in an effort to calm the furor brought about by modernist inroads, published the series of articles "The Fundamental Doctrines of Methodism," which laid special emphasis on evangelical doctrines of original sin, the Atonement, and the authority of Scripture, Francis McConnell contributed an article that basically denied what everybody else in the series had written.[18] McConnell identified Methodism's fundamental "doctrines" as Christian experience, sanctification, and the belief that children grew up Christians without having to experience a sense of sin.

McConnell later, in 1916, after he was elected bishop, expanded these ideas in the book *The Essentials of Methodism*.[19] McConnell's emphasis on the importance of conversion and sanctification must have sounded good to the readers of his day, but it was a strange and typically modernist reinterpretation of conversion and sanctification. For McConnell, conversion was to "surrender to divine forces which play around and upon him" and had nothing to do with original sin, the Incarnation, or the Atonement.[20] Indeed, the cross was not even mentioned in the book. Depravity was mentioned only to dismiss it as "not an essential Methodist doctrine." The key to Methodism, according to McConnell, was in experience. Sanctification was "bringing all parts of life under subjection to the law of the Kingdom."[21]

By 1920, modernism basically controlled Methodism, at least institutional Methodism, in both the north and the south. The colleges, the seminaries, the pastors' schools, the Courses of Study, the Church press, the Sunday school material, the Church agencies, and finally even the Council of Bishops were, or would soon be, in the hands of modernists. When Harold Paul Sloan and others made an heroic attempt at the 1924 and 1928 General Conferences to contain the spread of modernism and appeal to the Church not to forsake its doctrinal heritage, they were simply too late.

It must be emphasized that, even while this was developing, populist evangelicalism was largely untouched by modernism. This was observed by no less than *Christian Century*. In an article entitled "What Is Disturbing the Methodists?" the editors commented on Methodism's reputation for doctrinal disinterest.[22] Methodists might purge their rolls for lapses of conduct but never for charges of doctrinal heresy. Therefore, so stated the article, Methodists, or at least Methodist leaders, ridiculed the idea that their Church was disturbed by doctrinal and biblical matters, or, for that matter, by anything. To paraphrase Wesley, a member could do what he pleased theologically as long as his work prospered and his church wasn't disturbed. Bishops tended not to interfere in doctrinal matters except to keep men of premillennial views from places of importance. The editors commented that for years, articles on theological issues in Methodist magazines had been about as conspicuous as laudations of the liquor traffic.

However, the article went on to explain, it was hardly true to say that Methodists were not disturbed. The truth was that hundreds, perhaps thousands, of Methodist preachers were in a mood of incipient revolt, and it would tax the ingenuity of denominational leaders to make the organization function and not goad these ministers into open rebellion.

Bishops in the Methodist system, according to the editors, saw their job as keeping peace, denying that unrest really exists, and eliminating issues that might lead to problems. However, this was now no easy task. Ministers no longer believed bishops to be legendary creatures who appeared as often as Halley's comet. Now they were assigned to areas and were seen as mere mortals.

The present outcry was caused by a bishop (Bishop Edgar Blake) who had mentioned in an article that belief in the virgin birth of Jesus was not essential for salvation. The article explained: If the extent of this outcry had not reached the larger world, it was because of the unique way Methodists functioned.

Ministers, it was to be understood, came in three grades. The grades were actual, not technical. The upper grade consisted of bishops, secretaries of agencies, men in seminaries, men in detached services, and men who served the "big" churches. They were influential, prestigious men who had attended the seminary and ruled the denomination. They were also progressive and liberal. Through them, the liberal tone of Sunday school material had advanced beyond that of any other denomination, except perhaps for the Congregationalists. These men, trained as they were in historical studies, had no problem with new kinds of thinking.

The second grade, the editors continued, consisted of those men who aspired to be part of grade one, who had probably gained entrance to the itinerant ministry by the Conference Course of Study and pastored the medium-sized churches. The low grade consisted of men with limited education who served the churches with the slimmest of financial resources. These were lay pastors and pastors of churches in rural areas. Their numbers were not small. Thirty-five hundred of these low-grade pastors had not passed the seventh grade. Four thousand of these pastors made up the bulk of Methodist ministry.

The article now explained the problem: A rebellion was taking place in the middle and lowest grades. These ministers had not yet been caught up in the latest developments. Their rebellion was disturbing the Methodist tranquillity. And so the Methodists, like Baptists and Presbyterians, had not escaped the present controversies. Only they were disturbed in a different way.

Christian Century observed perceptively what has been called in this study the gap between populist evangelicals and the denomination's mediating elite. The article was written at a time when in the southern Church only 12 percent of the pastors had seminary training. It assumed, however, that the disturbances were only temporary until such time as Methodist clergy would be duly educated in the newer ways.

What *Christian Century* observed was confirmed by an extensive study published in 1929 by George Herbert Betts of Northwestern. In his study,

The Beliefs of 700 Ministers and their Meaning for Religious Education, Betts sought to determine what beliefs could be taught in religious education with any certainty.[23] Betts sought an answer to his question in the actual beliefs of ministers:

> All formal creeds aside, what do the ministers of our churches believe? Do they agree in the main on their beliefs within a single denomination? Do the denominations agree with each other on the great fundamental matters of the Christian faith? Can we of the masses find in our spiritual leaders a certainty of belief on the crucial questions of religion such as warrants our trusting their insight? On Sunday mornings the minister leads us of the congregation in a confession of belief called the Apostles' Creed. Does he expect and desire us to believe the assertions of this creed? Does he himself believe them? What, in short, have the clergy to teach us about belief by the simple and concrete method of telling us what they themselves believe?[24]

Betts sent survey sheets to 1,500 different Protestant ministers in the Chicago area. He received 700 returns, 200 of which were returned by students in seminary. The largest number of responders were Methodist, but Baptists, Congregationalists, Episcopalians, Lutherans, Evangelicals, and Presbyterians also responded, along with a group called "others."

Among the denominations, the Congregationalists were the most liberal, followed by the Methodists. The question regarding the virgin birth is illustrative. Ninety percent of Lutherans affirmed the virgin birth, followed by 80 percent of Baptists and Evangelicals, 69 percent of Presbyterians, 54 percent of Methodists, and 25 percent of Congregationalists.

Was Jesus' death on the cross the one act that made remission of sin possible? Ninety-nine percent of Lutherans believed so, followed by 78 percent of Evangelicals, 75 percent of Baptists, 67 percent of Presbyterians and Episcopalians, 60 percent of Methodists, and 20 percent of Congregationalists.

Betts was concerned that whatever denominations believed they be somewhat consistent within themselves. In this category, Methodists were dead last of the denominations. Eighty percent of Lutherans could agree on forty-four of fifty-six items and were the most unified. For Methodists, however, 80 percent could agree on only eleven items.

What evangelicals might conclude from this study is that the state of the Church was in chaos. Betts, however, drew a different conclusion:

"From this showing within denominations one conclusion can be reached: No denomination except perhaps the Lutherans has any right to demand that fixed creeds shall be taught the young. For the clergy of any denomination themselves do not subscribe to a common creed beyond belief in the existence of a God."[25]

The most revealing part of Betts's study was in the comparison in beliefs between seminary students and pastors of charges. Betts spoke about what the Church would be like in the next few decades based on the beliefs of the seminary students. His conclusion? "The beliefs of the students reflect a more distinct drift away from the older or orthodox positions and a tendency to be in accord with the scientific thought of the day."[26]

Seventy-one percent of pastors believed in the virgin birth, but only 25 percent of students did. Seventy percent of pastors believed that Jesus' death on the cross was the one act that made possible the remission of sins, compared with 29 percent of students. Fifty-three percent of pastors believed that persons are born with natures wholly perverse, sinful, and depraved, compared with 13 percent of students.

What were the implications of the study for the future teaching of the Church? Betts asserted that the Church cannot teach what its leaders do not believe. Therefore, a new system of beliefs should be constructed based on what ministers, the leaders of the Church, actually believe. Betts's new "minimum statement of belief" was indeed minimum and included items such as: There is a supreme being; God's relation to man is that of Father; Jesus on earth was subject to temptation as are other men; Jesus met his problems and difficulties using only those powers and resources available to all men; life continues after death; God operates on human lives through the agency and person of the Holy Spirit.

What was missing on Betts's list are references to sin, the church, Jesus Christ as the Son of God, the death of Christ on the cross for atonement of sin, and the necessity of the new birth. In other words, if Betts's recommendations were to be taken seriously, all of the doctrines that had once been considered essential Christian beliefs were to be considered essential no more. The Church had moved on to "higher" levels.

One can argue that Betts's study was not truly representative, at least not representative of Methodism. Methodism was still very much a rural denomination. Betts's study was concentrated on an urban area. Laypersons were not even polled, and supposedly they had something to say about what the church was actually believing. Indeed, to base the future on only the thinking of the clergy was just another example of the tendency to filter the course of the Church through the wisdom of its "mediating elite."

Still, the study was most revealing about what was ahead for Methodism and for the rest of mainline Protestant theology. Future bishops and seminary professors and large church pastors would come from the ranks of the seminary students polled. When Charles Keysor would write in 1970 that evangelicals had spent the previous forty years in Babylonian captivity, he knew whereof he spoke.

From the evangelical perspective of some years later, it is possible to make the following observations about the rise of modernism and official Methodism's casting aside of historic Methodist doctrine:

(1) The modernist impulse was primarily doctrinal in nature. It was doctrinal even as it sought to depreciate the importance of doctrine and shift the emphasis of religions to experience. It tended to cut the core out of Christian faith and substitute it with liberal culture religion.

A part of Methodism for a number of years had sought to find a place among the nation's intellectual, political, and business elite for the followers of Wesley. It took pride in Methodism's magnificent church structures, in its refined music, in its system of colleges that had passed all other denominations, and in the great number of business and professional leaders among its ranks. It was uneasy with orthodoxy's uncritical fascination with virgin births, Noah's arks, and bloody fountains. It disdained the emotionalism of revivals and camp meetings and Holiness gatherings. It also bridled under "old-fashioned Methodism's" preaching against worldliness, including prohibitions against card-playing, movies, theaters, cigarettes, and ostentatious dress.

Up until the time of modernism, however, whatever the other conflicts, Methodism had not been willing to compromise the cross of Jesus Christ in its quest for respectability. For modernism, it was not just the excesses of Methodism that were an embarrassment, it was the core of the faith itself: the Bible as the written revelation of God, original sin, the supernatural intervention of a transcendent God into human affairs, the Atonement, and the Resurrection.

Once the core of doctrine was compromised, liberal Methodism began to look and act and talk like the secular elitist culture into which it was being absorbed. In the new way of thinking, truth was truth wherever it was found; and if the Bible was in conflict with naturalistic science, it was assumed that the Bible, not the assumptions of naturalistic science, was wrong.

Education no longer stressed doctrinal truth and Bible knowledge, but stressed process, encouraging people to think for themselves and form their own beliefs. Sin was not rebellion against God, but ignorance. Salvation was not so much rescue from judgment as it was psychological wholeness. The work of the Church was not so much bringing people into a saving relationship with Jesus Christ as it was proclaiming "the kingdom," a political and economic order that felt and sounded very much like secular socialism. Modernism sought to remove the sharp edges of the gospel and in doing so reduced Christianity to the kind of bland religion-in-general that would characterize so much of United Methodism in years to come.

(2) Modernism was an elitist movement that sought to impose its ideology on grassroots Methodism by institutional control that disdained and disallowed much of the populist evangelical ethos that was Methodism.

American Methodism in its early days had been a movement in which spiritual power was directly accessible to every believer through the Holy Spirit. Truth did not have to be filtered or mediated through a pope or through educated clergy or through institutional curia. Spiritual gifts trumped educational degrees and institutional controls. This spiritual immediacy is what made Methodism so appealing to black believers, to people on the frontier, and to the uneducated and the poor.

There had been inceasing reaction to this sort of unrestrained populism throughout the nineteenth century, but with the rise of modernism, the reaction took the urgency of a campaign. Methodism had to be directed and controlled by those more qualified to lead it. In matters of doctrine, people such as Borden Parker Bowne led the way:

> The Church has need of a body of scholarly investigators to do its intellectual work. They will have the function of formulating the spiritual life so as best to express it and keep it from losing its way in swamps of ignorance and superstition. They will have to adjust religious thought to the ever advancing thought of cultivated intelligence so as to remove endless misunderstanding.[27]

For Bowne personally, it was not only uneducated laypeople who were placed in the "swamps of ignorance and superstition." Bowne was willing to place the conservative clergy and bishops in such swamps as well and presumably the whole evangelical world who did not agree with him.[28] Before modernism, Methodist prophets railed against unbelief and worldliness and coldness of heart. Modernists turned the message upside down: It railed against narrow belief, lack of appreciation for the world, and emotional excesses. Its sharpest barbs directed not at the secular world, but at Christian orthodoxy and the unwillingness to change: "Orthodoxy has frequently been a synonym for ignorance, dullness, narrow mindedness and narrow heartedness generally. . . . Crass obstinancy and inertia or stupidity will be found in the conservative camps as a matter of course."[29]

Modernists saw themselves as the enlightened leaders who should control the future of the church. Orthodox doctrine was not only a crude anachronism and thus irrelevant, but also a stumbling block to progress. Modernist ideology, instead of being one option among several, was to be made "official" Methodism and all other points of view were to conform or be considered disloyal.

The 1920s were not days of easy tolerance. The struggle over doctrine in the mainline denominations was referred to as the fundamentalist-modernist controversy. Fundamentalism, usually associated with Presbyterians and Baptists, was an orthodox reaction against the liberalism of the times and carried features far in excess of the evangelicalism of the nineteenth century.[30] Modernists were accused of apostasy and unbelief. In return, modernists declared fundamentalism an outdated theology that should be purged from the Church. *Christian Century* argued that modernism and fundamentalism were incompatible. They were two worldviews, two sets of moral ideals, two systems of personal attitudes, and two separate religions. They could not both be right.[31]

Under this assumption, modernists in The Methodist Church sought to control, first of all, books read by clergy in the Course of Study.[32] The sharpest conflict between liberals and conservatives in the denomination in the early twentieth century was over such books. Control over worship and educational materials soon followed. Within a few years, modernists dominated the seminaries, the educational enterprise (from colleges to Sunday school material), the Church press, and the church agencies.

The 1935 hymnal, a joint effort of The Methodist Episcopal Church, The Methodist Episcopal Church, South, and The Methodist Protestant Church, reflected the modernist revisionism. The number of Wesley hymns had already been reduced through several revisions, from 558 in the 1849 hymnal to 121 in the 1905 hymnal. The 1935 hymnal, finding less and less room for the Wesleys, cut the number of Wesley hymns to 56. Sections in the 1905 hymnal titled "The Need for Salvation," "Warnings and Invitation," "Christ's Ascension and Reign," "Judgment," "Retribution," and "Heaven" were eliminated (sections titled "Original Sin" and "Hell" had been removed from earlier hymnals). New sections included "Kingdom of God," "Service," and "Brotherhood." "Worship" replaced "Redemption" as a new focus. An important symbol of this shift was the replacing of "O for a Thousand Tongues to Sing" (a song about redemption, which had always been the first hymn in Methodist hymnals) as the opening hymn with a hymn of worship, "Holy, Holy, Holy."

Hymns centering on historic Christian faith were replaced with hymns about peace and brotherhood and loftier races and planting man's lordship firm and working for one's "fellow man." The Church's ritual was also changed significantly. References such as "redeemed by the blood" and learning the Apostles' Creed and the catechism were deleted in the baptismal service. Adults were no longer asked to "flee from the devil and his works" in the service of baptism, nor were they asked to confess the Apostles' Creed. Two creeds were added—"A Modern Affirmation" and "The Korean Creed"—both of which posited a Christianity without a cross.

Modernists had particular problems with the idea of sin, and for good reason. The idea that human beings cannot save themselves and are in need of an incarnate God and an atoning cross was repugnant to liberals, who saw such doctrine as a stumbling block to "man" as master of his own fate, to inevitable progress, and to the eventual kingdom of God on earth.

With this in mind, there was embarrassment over a Methodist baptismal ritual that up until 1912 spoke of "all men . . . conceived and born in sin" and those "in the flesh who cannot please God but live in sin committing many actual transgressions" and who "must be regenerate and born anew." In 1916, adult "men" still sinned but were not conceived in sin, and infants were neither conceived nor born in sin, but were partakers of God's gracious benefits. Within two decades, infants evidently didn't even need the gracious benefits because they were by birth "heirs of life eternal." Children and youth who were baptized did not confess to any sin in baptism, but they were asked to "put away" (by their efforts presumably) "every known sin." Adults had no sin at all according to the ritual but were simply responding to the invitation to be baptized. And, of course, adults no longer would renounce the devil and his work and all covetous desires of the same and the carnal desires of the flesh.

By this time, people might well have wondered what was the "gospel" anyway, if it had nothing to do with forgiveness, reconciliation, and salvation. The answer was clearly posited in the 1970 "official" confirmation materials in which "gospel" was defined as "the good news that we are all children of God by birth."

This revisionist ideology was imposed not only by controlling seminaries, ritual, and literature, but also by increasing institutional pressure in which the words "approved" and "official" were used to discount and prohibit expressions not in conformity with the new ways of thinking. Local churches were assumed not to be able to make Spirit-led and wise decisions on their own. They needed to be guided by a mediating elite. Evangelists used in local churches needed to be "approved." Sunday school literature needed to be "approved." Missionaries needed to be "approved." Seminaries needed to be "approved." In more traditional denominations, the purpose for "official" and "approval" was to guard against heresy. In Methodism, however, the purpose was to distance Methodism from its own past, namely revivalism, Holiness, and doctrinal. A new phrase, "the Methodist way," became the code word for the new reality. "The Methodist way" amounted to theological institutional liberalism. Those who disagreed were judged as disloyal or were discounted as "not really Methodist." Parachurch groups and ministries such as Sunday school associations, Holiness associations, union crusades, evangelistic ministries, independent publishers, independent missionary organizations, or (later) groups like Youth for Christ[33] were declared anathema and not appropriate for Methodists.

Perhaps liberalism's revisionist understanding of Methodism was no better exemplified than in the book *Why I Am a Methodist* by Roy L. Smith.[34] Smith had been pastor of First Methodist Church, Los Angeles, then known as "the largest Methodist church in the world." He had been editor of *The Christian Advocate* and had written approximately thirty books. He was a world traveler and was said to have spoken to more people than any other Methodist preacher at that time except for E. Stanley Jones.

What Smith celebrated in Methodism was the emphasis on a free pulpit, on the Church's commitment to education, its moral concerns, its publishing enterprises, its worldwide outreach, and its youth and women's organizations. In the chapter "Dedicated to Great Doctrines," Smith contended that the key to understanding Wesley was in "experience." Wesley, he believed, sought to convey to the Church not theology, but passion. On matters of doctrine, Wesley exhibited a liberal mind toward others, and doctrine was never as important in Methodism as it was in other denominations. Methodists were known for what they did, not for what they believed.

This, then, according to Smith, was the greatness of Methodism: the liberality of viewpoint. Methodists could rejoice that their Church had not been plagued by doctrinal or theological disputes. A study of the General Conference of recent years could reveal no doctrinal controversy. Smith asserted that the reason for no doctrinal controversy was in large part because of (1) the official literature used in Sunday schools and (2) the system used in choosing and training ministers. These, he averred, assured a uniform approach to spiritual truth.

According to Smith, the present generation of Methodists had come up under the same standards of education, instruction, and training because of the official material. Likewise, the theological schools offered essentially the same courses of instruction. Even if a student attended another accredited school, the Board of Ministerial Training chose the books students studied so that through a process of standardization, an impressive unity of viewpoints had been achieved. This continued through guided schools of study after ordination as well. The result was a body of clergy in excess of twenty-three thousand that presented a solid theological front. Because of this, the laity reflected the same spirit of uniformity. If there was heresy-hunting in the Church, it was in the areas of economics and social ethics, not in the area of doctrine.[35]

One might conclude from Smith's remarks that the mediating elite had won the day. Methodist Sunday school students, the clergy, and consequently the laity who took their cues from clergy had been guided from the top down by those more knowledgeable and capable in matters of doctrine so that Methodists walked in agreeable uniformity.

What Smith did not mention was that the Sunday school literature had been in the hands of modernists for thirty years and the seminaries for longer than that. Uniformity had come (if indeed it had come) because there was no challenge to prevailing liberalism. Evangelical truth had for all practical purposes disappeared, or was at least driven underground. It no longer was even discussed as an option. The institution, not the Holy Spirit, controlled the source of truth. Methodism had become civilized, respectable, and dead.

The Silent Minority

Still, for all of Smith's learning and supposed knowledge of the Church, his understanding was only one view of Methodism, and a limited view at that. Methodist clergy and laity were not nearly as much in doctrinal lockstep as Smith supposed. There was more to the story.

It was true that control of the denomination was in the hands of liberals. But what about common ordinary Methodists? How really did they react to modernism? It is possible to speak of four different responses.

(1) Some moved easily with modernism. Some cultured, educated Methodists felt modernism was the wave of the future. They were modernists by conviction. Numbers of clergy thought that the way to recognition in the denomination was to support the prevailing ideology.

(2) Another group—and perhaps this was the largest group of all—simply was not aware of, or failed to acknowledge, the radical difference between historic Christianity and modernism. They lived simultaneously in the evangelical world and the modernism world and saw no conflict between the two. They affirmed all and avoided conflict.

(3) Another group left the denomination. The 1890s saw a mass exodus of Methodists from the denomination over issues surrounding Holiness. Much of this was not conflict over doctrine as much as conflict over spirituality. It was primarily former Methodists who populated the Church of God, the Church of the Nazarene, and Pentecostal churches.

As modernism continued to make its inroads into the denomination toward the mid-twentieth century, numbers of other persons, influenced by the growing fundamentalist movement, left Methodism to be a part of growing evangelical churches. Many of these churches had come into existence out of mistrust of the denominations.

(4) A significant number of Methodists stayed the course. These believers knew and supported a different kind of Methodism. When Chuck Keysor wrote his article "Methodism's Silent Minority" in *Christian Advocate* in 1966, he was very much aware of a remnant that had always been faithful to Methodist doctrine, tradition, and ethos, who had not given up on The Methodist Church, and who defined loyalty not as obedience to an institution, but as faithfulness to the gospel as interpreted by John Wesley and other Methodists. These were people who had a different understanding of the Church, of the faith, and of loyalty.

Methodists in the last part of the nineteenth century were already major players in a new burgeoning evangelical subculture. The glue of this subculture was the revival and its language, the gospel song. It's leading figures were evangelists such as Dwight L. Moody and gospel hymn writers and compilers such as (the Methodists) Fanny Crosby, Ira Sankey, and Homer Rodeheaver. This Methodist subculture supported the YMCA, the YWCA, Christian Endeavor, newly forming missions agencies, and a proliferation of journals that were often pietistic and individualistic. Its cause was Prohibition, although it was also united in its preaching against card-playing, tobacco, and the theater. It gathered at camp meetings and Bible conferences.

One of the centers of this evangelical subculture was the Sunday school that was lay-led and often functioned like a church within a church. Organized Sunday school classes met social as well as religious needs. Sunday school associations crossed denominational lines and were organized on local, state, and national levels. For many years, the Methodist Sunday school would outdraw the preacher's worship service in attendance.

Many, perhaps most, Methodists had the unique ability to be little affected by what far-off leaders were saying and doing. To them, Methodism was the local church they attended, not the resolutions of the General Conference. Methodism was the revival (whether or not the evangelist was "approved"), the Sunday school class (whether or not the literature was "approved"), and the Methodist gospel songs (whether or not they were in the "official" hymnal). Methodism was other things as well: the potluck dinners, temperance, the Ladies Aid, offerings for the poor, and prayer meetings. It is less than fully accurate to describe The Methodist Church in the first half of the twentieth century as "modernist" when so many ordinary Methodists were so unaffected by modernism.

Methodism's unique tradition of calling and deploying its clergy, though based on a hierarchical system of authority, in some ways actually insulated parts of Methodism from institutional control. The rural and small-town churches in some conferences never did encounter the modernism of seminary-trained pastors. They were served by part-time and local pastors. Churches on circuits were often without the presence of a pastor and indigenous lay leaders directed congregational life. Even in the larger churches, pastoral changes were so frequent that pastors failed to gain effective control over their congregations. Numbers of churches, especially in rural and small-town Methodism, thrived quite well apart from denominational control.

In other words, modernism never did control the hearts and minds of many ordinary Methodists who continued in the tradition of John Wesley, Francis Asbury, Phoebe Palmer, William Taylor, and the many other laypeople and clergy down the years who believed and preached and lived historic Methodism. Sunday school classes continued to teach Methodist truth despite the official literature.

Methodist groups sang gospel songs regardless of official hymnals. Methodist Ira Sankey was song leader for Dwight L. Moody and compiled *Gospel Hymns* volumes 1 to 6. It is said that Fanny Crosby (1820–1915), a Methodist, with her eight thousand hymns, always with evangelical themes, did as much as any other person to define the ethos of Methodist evangelicalism during the last part of the nineteenth century. Henry Shepherd Date (1858–1915), Methodist evangelist and singer and founder and first president of the Young People's Alliance, the forerunner of the Epworth League, founded Hope Publishing Company and published *Pentecostal Hymns*, which for many churches became the unofficial Methodist songbook. E. S. Lorenz, sometimes called the father of gospel music, was United Brethren. Elisha Hoffman of the Evangelical Church, while serving as music editor for the Evangelical Publishing House, wrote numbers of gospel songs, including "I Must Tell Jesus" and "Leaning on the Everlasting Arms." George Bennard, Methodist evangelist, wrote "The Old Rugged Cross" in 1913. Thomas O. Chisholm (1866–1960), Methodist evangelist, wrote "Great Is Thy Faithfulness" in 1923. Homer Rodeheaver, song leader for Billy Sunday, was a faithful Methodist who popularized such songs as "He Lives" and "In the Garden," and founded the Rodeheaver-Mack publishing company.

Even as modernism was claiming the seminaries and driving out evangelicals from places of leadership in the institutional Church, Methodists in the twentieth century continued to define American evangelicalism in areas away from the intellectual centers. In music, in revivals, on the mission field, in prayer meetings, and in Sunday schools, populist evangelicalism persisted. And despite the different forms populist evangelicalism took, there was common understanding and common cause around the essential doctrines understood in their classical meanings: original sin, the Incarnation, the Atonement, and the new birth. Out of this evangelical subculture came the Good News movement and a renewed struggle for the soul of Methodism.

CHAPTER FIVE

MISSIONS WITHOUT SALVATION

In October of 1971, Philip Hinerman, pastor of Park Avenue Church in Minneapolis, attended as chair of the Good News board the annual Board of Missions meeting in Minneapolis. Hinerman, who until that time had spent most of his Methodist life cloistered in the evangelical subculture, was, in his words, "shocked." He wrote his reactions in the January-March 1972 issue of *Good News* magazine in the article "Missions Without Salvation": In five days "I heard or read not one word about the need to reach men who are forever lost without Jesus Christ."[1] He noted that the World Division had indicated it was making Latin America the focus of its mission and that the Church was to gear up for social justice.

Despite the liberalism that characterized establishment Methodism throughout the twentieth century, the Board of Missions represented a safe haven for evangelicals through the 1950s. The seminaries had been captured by modernists. Church school curriculum disdained teaching about sin and salvation. The Church's social stands were supportive of socialism. Still, evangelicals were welcomed to carry the gospel to the uttermost parts of the earth. Seminary classes on missions through the 1950s dealt a great deal with social and political issues, especially on the movements for national independence, but did not denigrate evangelism and were not as yet places of advocacy for various forms of Marxism.[2]

This is not to say that various mission societies were united in what it meant to spread the good news. The mission societies of mainline denominations, even from their beginnings, had operated with a vision that through education, evangelism, and economic development, the world could be Christianized. Human betterment, the way of Christ, and democracy would lead to a new society, a kingdom of God on earth.

World War I brought a dampening spirit to this vision. For one thing, if the world had been saved for democracy, the world did not seem to appreciate it. Progressive-era optimism turned to self-doubt and criticism. The European nations that had supported the vast majority of missionaries could no longer sustain their vision of a world united by Western civilization, nor could they continue to support missionaries under any vision, because of the devastation of the war. In 1910, out of twenty-one thousand foreign missionaries, only 30 percent were Americans. By 1968, out of forty-five thousand foreign missionaries in the world, 70 percent were Americans.

The Communist revolution in Russia brought another challenge to missions. Perhaps the political and economic systems of the Western nations were flawed. Perhaps communism or socialism offered a different and better route to the kingdom.

More significant, theological modernism caught up with the whole missionary enterprise and leveled a scathing attack against missionaries and traditional mission societies. There had previously been tensions between those who emphasized evangelism and those who emphasized education as the most effective means for spreading the faith. But the issues posed by modernism were more divisive than education versus evangelism. According to modernists, fundamentalist missionaries who still believed in prayers for rain and that God created the world in seven days were scarcely more civilized than the superstitious natives they were trying to convert. The claim that Christ was the only way to salvation was indefensible in a tolerant age. Modernists suggested that uprisings and resentment against missionaries around the world were justified. If there was value in missions work, it was in working with all religions to discover universal values, in offering education without sectarian doctrine, and in humanitarian work.

In 1932, an independent committee formed under the influence of John D. Rockefeller Jr., authorized by eight major denominations, chaired by William Ernest Hocking of Harvard, and dominated by modernists, issued a report entitled *Re-Thinking Missions*. Working under the modernist assumption that Christianity has no claim to exclusive truth and that no true seeker of any religion would be eternally damned, the report then asked:

> Many elements of progress formerly dependent on mission effort are now more effectively promoted by other agencies. Science and the scientific habit of mind dispel superstition more certainly and finally than does the mission. The spread of education, the emergence of womanhood, the promotion of general concern for the lot of the common man, all these are now taken up in some degree by various secular and general interests or by other religions. The question arises whether these agencies, now working together with the mission, can or should in time dispel it.[3]

The report concluded that there may be a place for missions, but its purpose would be not in advancing the cause of Jesus Christ, but in seeking to counteract a growing secularization in the world.

Despite the devastating criticism of missions by secularists and religious liberals on the one hand, and by militant fundamentalists on the other hand, missions operations in the mainline denominations—and especially for Methodists, United Brethren, and Evangelicals—in the 1920s, 1930s, 1940s, and 1950s continued pretty much in their traditional ways. Missionaries on the field were not greatly influenced by debates carried on in American classrooms, and mission agencies did not have great control over the everyday activities of missionaries. Furthermore, liberals in any denomination were hardly inspired, let alone called, to give up everything at home and travel to far-off lands to counteract what some were describing as the growing secularization of the world so that persons of other cultures find enduring values in all religions. Evangelicals still dominated the missionary forces.

In 1938, even in the midst of the Depression, Methodist Episcopal missionaries numbered 1,453 (second only to the United Presbyterians who claimed 1,700). By 1960, the number of Methodist foreign missionaries had increased to 1,742—more than any other denomination or group. And the purpose of missions was still to win persons to Jesus Christ. In 1956, the Board of Missions of The Methodist Church sponsored an interfield consultation of missionaries at Epworth-by-the-Sea and declared at the close of the conference: "At the deepest level missions and evangelism are one. They are not optional, but mandatory; not the special interest of a minority, but the central concern and privilege of us all."[4]

This emphasis underwent radical change in the 1960s. "Death of God" theology became a fascination on college and seminary campuses. There was growing criticism of the Church's complicity in the society's racist attitudes. Globally, growing independence movements led to an intense criticism of what was considered American and European imperialism. Institutional Christianity of any variety—liberal or evangelical—was accused of being irrelevant and outdated, at best, and a hindrance to progress, at worst. The future, at least it seemed to these radical thinkers, lay with the revolutionary movements breaking out in many places of the world.

The new way of thinking had radical implications for the cause of missions. Missions leaders from liberal denominations began to speak of traditional missions, or "old style" missions, as associated with a discredited imperialism. Revolutionary leaders in developing countries were denouncing "paternalism" and "capitalism" and linking missionaries with repressive political and social structures, and mainline liberal mission agencies were agreeing. God's call for a new social order demanded a different approach.

A significant symbol of the new way of thinking was in the dropping of the "s" from missions, changing "missions" to "mission." Traditional "missions," following Matthew 28:19 ("Go therefore and make disciples of all nations"), implied a sending out of specially called persons who would propagate Christianity by making converts and establishing churches. That was too narrow an understanding for liberals who wished to cover everything the Church did as its "mission," whether signing a petition to denounce racism, supporting a community center (whether church-related or not), or even painting the church hall. Armed with this new understanding, mainline mission agencies broadened the scope of their responsibility to cover what had formerly been assigned to social concerns, evangelism, education, and spiritual formation.

The Board of Missions and later, after 1972, the Board of Global Ministries soon began to see their responsibilities as all-encompassing. Did the Board of Evangelism wish to do evangelistic crusades overseas? If it did, it would have to be cleared through the Board of Global Ministries. Congregational development? That was the responsibility of the Board of Global Ministries. Social concerns? The Board of Global Ministries would spend much of its time addressing social issues.[5] An editorial in the May 31, 1985, issue of *United Methodist Reporter* asked, "Why have a social action agency?" if, in fact, the work of church and society is pre-empted by a bigger and more powerful Board of Global Ministries.

As the Board of Missions plunged ever more deeply into social action, the number of missionaries it was sending began to decline alarmingly, a decline shared with other liberal mainline denominations. From 1969 to 1975, the number of overseas missionaries associated with the Department of Overseas Mission (DOM) of the National Council of Churches decreased 31 percent (from 8,000 to 5,000). If that rate had continued, the work of 150 years of missionary efforts would have been wiped out in two decades in the mainline churches.

The Methodist-EUB merger in 1968 and the subsequent denominational restructuring facilitated the dismantling of the traditional understanding of missions and the establishment of the new ideology. A key to the imposition of the new ideology was in the consolidating of power within the mission board in deference to the Women's Division. The Women's Society of Christian Service of The Methodist Church, since its beginning, had operated pretty much as an independent missions agency. This grated on the Church's corporate managers who believed, for the sake of efficiency and coordination and strategic planning, that all mission work should be brought under the control of one agency. The women were suspicious of a male-dominated missions board and would agree to consolidation only if they were assured a guaranteed and significant presence.

In 1964, a deal was negotiated that would have far-reaching implications for the future of missions. The Women's Society would give up their own missionaries and the running of their own institutions. The support of these missionaries and institutions would be integrated into the larger board. In exchange, a new Women's Division would be organized, and, in a complicated formula, one-half of all of the other divisions would be composed of women, the majority of which would be Women's Division members. It is quite probable that no one understood the far-reaching practical results of this restructure. The new arrangement not only assured the presence of the women of the Women's Society—now Women's Division—but also led to a power shift in which the Women's Division, which was able to handpick its own representatives and whose considerable financial resources were now freed up to influence, if not mandate, policy, would now dominate the board. As the Women's

Division came to be controlled more and more by social and theological radicals, the missions program of the Church was ripe for upheaval.[6]

At the same time, Methodist seminaries, caught up in the radicalism of the age, began to redefine such words as "salvation," "commitment," and "evangelism." Professors began stressing that the kingdom of God was this-worldly and was related to political and economic justice. There was cynicism and sometimes outright hostility toward local churches rutted in the thinking of the past. The seminaries became centers of criticism for those who stressed a "personal" rather than a "social" gospel. In the ensuing controversies, traditional evangelism was often pitted against social justice and the battle to eliminate racism. These controversies carried over to the missionary outreach of the Church. The Church, it was maintained, needed to send out new and different kinds of missionaries, if it sent out missionaries at all.

During these developments, the Good News board, still in its infancy, was too far removed from the bureaucratic centers of power to be abreast of the latest ideological currents. Many evangelical churches were supporting missionaries from independent boards, in addition to Methodist missionaries. They were traditional in their understanding of missions; that is to say, they still believed that missions was about proclaiming Jesus Christ.

And this was true not only of evangelical churches. A study done by Dwight Busacca, field representative for the board in the North Central Jurisdiction in the early 1980s, revealed that the two major motivations among United Methodists for giving to missions were: (1) to meet human need and (2) a desire to save souls.[7]

Good News's major concerns about missions in the early days of the movement were directed primarily to the lack of fervor in the local church. Articles in the magazine between 1967 and 1971 dealt with missionary stories of inspiration and featured local churches with strong missionary programs. When the Good News board set forth its agenda for the Church in the fall 1967 issue of the magazine, not one of the fifteen items mentioned missions. From still a populist movement, the list included concern for discrimination against supply pastors, the gap between leaders and the people, the failure to uphold doctrine, imbalance in ecumenical relationships, decay in spiritual disciplines, literature and publishing, bureaucracy, but nothing about missions.

This would quickly change. Hinerman's article in the January-March 1972 *Good News* magazine was followed by "Missions Without Salvation,

Part II" by David Seamands in the April-June 1972 issue. The second article was the text of an address given to seventy-five missionaries and twenty-five general board staff members at Otterbein College in Westerville, Ohio. Seamands, part of a well-known missionary family, had spent sixteen years in India, was a member of the Good News board, and had been noting with alarm the seismic ideological shifts in mainline mission philosophy. He wrote, "A new concept of mission which, as far as we evangelicals are concerned, vitiates the very premises of the Gospel as found in the Scriptures."[8]

Seamands delineated the ideology that accompanied the new concept of "mission":

(1) Mission proceeds not from the Great Commission, but from sovereign activity of God in the world. God's intervention in world events turns world history into salvation history. Salvation now means something quite different from what it has always meant. Salvation has to do not with God reconciling sinners to himself, but in the this-worldly overcoming of evil powers.

(2) The Church is purely a sociological organization. The only difference between the Church and the world is that the Church has knowledge of the saving goal of history.

(3) The new concept of mission sees no relevance in reaching the unevangelized. God is most active in the sociopolitical revolutionary movements of our time.

(4) Christ is not the atoning Son of God, but the one who started the whole process of secularizing and humanizing world history. This is what is meant when the phrase "Jesus as the man for others" is used.

Seamands also raised the matter of a declining missionary force. The board had five persons working in the area of missionary recruitment. If the board was committed not to recruit missionaries, Seamonds argued, let the five go.

What Hinerman and Seamands articulated helped make sense out of the uneasy feelings other evangelicals, including a number of mission-supporting churches, were having about the new Board of Global Ministries. The number of foreign missionaries had dropped from 1309 to a force of 870 in four years. Of special concern was the claim that it was specifically evangelicals who were not being accepted as missionaries and evangelicals on the field who were not being returned.

Good News magazine articles struck a responsive chord with numbers of people. Missionaries on the field—some of whom asked that their names not be used—confirmed the allegations. Additional stories were shared of missionary candidates being turned down for service because— or at least it so seemed even though this was never the stated reason—of their evangelical convictions. Along with the other "crises" in the Church—a curriculum crisis, a doctrinal crisis, a faith crisis—Good News began to speak of a missions "crisis."

Were evangelicals to do nothing but sit and wring their hands? After a period of prayer and searching, an invitation went out from David Seamand's in November 1973 to seventy pastors and laypersons to meet at Sharon Lake Retreat Center in Dallas, Texas, in February of 1974 for a missions consortium. So that those who received the letter might know the concern behind the invitation Seamands expressed the conviction that the current missions problem was not devaluation of the missionary dollar or nationalization of the overseas church (reasons given by the board for retrenchment of the missionary force), but the de-evangelization of the board's missionary emphasis and the secularization of the missionary philosophy.

In compiling the list of those to be invited, Seamands was wise enough to realize that the task before them was greater than Good News's populist and rather narrow constituency. Seamands included some large-church pastors and persons who otherwise had been cautious about identifying with Good News. He made it clear that though Good News was initiating the event, there was no preconceived Good News agenda. This was a concern for all who loved the Church and particularly for those churches and persons who were committed to missions and the spreading of the gospel to all people.

The retreat brought together in a marvelous way the hearts and minds of a large, diverse group. The group agreed that what the predecessor bodies of The United Methodist Church had committed themselves to for nearly two hundred years ought not so easily be given over to alien ideology. Those in attendance formed themselves into the Evangelical Missions Council, pledged themselves to the cause of missions, and agreed to seek conversations with the newly formed Board of Global Ministries.

The Board of Global Ministries was itself working out kinks as the result of the restructuring brought about by the 1968 Evangelical United Brethren and Methodist merger. The merger and the subsequent restructuring came at the very height of radical influence in the Church. According to this radical influence, doctrine was irrelevant. Marxism was the wave of the future. The Church needed to let the world set the agenda. Meanwhile, the nation was experiencing riots over Vietnam and racial matters.

Good News was still too young and too inexperienced and too politically naive to have any influence on the outcome of the 1970–72 restructuring, or even to know what to suggest for structure if it did have influence. Evangelical Methodists were hoping the more moderate Evangelical United Brethren (EUB) might contribute to some evangelical presence in the new merged denomination. Evangelicals who were former EUB felt overwhelmed by the merger and were skeptical about any good that might come from linkage with the Methodists.

The EUBs were simply swallowed up. The EUB contribution to the structure—the Council on Ministries, an outgrowth of the EUB Program Council—would become a giant agency without power or influence, especially over the four major super boards. The plan that eventually came to the 1972 General Conference for approval elevated social concerns to board status in the new Board of Church and Society, devalued evangelism and church school education by removing them from board status to "divisions" within the new Board of Discipleship, consolidated control over the ministry by placing it with higher education in the new Board of Higher Education and Ministry, and created the supercolossal Board of Global Ministries that gathered to itself seven divisions. These divisions included ecumenical concerns and all health and welfare ministries as well as the Women's Division and the National and World Divisions. All of this came with a mandated quota system.

> At-large membership shall be elected by a board in order to perfect the representation of ethnic minorities, youth, and young adults, and to bring into the board special knowledge or background. Not less than 20 percent of the total membership of each board shall be under 35 years of age, with not less than 10 percent between the ages of 25 and 34, not less than 5 percent between the ages of 19 and 25, and not less than 5 percent 18 years of age or under at the time of election. Among the at-large members of each board, it is recommended that there be no less than two of each of the following: Asian Americans, Blacks, Hispanic Americans and Indian Americans.[9]

The church structure was ready-made for those committed to a radical social and political agenda. In the midst of staff changes (among other things, former EUB staff and former Methodist staff needed to be amalgamated into one system) and power shifts within the board, the Evangelical Missions Council had its first "conversations" with the newly formed Board of Global Ministries. The April 12, 1974, issue of *The United Methodist Reporter,* in the article "What Is 'Evangelical Missionary'?" by Bill Buchanan, offered an insight into problems that lay ahead.

According to the article, the Evangelical Missions Council requested as one of its first concerns a rationale for why more evangelical missionaries were not being sent by the board. BGM responded by wanting to know what EMC meant by "evangelical missionaries."

Beyond the response was an assumption that all associated with the board, including staff, were "evangelical," that all the work of the board was "evangelistic" in the way the board understood that term, and that there was therefore no legitimate "evangelical" concern.[10] Eugene Smith, former head of the World Division and member of the conversation team, asked, "Who is going to play God and say that this person is evangelical and this person is not evangelical?" "And," Smith continued, "what are you going to do with the people you decide are not evangelicals?"[11]

The meeting was not a hopeful start for those who believed dialogue would aid understanding and working together by an alienated constituency. EMC representatives were disturbed at what appeared to be either deliberate obfuscation to avoid having to answer the issues or total ignorance of the issues being raised by evangelicals, all in a climate of hostility and condescension. EMC proposed a functional secretary of evangelism and church growth within the World Division, who would be given some freedom in the job and not a "tacked on" position to quiet a constituency. Smith was quoted as saying in response: "There is a negativism about this. . . . A mentality here of cutting up the seamless robe of the gospel."[12] The implication was that the board was proclaiming a "whole" gospel and there was no need to single out evangelism and church growth.

The board representatives intimated that they suspected EMC was really coming with another agenda. The board was already under fire for its radical political and social positions. It was, after all, a time of turmoil during the Vietnam War and in the aftermath of racial incidents. The board seemed convinced that criticism was really motivated by an outdated gospel at best, but more likely by political opposition to programs of racial and social justice.

This was articulated clearly by Theressa Hoover, associate general secretary of the Women's Division, in an address at the pastor's school at Candler School of Theology in January 1976. An issue before the 1976 General Conference was whether to include evangelism as one of the Church's "missional priorities." If the General Conference declared evangelism a priority, it meant that church funds, programs, and efforts would be directed toward reaching the lost for Christ. In what appeared to be a departure from her written text, Hoover commented on the proposal that evangelism be declared a priority and then linked that with opposition to the programs of the Women's Division and the Board of Global Ministries. "We will," Hoover declared, "not be deterred by criticism." Hoover continued: "How could we. . . . How dare we. . . . " revert to the racism and the reactionary thinking of the past. That, she declared, was really behind pushing "evangelism" as a missional priority.[13]

In just twenty years the board had shifted from the declaration that missions and evangelism are one, to the view that "evangelism," at least as traditionally understood as winning persons to Jesus Christ, was, in fact, a hindrance to the real work of the Church.

For the Evangelical Missions Council, "dialogues" with the board served as a reality check. GBGM did not see Good News or the Evangelical Missions Council or evangelicals (which many preferred to label "fundamentalists") as having any legitimate contribution to make to the task that GBGM had outlined for itself in the world. Indeed, these so-called evangelicals were better understood as a negative influence.

The Evangelical Missions Council needed to do some serious reassessment. They were United Methodist. The *Discipline* of the Church was in place. The history and tradition of the missionary enterprise was far too rich to abandon. Furthermore, much of the work of GBGM was positive, and evangelical missionaries, despite the barriers often placed in their paths, were involved in significant and well-supported ministry.

At this stage in the Good News and Evangelical Missions Council history—while there was talk about a supplemental, independent missions agency—there was still a commitment to work with and through the GBGM. If it were true, as had been declared, that one of the main reasons there were not more missionaries was because of a shortage of funds, EMC could deal with that problem. For two years, EMC operated out of David Seamand's office at First Church, Wilmore, and operated as a free-standing committee within the Good News board.

A June 27, 1975, editorial in *The United Methodist Reporter,* entitled "EMC 'Agency' Is Dangerous Precedent," commented with some dismay about what it saw as a possible independent missions-sending agency sponsored by EMC. The issue, according to the editorial, was not evangelism versus social action, but constructive versus destructive methods of making a group's voice heard in the Church. Change could come, according to the *Reporter* editor Spurgeon Dunnam, but it should come about through the established Church procedures.

But what if "established procedures" were so manipulated that true change could not take place? Numbers of moderate United Methodists, including several bishops, were alarmed at the actions of the GBGM but were more alarmed at the possibility of an independent agency. EMC itself, while seeking publicly to say positive things about the "dialogues," was growing impatient.

In 1976, Virgil E. Maybray, pastor of First Church, Irwin, Pennsylvania, was invited to become EMC's first full-time staff person. Virgil would spend the next eight years in a job he dearly loved, traveling through the country to speak of reaching the lost for Christ. Virgil's task was not to be embroiled in the ideological controversies related to missions, but to build positive support for evangelical missionaries and evangelical causes that were functioning within the board.

What appeared at first glance to be a positive development took place in 1976 when the board agreed to bring on executive staff of the World Division a person to serve as Functional Secretary for Church Development and Renewal. The person selected was Dr. Malcolm McVeigh, a highly respected and veteran missionary in Africa.

However, McVeigh and EMC hit another reality check. McVeigh resigned in frustration after two years. He explained:

> The reason my position was frustrating was that its real purpose was window dressing. It was set up to say that we were doing something when it was obvious that there was no real intention of doing anything. My major job there was to try to persuade people who weren't interested that we ought to do something. Talk about spinning wheels.
>
> Because of past experience and because of the present staff alignment in the World Division, the fact that the Board has referred the issues to the Divisions and subunits for study means nothing . . . absolutely nothing. You could refer the issue of "unreached peoples" to the World Division one hundred times a year, and at the end of ten years, you would be exactly where you were at the start. That is true because the

staff of the World Division (with a few non-vocal exceptions) are simply not interested. The only way the World Division can become a possibility in the future is through a radical change of staff, and that doesn't seem to be very likely.[14]

If the World Division was not interested in evangelism, it was because it was focused in other directions. This focus was illustrated by the article by Dow Kirkpatrick in the July 22, 1977, issue of *The United Methodist Reporter* "Castro and Wesley." Kirkpatrick had been a friend of the GBGM for years and had in fact been the chair of the General Conference Restructure Committee that had given superpower status to GBGM. Kirkpatrick was given missionary status with the board where he lived in Atlanta and traveled mostly to Latin America with the responsibility of "interpreting issues" to North American churches. Speaking out of his exhilarating experience of being in Cuba on May Day, Kirkpatrick commented:

> Fidel and his people celebrate the revolution they caused; we (Wesleyans) commemorate the ones we prevent. Cubans believe their lives are vastly better because of their revolution. Hunger, poverty, unemployment, racial discrimination and illiteracy have been eliminated. Quality health care is universal. Slums are being replaced by new housing. Dignity has been given to every human being.
>
> Wesley's movement improved the lot of depressed 18th century England. Cuban Christian Marxists say, however, it failed because it was not radical. Like all gradualist proposals it left the roots of injustice untouched.
>
> We can learn what evangelism is from Cuba. Why is Marx believed more adequate than Wesley by millions of people today? . . . The Cuban Revolution—in contrast to the Christian Church, [Castro] believes—is one "that is with the poor" and "he who condemns a revolution like this one betrays Christ."[15]

Kirkpatrick went on to argue that the clearest statement of evangelism in Cuba had been by Sergio Arce, rector of the Evangelical Seminary in Matanzas, who was quoted as saying: "The first task of evangelism is to confront Christians who are not atheists of the head, but are atheists of the heart. Marx was an atheist of the head, but not of the heart."[16]

An article in the September 9, 1977, issue of *The United Methodist Reporter* quoted Arce again as he elaborated on evangelism: "It is more important today to be a Marxist than a Christian."[17] Arce argued that

Christianity and Marxism are interchangeable and he had no interest in converting Marxists to Christianity.

Because the "official" Church press, always in service to the denominational establishment, almost never asked questions about the appropriateness of church actions or the use of funds, the average United Methodist was uninformed about issues that might otherwise raise questions. And, some have suggested, the average church member might not care even if disclosures were made. Apart from *Good News* magazine, only *The United Methodist Reporter* seemed willing to probe into the more controversial matters of mission policy and use of funds. This was to change with the Jessup Report and the founding of the Institute of Religion and Democracy and the Mission Society for United Methodists.

CHAPTER SIX

SEEKING TO OFFER BALANCE

In 1979, David Jessup, a layman from Virginia, became interested in the funding patterns of agencies of The United Methodist Church. As he explained:

My interest . . . began when my wife and I started to attend services at Marvin Memorial Methodist Church in 1977 not long after moving to the Washington, D.C. area from the West Coast. My wife is a family nurse practitioner whose grandfather was a Methodist minister. I am employed by the AFL-CIO. We had been active in the Peace Corps in Peru, and in the civil rights and farm worker movements in California, and we were interested in becoming involved in church related projects such as refugee assistance. When my children brought home Sunday school appeals for wheat shipments to the government of Vietnam, and the controversy over Methodist support for the Patriotic Front in Zimbabwe became public, I was troubled, but not persuaded that these projects represented anything more than minor aberrations from a more consistent tradition of Methodist support for democratic values. . . . I am no longer so certain.[1]

At first out of curiosity, and on his own, Jessup decided to do some investigating. Was it true that the Church was involved in heavy political activity? How much was it involved? What was the reason? The answers were not easy to come by. Initial contacts with both the Board of Global Ministries and the Board of Church and Society did not yield a lot of information. Staff members were tight-lipped, even hostile to Jessup's inquiries. But Jessup had been trained not to give up so easily. He was moving in his area of expertise. His job with the AFL-CIO was to identify for the unions radical groups that would undermine the cause of labor and democratic values. He visited the United Methodist center in Washington and made trips to New York and persisted until he had gathered what he believed was credible evidence of Church involvement with organizations fronting for Marxist, communist, and revolutionary political activity.

But what should he do with the information? Jessup was not interested in a sensational exposé. He really believed, at least at that time, that the Church would not have done these things willingly, and if the agencies knew what sort of organizations they were supporting, they would make necessary adjustments.

No one that he spoke with, however, seemed willing to be involved or to suggest how the information might be used. United Methodist loyalty, it seemed, precluded involvement with anything that might be considered an attack on the Church. Then he was referred to a Good News couple, Don and Virginia Shell. The Shells were one of those couples with a combination of experiences and gifts that over the years proved invaluable to Good News.[2] Virginia knew about revolution in third world countries, about the United Methodist bureaucracy, about missions, and about controversy. Her first husband, Burleigh Law, had been martyred in the Belgian Congo in 1964 as a Methodist missionary during revolutionary activity.

Virginia later became a staff person with the United Methodist Board of Discipleship and developed the Marriage Enrichment program. She was a speaker at the 1971 Good News Convocation in Cincinnati, where she commented that her two sons who grew up in Africa and knew the languages and the culture had applied to the Board of Missions to be missionaries. Though they had been requested personally by the African bishop, they had not been accepted for service by the board. For public remarks critical of the Board of Missions, Tracy Jones, general secretary of the board, sought to have Virginia Shell fired from the Board of

Discipleship. Jones argued there was a policy against criticizing another agency of the Church. Virginia was defended by Joe Yeakel (later Bishop Yeakel) and the Board of Discipleship. In 1973, she became convinced that renewal in The United Methodist Church would have to come outside of the official structures of the Church and joined the Good News board.

Don Shell, Virginia's husband, was a retired computer executive from General Electric with exceptional leadership skills. The Shells together had committed themselves to head the Good News's strategy team at the 1980 General Conference, and later Don would chair the Good News board. The Shells knew what to do with the Jessup information. The 1980 General Conference was only months away. What Jessup had discovered should be in the hands of delegates. The Shells brought the information to Good News, and Good News did the printing and the mailing and rendered office and publicity support.

The "Jessup Report" that was shared with conference delegates was a well-documented twenty-seven-page paper identifying grants and involvements, mostly by the Board of Global Ministries and the Board of Church and Society, to numbers of organizations, fronts, and political groups associated with the far-left, including groups with communist links and revolutionary intentions. Jessep identified not only grants, but also sponsorship of events, in-kind support, and statements of support. He called his report "preliminary" because he suspected he had touched only the tip of the iceberg. He mentioned, though he did not explore it more fully, a number of the projects also involved the National Council of Churches. The consistent theme through much of the United Methodist material, according to Jessup, was "the evil nature of American society." Support of "human rights" seemed almost always linked with capitalist exploitation and not with the more traditional understanding of human rights associated with religious freedom, freedom of expression, and freedom of assembly.

Jessup summed up his report with these words:

> The fundamental question posed concerns about the direction of political activity, and whether the membership has any say in determining that direction at the all-important level of staff and funding decisions. In other words, it is a question of accountability. It is the same question that was faced by the labor movement of the 1930s, when many trade unionists had to reach an internal decision over the question of whether

their organizations would represent their own aspirations or those of the defenders of the Hitler-Stalin pact.

The report, to the disappointment of Good News insiders, did not attract any outward attention at the General Conference. Though in the hands of the delegates, it did not relate specifically to any agenda item. Furthermore, delegates were already overwhelmed with material. The official Church press, always in service to the institution, noted the report but made no efforts to follow up on the accusations.

When published reaction came—after the General Conference—it came through the pages of *Newscope*. *Newscope* noted the report and then printed lengthy critical responses from church leaders. Instead of indicating any interest for further inquiry into whether church funds were being used other than how they were represented to church membership, the responses spoke darkly of a right-wing conspiracy, a "McCarthyite witch hunt," and questioned Jessup's motives.

On October 17, 1980, a major white paper was mailed by United Methodist Communications (UMCom) to clergy in The United Methodist Church and others. The paper, entitled "The Use of Money in Mission—An Opportunity for Understanding," was a six-page defense of the ideology of the general boards, arguing: "The gospel of the presence of the Kingdom of God cannot become the servant of any particular political or economic system."[3] Then the white paper, while supporting the activities of the general boards of Global Ministries and Church and Society, in a section entitled "Dealing Responsibly with Controversy," launched into a frontal attack on David Jessup and, by extension, on those who had supported him:

> We are not simply discussing some apolitical need for theological and political "balance" in our denomination. We are nearing the center of a debate between different worldviews. As change swirls around us, some persons cling to an understanding of history and the role of our nation that seems to be fading. Such persons are deeply troubled by the shifting of power they see in the world and are fearful. . . .
>
> On many pastors' shelves one might still find copies of important books from the 1960s: Harry and Bonaro Overstreet's *The Strange Tactics of Extremism*, or Forster and Epstein's *Danger on the Right*, or Littell's *Wild Tongues*, or Walker's *The Christian Fright Peddlers—Radical Right and the Churches*. These references are useful for a beginning understanding of today's right wing extremism in its use of the church and of

individual Christians, as well as the media and the governmental processes. A recent book is *The Fear Brokers* by Thomas J. McIntyre.

In public debate and political action, persons and groups holding extremist positions often claim that they have the correct, biblical answer and that those who disagree with them are not suited for public or church office. Such tactics must be analyzed and exposed.[4]

The white paper came with all of the weight of the institutional church. A cover letter by Roy C. Nichols introduced the paper.[5] The paper also identified the Board of Global Ministries and the Board of Church and Society as agencies along with UMCom who had prepared the paper.

In December 1980, Jessup responded to the *Newscope* criticism and "The Use of Money in Mission" in another fourteen-page paper entitled simply *Response to Newscope*. By this time, Jessup had uncovered more information: church pronouncements in support of Ayatollah Khomeini and the "students" holding hostages in Iran; further discussion on the Cuba Resource Center, the Nicaraguan Literacy Program, and the North American Congress on Latin America (and their monthly newsletter devoted to Che Guevarra), groups that had been monitored closely by the state department of a Democratic administration.

Jessup was willing to discuss his motives:

> Because my report has been publicly attacked as a "McCarthyite witch hunt" by several Church officials, it is necessary to repeat that I am not questioning the right of any group or individual to speak out and orga-nize for any cause, no matter how offensive it may be. The only ques-tion is whether the majority of churchgoers wish to foot the bill for such causes. As a member of a democractically structured church, an indi-vidual has a perfect right to disagree with Church funding policy and to work with others in getting that policy changed. To discredit such legit-imate concerns as "McCarthyite" is to demean the concept of pluralism, and discourage donations to other church benevolences that deserve support. After many years of past and continuing involvement in pro-labor, liberal and Civil rights causes, I am more than ever convinced that there is nothing "reactionary" about trying to redirect Church resources toward a more consistent support of democracy in all societies, left and right.
>
> In carefully reviewing the responses [to the Jessup Report], printed in *Newscope*, I have concluded that none of my descriptions have been convincingly rebutted. Furthermore, *my conclusions have been reinforced*

by events within the Church that have come to my attention since the paper was written. These include announcement of a cooperative project with the Cuban government to send Cuban teachers to Nicaragua, the formation of a U.S.-Soviet Citizens Dialogue Committee, the assistance given to pro-Khomeini Iranian student demonstrators, the funding of National Division participation in the Theology in the Americas conference that urges the "socialist option" of radical social change, and the use of pro-Cuban texts for the Women's Division's School of Christian Missions. It should be noted that in nearly all these cases, *the Church's political orientation is revealed not only by grants to outside organizations, but by expenditures and projects of the church agencies themselves.*[6]

Jessup went on to comment that he did not see evidence that church funds were being used to further democratic values. If the AFL-CIO could support democratic values, why could not The United Methodist Church? Why would the Church condemn human rights abuses in right-wing dictatorships, but at the same time make excuses for alleged abuses in Cuba, Vietnam, the Soviet Union, and Iran?

The Evangelical Missions Council and Good News reviewed these developments with consternation. Church involvement with the radical left went beyond what even they had suspected. The reports confirmed their suspicion that money given for "missions" was not being used to send missionaries or, in many cases, even to support church projects, but was being given to secular groups with a political agenda, indeed, to groups with a far-left political agenda.

Good News board discussions centered around what to do with the information. As in the past, Good News had to ask whether it wished to become involved in political and social issues that would divert it from its task of promoting spiritual growth and doctrinal integrity in the Church. The murky world of international politics and revolutionary movements seemed far removed from their populist, evangelical world and beyond their level of expertise. Washington, D.C. was a far different world from Wilmore, Kentucky.

But there were persons who took note of the Jessup Report who did have a level of expertise in the murky world of international politics and revolutionary movements. David Jessup was not the first to have raised concerns about the involvement of mainline churches with the radical left. These persons had noted with alarm that some of the revolutionary movements of the world that were not only anti-capitalist, but also anti-democratic and even anti-Christian, were being supported by mainline money and rhetoric. At the same time these persons were cautious about aligning themselves with reactionary and dictatorial governments and movements, especially if they were linked with South Africa.

David Jessup's report and the publicity generated by Good News opened a door for the coming together of a number of these individuals in Washington in April 1981. They were not persons associated with the Moral Majority or with the political far right. Jessup himself had credentials as an activist Democrat. Many, though not all, were from the evangelical subculture. What they shared in common was a concern for religious rights and a desire to offer a responsible but religious-based ideological balance to that offered by mainline groups and the National Council of Churches.

Good News involvement came with Ed Robb (who along with David Jessup was instrumental in calling the interested people together), Paul Morrell, and Virginia Shell. Well-known and respected persons such as evangelical leader Carl F. H. Henry and Catholics Michael Novak and George Weigel lent their support. Penn Kemble (a friend of David Jessup), J. Ellsworth Kalas from Cleveland, Diane Knippers, James Robb (who would soon become associated with Good News), Paul Stallsworth, John Bryant (chair of the Ed Robb Association), and Ruth Bieler White joined the cause. The Sarah Schaife Foundation and the Smith Richardson Foundation gave initial grants. The group gave itself a name, the Institute of Religion and Democracy (IRD). Richard John Neuhaus wrote the founding document entitled "Christianity and Democracy," which set forth the basic philosophy of the new group:

> It is our purpose to illuminate the relationship between Christian faith and democratic governance. It is also our purpose to oppose policies and programs in the churches which ignore or deny that relationship. With the prayer that we may always speak the truth in love, we will not hesitate to specify policies, programs and persons when we believe they are demeaning the Church's witness and obscuring the sufferings of the poor and oppressed. . . .
>
> Arguments for oppression are evident in our several churches, in some churches more than others. . . .
>
> Apology for oppression is sometimes passionately anti-Communist. . . .
>
> Much more [despicable] . . . is apology for oppression that excuses injustice as necessary for the eventual creation of a new and, it is claimed, more equitable social order. . . .
>
> Another form of apology for oppression asserts that we have no right to impose our values upon others. . . .

It is also an apology for oppression to claim that, faced with repressive oligarchies or militarisms, people often have no alternative to Marxist-Leninist revolution. . . .

Some even excuse the denial of elementary religious freedom. . . . It is said that securing social and economic rights requires the sacrifice of formal, "bourgeois" freedoms—including the freedom to assemble for worship without penalty, to proclaim the Gospel publicly, or even the freedom of parents to instruct their children in the faith. . . .

The debate is not between liberals and conservatives, between left and right. The debate is between those who do believe and those who do not believe that there is a necessary linkage between Christian faith and human freedom.[7]

IRD would be committed to democratic values, with special concern for religious freedom. The group noted with dismay the lack of concern on the part of the liberal religious community as well as the secular press for the persecution of Christians in many of the totalitarian regimes of the world.

The fledgling organization soon let its influence be known. Publishing the monthly newsletter *Religion and Democracy*, IRD soon built up a mailing list of 2,500. *The Washington Post* and *The New York Times* did several stories on IRD. The secular reports noted the differences between the ideology of mainline bureaucracies and the persons in the pew.

The church agencies were not pleased. Was this not a revival of Circuit Riders[8] and other right-wing, big business, anti-communist organizations of the 1950s? Some of the suspicions verged on paranoia. Roy Beck, reporter for *United Methodist Reporter*, commented on IRD, the meeting of the Council of Bishops, and a secret investigation:

> Late that evening, I tracked down one of the bishops who had been in the meeting. We had to meet clandestinely out of view of the others so he wouldn't be discovered. . . . [The bishop] explained that the secret meeting was to discuss strategies for counteracting the Institute of Religion and Democracy. . . .
>
> I knew [IRD]. Just the previous week I had reported that a meeting of the NCC had included the unveiling of a previously secret, $6,000 study of the IRD by United Church of Christ and United Methodist national agencies. For three months private investigators had undertaken to find out who was really behind the IRD.
>
> Like so much of the conspiracy-tinged work around the church, it just seemed overdone to me. Why do it in secret? I had covered the founding

meeting of the IRD and had gathered much of the information openly that the secret study had gotten. The church leaders in IRD charged that it was more than overdone and had involved "subterfuge and Watergate-style" tactics.[9]

By this time, more people were taking note of IRD research. In December 1982, *Reader's Digest* carried the article "Do You Know Where Your Church Offerings Go?" On January 23, 1983, the CBS program 60 *Minutes* aired the segment, "The Gospel According to Whom?" Both the article and the TV program were sensationalized versions of the Jessup Report and IRD research. Both, however, had gone beyond United Methodist family concerns to involve the National Council of Churches and other mainline denominations. *Time* magazine reported on controversy in its March 28, 1983, issue under the heading "Warring Over Where Donations Go":

> For months national leaders of old-time liberal Protestant churches have feared that what amounts to a counterrevolutionary civil war is about to break out among their flocks. They have good cause for concern. In the most thoroughgoing attack since these churches were daubed with a pink brush during the McCarthy era, conservative critics have mounted an anti-Establishment research-and-destroy campaign. Their charge: collection-plate-donations are being misused by Protestant officials and agencies who have become unduly partisan on behalf of left-wing, even Marxist, causes. . . .
>
> (The reports) relied heavily on evidence supplied by a small, neo-conservative group called the Institute on Religion and Democracy, which set off the present furor. . . .
>
> From their shared New York City headquarters, the "God Box" to insiders, the accused Protestant agencies have fought back with a barrage of publicity, defensive polemics and at least 36,000 explanatory packets sent to local church leaders. N.C.C. General Secretary Claire Randall admits no serious mistakes in the council's political judgments and believes the attacks result from "our firm and unwavering adherence to Gospel as our churches interpret it." Says the Rev. Randolph Nugent, who runs the Methodists' Board of Global Ministries: "Our only bias is toward the Gospel of Jesus Christ, not any political system. Jesus Christ and the Gospel do have a bias toward the poor."[10]

Now people in the pew (as well as those who seldom ever saw a pew) were beginning to respond. What was happening? Was it true? Bishops and district superintendents were besieged with angry letters. It was no longer possible for the Church to ignore the kind of information uncovered by the Jessup Report. The official Church press became fully engaged in efforts of damage control. Even before the *Reader's Digest* article, *Response,* representing the Women's Division, in an editorial written by Betty Thompson, asked: "If You See It in the Digest, Virginia, Is It So?"[11] The article spoke of *Reader's Digest* as "vicious, even slanderous," and dredged up images of the McCarthy era. Before the article had even appeared, *Response* was arguing that it could not be believed.

Following the *Digest* article and the *60 Minutes* program, there was a flurry of National Council and denominational rebuttals. The National Council of Churches called the portrayals biased and unfair and accused the Institute of Religion and Democracy—specifically Richard Neuhaus, Ed Robb, and Michael LeSaux (the United Methodist pastor featured in the CBS program)—of having a political agenda that existed solely to attack mainline Protestant churches. The National Council claimed that it was accountable to the membership churches while IRD was accountable only to a self-selected thirty-member board.[12]

The official United Methodist press ran its own public relations rebuttals, which insisted that both the article and the program were overdramatized and misleading interpretations of what the Church was about and therefore should be discounted. Packets were sent to all clergy in the United Methodist connection. No one within the official Church press asked, at least publicly, whether beyond the misleading sensationalism was a core of truth that needed further examination.

The United Methodist Reporter, however, under its editor Spurgeon Dunnam, was one paper not controlled by denominational leaders. It was highly respected not only for its fairness, but also fot its willingness to investigate bigger issues and, when necessary, expose the foibles of both conservatives and liberals. It was also the highest-circulation Protestant newspaper in the nation. How would *The Reporter* cover the stories about IRD, *60 Minutes,* and *The Reader's Digest?*

Along with a number of others, *The Reporter* expressed its dismay at the sensationalism and misleading presentation of *60 Minutes.* The staff, however, was also troubled by the angry defensiveness to the *60 Minutes* assault. Church resources seemed directed only at rebutting *60 Minutes,* with no acknowledgment that some of the criticisms deserved to be probed in a more thoughtful way.

The Reporter finally was to launch an investigation of its own, not of the accusations of IRD and *Reader's Digest,* but of the workings of the

National Council of Churches (NCC). The probe, perhaps the most extensive ever done of the NCC, when finished, reported: "The 'leftist-tilt' of which the NCC has so often been accused by critics, and which its defenders have so often denied, was shown by the Reporter's analysis of the NCC's own statements and citations to be undeniably real."[13]

By now the bishops could no longer pretend there was no issue, and so the Council of Bishops authorized its own study of the NCC. Even the secular and liberal *New Republic* joined the issue. A June 13, 1983, article, "Pliant Protestants," by Joshua Muravchik, addressed whether what *60 Minutes* had done could be identified with McCarthyism. It was interested not so much in ideology as in the tactics of *60 Minutes*. Was there "guilt by association," "innuendo," and "unsupported charges"? The article basically said no and defended *60 Minutes:*

> What lobbying [the mainline churches] does often seems amateurish by comparison to some of the special interests. But they may have a great deal of influence on the ideas and values of electorates and leaders. This is why the *60 Minutes* examination of the churches is so important, and another reason why the charge of McCarthyism is so out of place. At issue is not anybody's loyalty or qualification for government service, the questions around which McCarthyism revolved. At issue are the merits of the foreign policy positions advocated by the mainline Protestant church establishment. To weigh this question, it is instructive to know that much of this establishment has looked into the face of the cruelties of Castro and Le Duan and come away smiling or muttering excuses. This shows a critical failure either of values or perceptions.[14]

Christianity and Crisis, a journal of liberal opinion (supported in part by grants from the Women's Division) devoted its March 21, 1983, issue to "politics, faith, and polemics." A large portion of the issue was given over to the conclusions of the secret study of IRD.[15] The editorial "I Am Not Making These Charges" took a serious look at the IRD philosophy as set forth in Richard Neuhaus's "Christianity and Democracy" and then identified what for many was the major complaint against IRD:

> [Neuhaus] does not use Reaganite rhetoric; he does endorse the Reaganite notion that the *overriding* goals of the U.S. in deploying its wealth and power in the world must be opposition to Soviet influence, the diminution of Soviet power, if possible the dismantling of the Soviet empire.
>
> We don't think it's sinful to hold that view; we do strongly disagree

with it. Countering Soviet influence and matching Soviet military capabilities are important American responsibilities. An overall policy in which everything else is subordinated to anti-Sovietism introduces distortions into the domestic political economy and will be counterproductive to the cause of democracy and human rights abroad—for example, in southern Africa, in Central and South America and in the Middle East. Most importantly, obsessive concern about Soviet capacities and intentions makes it impossible for this country either to *appear* to be or to *be* committed to the control of nuclear arms.

Who's right about this? Who knows? It's only in part an argument about facts. In larger part, it's an ideological dispute. Along with most *C & C* readers, we don't claim a detached, above-the-battle perspective.[16]

In addition to printing a history of IRD and this editorial, the issue of the magazine went into great detail regarding how IRD had been funded by conservative foundations. There was never a denial that major funding for IRD came from conservative foundations. And it was further true that in the case of IRD, Good News was linked with an organization much more political in nature than the parent group. But the criticism was taking place at a time when evangelicals in general, and Good News in particular, were being criticized for emphasizing only a "personal" gospel without any social or political involvement. On the one hand, the Good News people were criticized for having only a "personal" gospel that shunned social activism. On the other hand, these same Good News people were being criticized for having hidden political and social motives.

The "secret" apportionment-supported study of IRD became an issue at the February 1984 meeting of the General Board of Church and Society. When the secret study was finally made public, not all of the members of the board were pleased. As reported in the February 24, 1984, issue of *Newscope:*

James M. Dolliver, a state supreme court justice from Olympia, Wash., challenged the inquiry and report as "questioning the integrity of an organization rather than fighting it on its merits." "The principles that apply to those we love should apply also to those with whom we disagree," said Dolliver. "I know of no other group about which we have felt compelled to mount a full-scale investigation . . . until we took this action I have never been ashamed of this church. I am now."[17]

Good News leaders also raised questions in response to the secret study: Even if it were true that IRD was operating from a conservative political and social and economic agenda, would that be reason enough to condemn it as unacceptable for United Methodists? Was there only one political point of view acceptable, that of extreme liberalism? And would the average United Methodist politically be more in tune with IRD than with the extreme leftist agenda of the Board of Global Ministries and the Board of Church and Society?

The 1983 book *Drifted Astray* by Ira Gallaway, pastor of First United Methodist Church Peoria, Illinois, the largest church in the North Central Jurisdiction, serves as an insight into evangelical United Methodist motives and agenda at the time.[18] Gallaway, former head of the Board of Evangelism of The Methodist Church, was associated not only with IRD and UMAction—the United Methodist division of IRD— but also later with the Mission Society for United Methodists and the Confessing Movement.

Drifted Astray recounted those things that made United Methodism a great movement—polity, doctrine, social outreach, and spiritual life. It was a call to be faithful to that heritage. It was only after a hundred pages of affirming that which was good in the Church that Gallaway finally approached the issue of "covenant trust" and the "credibility gap" between the grassroots church and the leadership and programs of the national boards and agencies. Gallaway continually reminded the reader that the gospel should not be identified with any one form of government or economic order. He then charged the Board of Global Ministries with an unbalanced ideology, in which the evangelistic call to make disciples of Jesus Christ had been eclipsed by leftist political advocacy. He concluded his book with encouraging examples of local churches that were making a difference in the world because of a more balanced understanding of a holistic gospel.

In that same year, 1983, Bishop Ole Borgen, who had been one of the bishops participating in the dialogue between the Evangelical Missions Council (EMC) and GBGM, gave an address at the Good News Convocation at Anderson, Indiana, entitled "One Mission—One Missional Purpose." Bishops, or at least American bishops, seemed committed through what some have called "a conspiracy of silence" not to criticize publicly other bishops or church agencies. Borgen, however, being from Norway, evidently felt no such constraints. His message grew out of the distressing trends he observed in the GBGM:

Historically (evangelism) has been generally conceived as preaching the Gospel of sin and grace and forgiveness, leading persons into a living relationship with Christ. Now it has . . . been corrupted to mean receiving members into the church whether they have committed themselves to Christ or not. . . . Likewise "conversion" now indicates any turning around or change of mind or attitudes, and not the traditional meaning of turning away from sin to God's mercy and forgiveness. "Salvation" no longer indicates the new relationship with God, but just as much any kind of "salvation" within the socio-political realm.

We have almost imperceptibly moved to a position which, drawn to its uttermost consequence, will end up in a socially defined humanism where faith concepts are used, but where man himself is the acting and redeeming agent.[19]

Bishop Borgen's presentation lifted up a number of concerns that had already been expressed in the Evangelical Missions Council (EMC) and General Board of Global Ministries dialogue. The purpose of "dialogue" supposedly was to increase understanding, resolve differences, and find common ground for mission. Members of the evangelical dialogue team after ten years of sessions were not experiencing understanding, resolution, or common ground. The GBGM team was still challenging the use of the term "evangelical," questioning whether EMC really spoke for any legitimate constituency, and defending board policies and actions as a faithful fulfillment of *The Discipline*. To make matters worse, there was no way of discussing the issues outside the dialogue meetings since there was an agreement of confidentiality about the substance of the talks.

The position of the GBGM board was that missionaries were not being sent because there was a lack of funds and because they were not being asked for by overseas churches.[20] Furthermore, effective evangelism was being done by indigenous Christians. Missionaries who proclaimed the gospel were not needed, and justice ministries, even when identified with political groups and not distinctively Christians, were a form of evangelism.

That there was a problem in the way the whole missionary enterprise was viewed was being noted by a number of persons. In the March 18, 1981, issue of *Christian Century* in the article "Crisis in Overseas Mission: Shall We Leave It to the Independents?" Richard G. Hutcheson Jr., observed:

In no area of church life is the contemporary confrontation between mainline liberals and the increasingly powerful evangelicals more troublesome than in overseas mission. Missiologist David I. Bosch suggests that the international mission movement today is in "a crisis more radical and extensive than anything the church has ever faced in [its] history." He analyzes that crisis in terms of fundamental differences between the "ecumenical" and "evangelical" understandings of mission. In one sense the confrontation is a tragedy of miscommunication. The whole situation is seen so differently from the liberal and the evangelical perspectives that in their disputes liberals and evangelicals are seldom talking about the same thing.[21]

Hutcheson went on in the article to comment on the significance of the dropping of the "s" from "missions," which was symbolic of the differences. Evangelicals want to evangelize. Liberals believe "evangelizing" smacks of the old colonialism. They wish to see life improved in overseas settings by political and social reform. He also noted that from 1969 to 1975, the number of missionaries serving overseas under the auspices of denominations constituting the Department of Overseas Mission of the National Council of Churches decreased from 8,000 to 5,010 (21 percent decrease); the number serving under independent agencies increased from 12,500 to 14,000.

Evangelicals in The United Methodist Church were well aware of these philosophical differences. On November 28, 1983, thirty-four persons gathered in St. Louis at the invitation of Ira Gallaway and Bill Thomas, pastor of First United Methodist Church, Tulsa, and covenanted to form a supplemental mission-sending agency within The United Methodist Church. Among those present was Gerald Anderson, former missionary, former president of Scarritt College, director of the Overseas Ministry Study Center, editor of the *International Bulletin of Missionary Research*, and perhaps the foremost missiologist in the denomination. Dr. Anderson, just a month before, had presented a paper to a number of pastors in Dallas, Texas, entitled "Why We Need a Second Mission Agency." At the meeting in St. Louis, he commented: "[It is] difficult to discern that those who are now responsible really believe that it makes any difference whether or not one believes in Jesus Christ as Savior and Lord. Further, that their programs do not reflect this belief."[22]

David Seamands reported on the failure of ten years of EMC-GBGM dialogues. In addition, the group heard additional reports from missionaries on the field and from the gathering of missionaries in the summer jurisdictional meetings. Some of the frustration was with the failure to send the missionaries requested by overseas churches. There was additional concern that missionaries who were sent were engaged in kinds of ministries not requested by overseas churches (often "justice-type" ministries). Sometimes missionaries were sent without consultation of the receiving church. While this was taking place, the general board was neglecting evangelism.

However, the main precipitating factor that led the group to believe that evangelical concerns were making no inroads into the thinking of the GBGM and that it was now time for a new agency was the selection of Peggy Billings to head the World Division. The selection had been made just prior to the November 1983 meeting. Several persons had determined ahead of time that the appointment of the new World Division secretary would be an indication whether the board was ultimately interested at all in working with the evangelical constituency of the Church. They considered Billings's appointment as an in-your-face put-down of everything that had been discussed in the dialogues.[23]

Peggy Billings was an assistant general secretary with the Women's Division, responsible for Social Concerns, whom those who supported the formation of a new agency perceived as an outspoken critic of traditional United Methodist doctrine and of traditional missionary efforts. Billings, a former missionary to Korea, had been involved in organizing a trip by GBGM staff to Korea without the knowledge of the Korean Church. The trip was highly resented by the Korean bishops. Billings then published with Friendship Press the mission study material on Korea entitled *Fire Beneath the Frost,* to which the Korean Church (which it supposedly covered) acted with dismay and anger. The study promoted "Minjung theology"—a kind of liberation theology so obscure that most Korean Christians had never heard of it—made almost no mention of the explosive growth and evangelism of the Korean Methodists, and was highly critical of the Korean government and the Korean churches. Billings refused to identify her sources in Korea.

In addition, it was Billings who put pressure on the AFL-CIO regarding David Jessup after he published the "Jessup Report" critical of Women's Division grants to secular and political organizations.[24] She was also highly critical of the Evangelical Missions Council (EMC), labeled EMC divisive, and used her influence to cut off support to overseas churches that sought help from EMC. Inside observers noted that the Billings appointment came on the heels of a power struggle within the general board in which the voices of moderation lost.

With the Billings appointment it was apparent that GBGM was not intending to take the evangelical concerns seriously. Thus, a new supplemental agency would be formed. The name for the agency would be the Mission Society for United Methodists. Those present at the first meeting covenanted to raise the $130,000 that would be needed to launch the agency. Support and encouragement came from a number of quarters. H. T. Maclin, field representative for Mission Development in the Southeast Jurisdiction, resigned his job with the Board of Global Ministries and became the first executive secretary.

Maclin, a student of missions history, believed that a supplemental agency would strengthen the outreach of the church. There were precedents for multiple sending agencies, in the Church of England primarily, but even in the early years of Methodism. William Taylor, before he became bishop in 1882, had established Methodist mission work in India and South America under his "self-help" mission society.

Indeed, the Women's Division itself was once a separate sending agency. After the Methodist Missionary Society of The Methodist Episcopal Church in 1869 refused to send women doctors to India to work among women there, women interested in missions formed the Women's Foreign Missionary Society (now United Methodist Women) as an independent and unapproved sending agency. Bishops at the time accused the women of being divisive, not accountable, not connectional, and diverting funds from the "official" agency.

Wade Crawford Barclay in his *History of Methodist Missions* records early developments of the Women's Foreign Missionary Society in this way:

> From this point events moved rapidly and decisively. Decision was made to publish a periodical in the interest of the Society, and the first issue of the Heathen Woman's Friend appeared in May. On May 7 (1869) John P. Durbin and William L. Harris met members of the new Society in the Bromfield Street Church, Boston, "for the purpose of coming to a more definite understanding with regard to . . . object and aim" of the new Society. The brethren were apprehensive. The "secretary of the new society recorded that 'Dr. Harris inquired solicitously how the ladies proposed to raise money, stating his fear that their success would interfere with the receipts of the Parent Board.'" Dr. Durbin again proposed that the women raise the money and let the Board administer it. Both of the Secretaries were ready to grant the "missionary spirit manifest" by the women "worthy of all commendation, but (they) were apprehensive of collisions at home and abroad." Dr. Durbin emphasized the importance of "unity of administration" both at home and on the mission field. Speaking for all the women present Mrs. John H.

Twombly asserted: "We women feel that we have organized an independent society. We will be as dutiful children to the church authorities, but through our own organization we may do a work which no other can accomplish." The women felt that ample justification for their position was to be found in the experience of the Women's Union Missionary Society which was beholden to no men's organization but wholly independent. The Secretaries argued that independence was incompatible with Methodist connectionalism.[25]

Not until 1884 at the General Conference was the work of Women's Foreign Missionary Society recognized as valid expressions of ministry and given official status.

The Mission Society was very careful in its organizing literature to affirm most of the work the GBGM was doing. It would seek to act not in competition with, but alongside the official mission board. It would in no way seek to divert apportionment money or advance money from the GBGM. It would enter no area without a specific invitation of the bishop and the national church.

The positive response on the part of numbers of pastors and local churches was overwhelming. The new society would be a way to augment United Methodist work around the world. If the reason missionaries were not being recruited and sent was lack of funds, the new society would raise those funds. Overseas bishops who had continually been requesting missionaries would now have missionaries available.

The Good News board rejoiced at the news of the new society. It voted immediately to disband the Evangelical Missions Council so that the Council could integrate itself fully in to the new society. It released Virgil Maybray from his staff responsibilities with Good News so that he could work with H. T. Maclin in the Mission Society.

Not all in the Church, however, were pleased. Within a few months, the 1984 General Conference would be meeting in Baltimore, and the Mission Society would be an issue. Some wished to make the Mission Society "official." Key leaders of the Mission Society were cool to the idea of being declared "official." "Official" would carry with it restrictions, political compromise, and bureaucratic entanglements, the very thing the society wished to avoid. Others at the General Conference desired an expression of condemnation. The conference finally passed a statement affirming the general board as the only "official" sending agency in the Church but also adding this statement: "In fairness to the concerns of those who feel the necessity for a second agency, we urge that measures be taken to assure our people that evangelization and evangelism are a vital part of the philosophy and practice by the Board and its staff is committed to Wesleyan theology."[26]

The General Conference also directed that directors and staff persons of the GBGM confer with directors and staff persons of the Mission Society to enhance the witness of Jesus Christ. Bishops were asked to serve as mediators in the discussion of mission philosophy. The "dialogue" that had begun between the General Board of Global Ministries and the Evangelical Missions Council would continue.

When the date was set, May 7, 1985, at Highland Park Church, Dallas, for the commissioning of the first missionaries from the Mission Society, Bishop James Thomas, president of the Council of Bishops, made arrangement with three other bishops to be present and participate in the commissioning service. It was customary to participate in such commissioning when United Methodist missionaries were being sent to do United Methodist work in partnership with United Methodist churches. However, strong voices in the Council of Bishops, who wished to use the power of the institution against the society, prevailed against Thomas and made him renege on his promise.[27]

This action of withholding the blessing of the bishops was followed by the bishops' resolve not to give special appointment to any clergy who would seek service with the Mission Society. In light of the practice of giving special appointments to almost everyone who asked, even to agencies that had no contact with the Church, the action could only be seen as punitive and was a reminder of other actions taken by bishops and the Church against those who sought to serve Christ apart from "official" structures. The message of GBGM and the bishops to churches was plain: Do not support United Methodist efforts to win persons to Jesus Christ unless properly authorized by the "official" agencies.

And yet the ideology of the General Board of Global Ministries was so extremely one-sided that even moderates and institutionalists were finding it difficult to support some of the actions of the board. In fall of 1985, the Curriculum Resources Committee of the Church withheld approval of the mission study books sponsored in large part by the Women's Division and published by Friendship Press.[28] Since all educational materials for use in local churches needed approval by the Curriculum Resources Committee, the unwillingness to approve the material meant that the studies could not be considered "official" and were not recommended for use in United Methodist churches.

The specific books not approved were *Crossroads in Southern Asia* and *Technology in Tension with Human Values*, but considerable discussion in the committee was directed at previous studies that consistently extolled the virtues of socialist and Marxist systems and reflected "no concern for persons who are outside the gospel of Jesus Christ." In addition, the materials, especially those designed for youth, were not age appropriate and were educationally deficient.

The reasoning of the Curriculum Resources Committee was that the study books failed adequately to present differing Christian viewpoints on provocative topics. The style of the books was inconsistent with United Methodist pluralism. The response of Global Ministries officials was that theirs were the only mission materials being prepared for the Church, and without these no study materials would be available. Furthermore, the books were intended to be "cutting edge" and not representative of other positions, and there was no intention to change either the style or the approach or the content of the books. Staff of the Women's Division called for a face-to-face encounter with the editor of the Curriculum Resources Committee, Dr. Claude Young, and demanded the action be rescinded. The division declared the books would be promoted and used whether or not "official" Church approval was given.

The pressure to "approve" was really too great for the Curriculum Resources Committee, and a year later the materials were approved without any appreciable change in the approach of the books. There was agreement, however, that the work of the Nashville-based education people and the New York-based mission people needed to be coordinated.

This "coordination" failed to improve either the quality or the ideological balance of the study materials, and some of the women associated with Good News began to speak of raising up a Good News task force that might address women's concerns. As early as the mid-1970s, two women associated with Good News, Diane Knippers of the Good News staff and Helen Rhea Coppedge (Stumbo) of the Good News board, gathered some interested women and formed the Task Force on Women in the Church (or, WTF-Women's Task Force). The group functioned as a subcommittee within Good News and took on as one of its first tasks the editing of the newsletter *Candle*, which was first published in 1977. By September 1982, the circulation of *Candle* had reached twenty-one thousand.

The newsletter reviewed United Methodist Women (UMW) resources produced by the Women's Division, shared inspirational faith stories of women in mission, and sometimes carried supplemental study material ideas. The reviews were the most controversial part of the newsletter. *Candle* would regularly critique the liberal and often radical left-wing bias of the books it was reviewing. When Friendship Press published the study book *China: Search for Community* by Raymond and Rhea Whitehead in 1978, it was *Candle* that pointed out that the book appeared to be an apology for Maoism. Quoting favorably the British scientist Joseph Needham, the book on China reported:

> China is, I think, further on the way to the true society of mankind, the Kingdom of God if you like, than our own. . . . We don't know what back-slidings and failures will occur, but on the whole, I think they are more advanced.
>
> You will naturally ask about the situation of the Christian churches. They are exceedingly weak. . . . I don't believe there has been any great number of Christian martyrs. I am much more inclined to think that many Christians have felt that their aims were being implemented by revolutionary Chinese communism and that they ought to join up with it. . . .
>
> And so one comes to the great paradox that, as I see it, in China they are implementing the second great commandment far better than has been done by Christendom at any period, while at the same time rejecting altogether the first one. . . . I think China is the only truly Christian country in the world in the present day, in spite of its absolute rejection of all religion.[29]

The WTF sought to balance its criticism with helpful suggestions for supplemental resources. However, without guaranteed financial resources and staff time, WTF found it difficult to keep up with the task of producing a regular newsletter, interacting with women in local churches, and producing helpful resources. After several years of relative inactivity, the Women's Task Force was reorganized in 1988 under the name Evangelical Coalition for United Methodist Women (ECUMW). The word "coalition" indicated that this would be a joint effort among women from Good News, the Mission Society for United Methodists, and the Institute of Religion and Democracy. Key leaders included Diane Knippers, now with (IRD), Faye Short and Helen Rhea Coppedge (Stumbo) of Good News, and Julia Williams of the Mission Society.

By 1990, the ECUMW was registering a network of seven hundred individuals or UMW groups. By the spring of 1991, the list had increased to eleven hundred. ECUMW was producing by this time some Bible studies and suggestions for programs for those who wanted something more than the materials produced by the Women's Division. It also produced "Financial File," an exposé of Women's Division programs. In 1993, the coalition took on a new name, RENEW (Renewing, Enabling Network for Evangelical Women), and became the key evangelical voice in reporting and assessing the controversial RE-Imagining Conference that was held in Minneapolis in November 1993 (see chapter 11).

The efforts of ECUMW were not received with appreciation by the Women's Division. ECUMW had never asked for a separate women's organization, but only asked that the division consider the views of ordinary United Methodist women who sought to minister within their churches.

To the Women's Division, however, ECUMW, like Good News and every other renewal effort, was a divisive effort by right-wing malcontents. The Women's Division did not specifically address the concerns of ECUMW but made it clear that the Women's Division alone spoke for, to, and with United Methodist women in the churches. Institutional loyalty allowed no work but what had been approved and advocated by an inner core of mediating elite. Important distinctions were to be made between that which was "official" and that which was "unofficial." Only the Women's Division was official. This was the point made by Sally Ernst to the women at the 1990 UMW assembly in response to the formation of ECUMW: "Conference presidents have been reminded that the responsibility to educate, empower and equip United Methodist women belongs solely to the organization of United Methodist Women."[30]

For the Women's Division, even news sources were to be considered suspect unless approved by the official and proper persons. A white paper entitled *Interpreting the Women's Division/United Methodist Women Official/Unofficial Sources of Information* was issued by the Division on March 15, 1991.

After explaining that the Women's Division is the official national policy-making body for United Methodist Women, and delineating what and who the Women's Division is, the paper then contrasts what the official and unofficial sources of information are in the Church. The primary official sources mentioned were:

1. Women's Division directors and staff;

2. *Response* magazine;

3. publications of the Division;

4. press releases authorized by the Division; and

5. mailings prepared by the Division.

Secondary official sources included mailings, newsletters, and presentations by elected leaders or authorized by the Conference Executive Committee and articles and press releases of the General Board of Global Ministries or United Methodist Communications. *Interpreter* magazine and *New World Outlook* were also listed as official secondary sources.

Other sources, though, were "unofficial" and were listed by the paper:

1. *United Methodist Reporter* (except for supplements and columns edited by "official" UMW persons);

2. *Good News* magazine;

3. Mission Society for United Methodists;

4. Evangelical Coalition for United Methodist Women (ECUMW);

5. secular newspapers;

6. *Reader's Digest*; and

7. *Challenge* (publication of the Ed Robb Evangelical Association).

The white paper went on to discuss distortion and misrepresentation caused when persons or groups who disagree with the Women's Division offer their own "interpretation" of the Division and cause confusion. This occurs when:

1. disagreement with general church policy is directed toward the Women's Division;

2. division actions are not placed within the context of stated denominational policy;

3. unofficial groups recommend and promote their own resources and suggest financial procedures in opposition to Women's Division policy;

4. quotations of faction information are selectively used so that original meanings are changed; and

5. source of information is not documented, and "fact" and "opinion" are not clearly separated.

These actions did not greatly affect the evangelical consistency of the Church, because numbers of evangelical women, especially young women, were less and less attracted to the activities of the Women's Division and were working with other women's ministries. Membership in the United Methodist Women had fallen by about one-third from the merger in 1968 to 1991, although faithful United Methodist women continued generous financial support.[31]

In early 1988, the "dialogue sessions" between the Board of Global Ministries and the Mission Society mandated by the 1984 General Conference broke down and ended. The board had insisted that the meetings be closed and secret. When members of the Church press pointed out that this was in violation of the *Discipline*, and members of the Mission Society refused to continue banning the press, the bishops simply canceled the meeting and the whole dialogue. It appeared to a number of observers that the bishops thought it more expedient to violate the General Conference mandate than to make public the discussions. Ten years of efforts to find common ground had brought more alienation rather than reconciliation among the board and the EMC and then the Mission Society.

The dialogues did bring about one interesting by-product. In order to display its theological "pluralism" after the 1988 General Conference, the GBGM named in an at-large category of membership one self-identified evangelical to serve on its 177-member board, the chair of the Good News board, Helen Rhea Coppedge, a laywoman from South Georgia. Attending the New York meetings, she became acquainted with and eventually married John Stumbo, an attorney from Kansas who had represented the board on legal matters and was an early member of the GBGM-EMC dialogue sessions and a church activist and social liberal. Before the 1984 General Conference, Stumbo had also chaired a major general church task force dealing with how to make the General Conference more efficient. He was one of the most visible members of the General Conference and, in 1984, spoke a total of nineteen times from the floor, more than any other person.

The unlikely marriage, which appeared to be a match of theological and political opposites, created, if nothing else, a lot of hallway conversation. Eventually, it turned out that evangelical theology and social activism were a compatible combination.[32] John Stumbo, after years of being a political insider, was becoming increasingly alienated by an entrenched and heavy-handed institutionalism, was drawn more and more to evangelical theology, and, because of his considerable skills, soon found himself involved in a number of evangelical, reformist causes. The Stumbos helped bring about the successful spin-off of Bristol Books from Good News and eventually worked with Neil Alexander, president and publisher of The United Methodist Publishing House, to bring Bristol Books into a cooperative relationship with the publishing house.

John Stumbo would later play a key role in the Council of United Methodist Accountability (CUMA), a cooperative effort of Good News, the Confessing Movement, and UMAction. The purpose of CUMA would be to supply legal help when evangelical causes were involved in church law. Helen Rhea Stumbo would move from being chair of the Board of Good News to being chair of the board of the Institute of Religion and Democracy (IRD) in 1991, following Ed Robb. She served in that capacity until 1999, when Tom Oden, professor at Drew Theological Seminary, became chair.

The dire predictions of those who prophesied divisiveness, lack of support for the General Board, conflict on the mission field, and a loss of connectedness if the Mission Society were allowed to exist, never came to pass. The GBGM in the late 1980s and early 1990s used lack of funds as the reason more missionaries were not being commissioned, but there is no evidence that this was because of money being withheld by evangelicals. Indeed, at the end of 1998, it was revealed that not only was there not a lack of funds, but also, in fact, the GBGM had unrestricted reserves of $140 million, money that could have been used for missionaries.

The Mission Society for United Methodists served as a good outlet for those who wished to support United Methodist missions work (rather than other independent agencies) that they could trust would operate with evangelical integrity. At the close of the century, the society had 135 active oversees full-time missionaries supported by 16 administratively based staff persons (compared with the Board of Global Ministries 350 overseas missionaries and 400 administratively based staff).

CHAPTER SEVEN

VITAL PIETY AND THE MIND

Billy Graham was coming to Chicago. Some of us at the seminary I attended thought it would be good for the school, and good for Billy Graham, if he would speak in chapel or in some way be invited on campus to interact with students. With that in mind, several students spoke with the president of the seminary. The word back was that Billy Graham would not be invited, because "we do not wish to be identified with that kind of Christianity."

For those in a Methodist seminary during the 1950s, or, for that matter, during the 1940s, or 1930s or 1920s or 1960s or 1970s or 1980s, such response was common. If not outright hostility, there was either subtle discounting or, even worse, a failure even to acknowledge, let alone understand, the part of Christianity that maintained faithfulness to the doctrinal standards of the Church and understood itself to be part of the evangelical approach to the faith.

I spoke one day to the faculty person responsible for finding chapel speakers. I asked if it would be possible to invite a well-known evangelical to be "preacher of the quarter." He was cautious: Who was this "evangelical"? This was not the first time we had played word games at the seminary. He commented that at the seminary all were "evangelicals," so obviously I had another group in mind.

As a matter of fact, the Chicago area at that time was flush with evangelicals. A few months earlier, *Christian Life* magazine had named Chicago "the evangelical capital of the U.S.A"[1] and had identified a hundred different evangelical agencies in the Chicago area. I mentioned several persons who were well known and who I believed would make a positive contribution to the life of the seminary. He thought and then responded, "I believe you are talking about fundamentalists. Some of those persons have hurt us deeply in the past, and we would not be interested in opening our pulpit to them."

A couple of years earlier, when I was trying to decide what seminary to attend, I had sought the counsel of a number of persons—friends, pastors, and other people I respected. I heard horror stories about individuals who had gone to "liberal" seminaries and had graduated confused about faith and as cold and "formal" as the churches they would eventually serve. The Methodist counsel I received disputed those stories and argued that since I was Methodist, I should go to a Methodist seminary. It was sure to be a broadening experience. The advice given was that those who graduated confused were likely not mature to begin with.

When I mentioned to a district superintendent one day that I had tentatively made a decision to attend Fuller Seminary in California, he told me that Fuller was really in the category of a Bible school and I would not receive a good education there. Indeed, it was unacceptable, and if I went out there I should not expect to come back to the North Indiana Conference. I eventually ended up at Garrett Biblical Institute. Garrett had high academic standards, was close enough to Indiana so I could pastor churches in my home conference while in seminary, and was supposed to be—so everyone associated with the school assured me—diverse and open to many different points of view.

It was indeed academically challenging. And it was diverse. Some were convinced that pastoral counseling would save the world, others, that what the Church needed was liturgical worship. Still others, that the Church could never influence the world without social and political involvement—mostly fighting racism and exploitative capitalism. There was a group convinced of the primary importance of Christian education. Others were drawn to biblical studies and theology.

This was during the heady days when neo-orthodoxy and existentialism were the current theological fads. We read Karl Barth and Rudolf

Bultmann and Reinhold Niebuhr and discussed personalism and existentialism and process theology. The theological and biblical perspectives of the professors covered all of the positions that ranged from radically extreme liberal to extreme liberal to liberal to—as conservative as anyone got—moderate.

There were no evangelicals, at least as I understood the term. There were no fundamentalists. There were no conservatives. There were no Pentecostals. A large part of Protestantism simply did not exist in that seminary community, at least not in serious form. Its representatives were not invited on campus. Its books were not read. Its perspectives were not taken with seriousness. When it was recognized at all, it was almost always with negative implications. It was religion that was "privitized," "individualized," and "simplistic." It was referred to as "literalism," "fundamentalism," or "pietism." It was religion that existed in backwoods areas, among the uneducated, and among those fearful of modern times. The symbols of this unenlightened religion were Billy Graham, Norman Vincent Peale, Oral Roberts, the gospel song, unbridled enthusiasm in worship, and Sallman's head of Christ; and scarcely a day went by without a cynical remark made about one or all of these. Comments made were that as modern society became more educated and more sophisticated, these vestiges of a former age would simply fade away.

Furthermore, this "fundamentalism" was identified with an intolerant spirit that simply would not be tolerated. Early in my seminary life, I handed in a paper critiquing the professor's favorite author and had concluded that the man's views were heretical. The paper came back with an F. The professor then commented in class that papers judging the author's work not to be Christian had been submitted and such views simply would not be allowed. Here was a new understanding of "heresy." Heresy was no longer deviation from historic standards of doctrine, but rather believing that historic standards of doctrine mattered. So we learned early that ideas needed to be guarded, speech carefully chosen, and one's true convictions suppressed.

There were a few exceptions among the faculty. One of my favorite professors, William Hordern, had regularly been invited by Kenneth Kantzer and the Wheaton graduate school, an evangelical institution, to address and interact with students there. Hordern was then asked when we could invite Kenneth Kantzer to Garrett to interact with students here. He just smiled and commented that that would not be possible.

My seminary was evangelical, as long as the seminary could define what evangelical meant. It was Methodist, as long as it could define what Methodist meant. It was diverse, as long as it could define what diverse meant. It was faithful to the gospel, as long as it could define what faithful to the gospel meant. It was also open-minded, as long as it could define what open-minded meant. Open-minded in the seminary meant that we would be "stretched" and challenged by points of view from the theological left but did not need to hear anything from the theological right. We could invite Jews, Unitarians, and nonbelievers to speak in chapel, but never evangelicals.

The only person in the whole seminary community who seemed singularly untouched by this seminary ethos was Becky, the African American cook in the commons in the seminary basement and my personal heroine. Becky, whether she knew it or not, was a subversive element on campus. What was declared unacceptable upstairs was proclaimed with reckless abandon downstairs. Gospel hymns as bad music and bad theology? Becky sang them all and especially liked "When the Roll Is Called Up Yonder." Exuberant worship as appealing to emotions and not thoughtful response to a holy God? Becky banged pans as she sang. Talk of the devil as an outdated myth of a former age? Becky continually exhorted her preacher boys to avoid all of Satan's temptations. Miracles in the present age? Becky shared stories of answered prayers.

Most of the seminarians loved Becky. She was a genuine woman of God. But I was impressed that some who were the least enthusiastic about Becky's ministrations were African American students, who dropped remarks about "hoot and holler" religion and that Becky was giving blacks a bad reputation. In the seminary frame of reference, Becky's faith and worship style had not yet been "broadened" and advanced to the point of Christian maturity, and black students (to my disappointment) were agreeing. And it suddenly dawned on me that this attitude of condescension was a form of racism. Multiculturalism was not yet on the scene. African Americans, in the seminary frame of reference, were like anybody else but needed to become respectable. Black religion, which was really a form of evangelicalism, needed to "mature" and conform to white intellectual liberalism.

It was during a period of time when the school saw itself on the forefront in the battle for integration and equality. Many of us dealt with ugly forms of hatred and prejudice on a daily basis (sorry to say, from evangel-ical Christians), but here was a racism that was also demeaning.

With a few exceptions, administration and faculty at the seminary did not understand that they were operating from a parochial point of view. And, unfortunately, the attitude of the seminary was becoming the atti-tude of the larger institutional church, and especially of "the hierarchy," a phrase usually used pejoratively and signifying a system operated by a mediating elite of seminaries, bishops, and agencies. This mediating elite needed to filter and approve what was appropriate teaching or action for common ordinary Methodists. A professor commented one day that without a critical understanding of the Bible, supplied supposedly by seminary-trained pastors, the Bible in the hands of a layman was a dangerous thing.

It seemed impossible ever to present enough evidence, or any evidence that would be considered seriously, that would convince the seminary that it was culturally imperialistic, theologically biased, and—and this is the most important—not really faithful to its Methodist heritage. Methodism as a movement of the people, as "bottom-up" religion in which the filling of the Holy Spirit was more important than the refined mind, whose only purpose was to save souls—this understanding seemed foreign to the life and focus of the seminary. Nor did the seminary com-munity seem much interested in Methodism as holiness of heart and mind—Methodism that shunned worldliness and opposed the use of tobacco and alcohol, or Methodism as the people of one book.

This is not to say that the seminary experience was not appreciated, that learning did not take place, that the professors (and students who quickly learned to mimic the professors) were not in many ways person-ally gracious and academically qualified. It is to say, however, that the overall experience of seminary did not adequately prepare for ministry or for dealing with the actual culture and ethos of local churches or for the present currents of the Christian world at large. Even before they gradu-ated, student pastors found it difficult to communicate with their own congregations. Students were being prepared for an intellectual world of high culture and philosophy and politics and economics, and not for the world of the corner gas station. What they did not know about was life in the Spirit and the essentials of the faith and how to lead a person to Jesus Christ.

Many of us who graduated from these seminaries predicted that, given the pastoral leadership supplied by the seminaries, the mainline churches would soon face disintegration and decline. This, to our sorrow, was precisely what would happen in the years to come. Inasmuch as there was hope, it would come to us because of the evangelical influences apart from seminary. This, to our encouragement, is precisely what would happen in the months to come. One of those influences was the Good News movement.

What the Good News movement did for numbers of evangelicals was to provide safe space for persons to be themselves, to share their stories, to speak their language and give expression to their worship. Clergy and lay could talk openly about "the blood of Jesus," "being saved," the return of the Lord, answers to prayer, and the baptism of the Holy Spirit. Renewal group gatherings and national convocations became times of spiritual refreshment because the environment was open and accepting. "I never knew there were so many other United Methodists who shared my convictions" was a phrase heard over and over.

At these gatherings and in other relationships made possible by Good News, the church-related colleges and seminaries were often discussed. The accounts were not positive. Some of the best evangelical candidates had left the denomination. Seminary atmospheres were described as stifling and oppressive. There were some bright spots. Students who had attended Candler School of Theology could find encouragement from Dr. Claude Thompson. Others could relate to moderates such as William Hordern of Garrett and Albert Outler of Perkins, but beyond that, from top to bottom, in every geographical area, United Methodist seminaries offered a hostile environment to evangelicals.

Struggles over ministerial training were not new to Methodism. Methodism from its very beginning was a populist and egalitarian movement that valued the changed heart above the trained mind. At Methodism's organizing conference in 1784, preachers were advised never to let study interfere with soul-saving: "If you can do but one let your studies alone. We would throw by all the libraries of the world rather than be guilty of the loss of one soul."[2]

Between 1780 and 1829, during the period of Methodism's most rapid growth, forty colleges and universities were founded in the United States, mostly by Presbyterians, Episcopalians, and Congregationalists.[3] Hardly any were Methodist. While Presbyterians and Congregationalists were steeping themselves in classical studies so that they serve as the cultured and educated elite of the nation, Methodist preachers were organizing camp meetings, preaching revivals, and winning the hearts of the masses.

The Methodist message that all could be saved (unlimited atonement), that every person had value in God's sight, and that in God's sight the experience of the heart was more to be desired than the trained mind made it attractive to all people, rich and poor, black and white, sophisticated and unsophisticated.

Methodists were not necessarily anti-learning, but they were suspicious of "aristocratics," "formalists," and the cold intellectualism that was often associated with highly educated clergy who had lost the ability to communicate with common people. Methodism was a "bottom-up" religion rather than a "top-down" religion ruled by mediating elites.

The frontier preacher Peter Cartwright spoke for many when he said: "I do not wish to undervalue education, but really I have seen so many of these educated preachers who forcibly reminded me of lettuce growing under the shade of a peach-tree, or like a gosling that had got the straddles by wading in the dew, that I turn away sick and faint."[4]

In 1832, Congregational seminaries enrolled 234 students, Presbyterian seminaries 257, Episcopalians 47, Baptists 107, and the Methodists none. The first Methodist seminary opened in 1847. In 1859, the other denominations enrolled over 1200 students to the Methodists' 51. Yet Methodism claimed the allegiance of one-third of the entire American population.[5]

Methodist higher education was the result rather than the cause of its tremendous growth. Converted Methodist frontier persons became responsible citizens, then community leaders. A changing and more sophisticated America demanded an educated laity and clergy. There was a conviction that education did not have to undermine the gospel if it were the right kind of education, if it were an education sanctified and in service to Christ. Education was a logical next step in the desire to spread God's kingdom over all the earth.

Indiana Asbury (now DePauw University) was an example. At the very first session of the newly formed Indiana Conference in 1832, a committee was appointed to consider a college or conference seminary. The committee reported that education was to be desired, and it would be best if conducted under the auspices of the Church. Unfortunately, the present institutions in the state were in the hands of those whose "doctrines . . . we consider as incompatible with the doctrines of revelation." The reference was to Presbyterians; and the Methodists wondered why, if Methodists outnumbered Presbyterians in the state 25,000 to 4,000, Presbyterians controlled three colleges and Methodists none.[6] The report further commented: "Therefore, we think it desirable to have an institution under our control, from which we can exclude all doctrines which we deem dangerous, though, at the same time, we do not wish to make it so sectarian as to exclude or in the smallest degree repel the sons of our fellow-citizens from the same."[7]

The school was finally launched and selected as its first president a man who would later become "Mr. Methodist" of the nineteenth century, Matthew Simpson. At his inaugural address in 1840, he laid out the philosophy of the school:

> The precepts of the Bible is the standard we adopt in morals, being fully convinced that, apart from the influence of the Christian religion, no truly great or virtuous character can be formed. The observance of the Sabbath, attendance at public worship in such churches as may be selected by the students or by their parents, together with such other religious exercises as are instituted in connection with the college, will be strictly enjoined. . . . But the startling cry of "Sectarianism" may perhaps by others be echoed throughout the land. Nay, we expect it, because it has always been the favorite resort of infidelity. Eighteen hundred years ago Christianity was the sect everywhere spoken against, and from that period to this "Schism and Sectarianism" have ever been the cry of its relentless opponents.
>
> If by sectarianism be meant that any privilege shall be extended to youth of one denomination more than another—or that the faculty shall . . . dwell upon the minor points controverted between the branches of the great Christian family—then there is not, and we hope there never will be, sectarianism here. . . . But if by sectarianism be meant that the professors are religious men, and that they have settled views upon Christian character and duty, then we ever hope to be sectarian. . . . If it be sectarian to differ from one man's religion, then it is equally sectarian to differ from that of another. Where shall we pause? We must not believe in a future state of rewards and punishments, for that is sectarian. We must not teach that the Messiah has appeared, or the Jew cries out "sectarian." We must not claim the Bible as inspiration, or the Deist is shocked at our illiberality. We must not deny the existence of pagan gods, or Nero's torch is the brilliant argument against sectarianism. Nay, we must not admit the existence of a God, or the Atheist will rail at our want of liberal feeling and sentiment. What then shall we do? Whether professors are Pagans or Atheists, Mohammedans or Jews, Deists or Christians, still they are sectarian. The only persons who are properly free from sectarianism are those who either believe *all things*, or who believe *nothing*.[8]

Simpson never wanted the Church to lose its zeal. He encouraged and always responded positively to invitations to preach revivals and camp meetings, but Simpson saw Methodism's future in education:

> If there is a single point on which the public regard us unfavorably, it is in the matter of education. They acknowledge our piety; they know our numbers; they admit our energy and enterprise; but they have not given us credit for being deeply interested in education. . . . But if, at this time, standing at this point of our history, we put forth our energies in behalf of Christian education, the world will recognize the fact that Methodism, spiritual religion, that religion which touches the hearts, the affections, and the emotions, does not pass by the intellect, but, calling fire from heaven, kindles in the intellect the highest thoughts, and exalts its power. I look into the Methodism of the future and I recognize all this. I see a people vast in number—a people whose hearts swell with gratitude to God—a people with intellects educated, with tastes refined, artistic, lovely, energetic, and expressive—going forth preaching the Gospel in all languages, and conquering the world unto God.[9]

For Simpson and many evangelical Methodists, one did not have to choose between revivals and education, between commitment to the Bible and commitment to science, between the common and the cultured, between sectarianism and a common Protestant vision; all could work together for good, toward "conquering the world unto God," and, ultimately, for millennial glory (postmillennialism).

With that in mind, Methodism, with organizing and fund-raising skills, began to establish colleges and seminaries with abandon. Education became the great hope that could bring in the coming kingdom. Knowledge would be pursued for its own sake; truth would be sought wherever it could be found. Religion would contribute moral and ethical direction. Leaders could speak of "educational evangelism," which referred to the making of Christians through learning rather than through revivals and crisis experiences.

But "educational evangelism" proved to be spiritually barren. There was no direct link between enlightening the mind and changing the heart, especially when enlightening the mind became associated with rationalism, the scientific method, and a growing conviction in the academic world that religion was to be equated with superstition. Though many of the early Methodists envisioned education as an extension of the mission of the Church, others found Church oversight much too constricting. To need to be committed to Methodist doctrine and morality, especially if that doctrine and morality reflected Methodism's preenlightenment tradition, would inhibit the search for truth.

By the turn of the twentieth century, Methodism's leading educators were making the transition from a populist and revivalist understanding of the faith to an approach that was reasoned, in tune with the latest developments in the social sciences, and at home with the respectable leaders of society. By this time, Methodism itself had also established more colleges than any other American denomination. And in addition to its denominational colleges, it had launched a number of significant universities: Boston University, Northwestern, Southern California, Duke, Emory, Southern Methodist, and Syracuse. It was aided by wealthy businessmen zealously courted by Methodist bishops and pastors. Cornelius Vanderbilt gave $1 million by 1877 to fund the Methodist Vanderbilt University. James B. Duke endowed Trinity College, which changed its name to Duke University in 1924. Indiana Asbury was renamed DePauw University in 1884 after a major gift by Washington T. DePauw, a wealthy glass manufacturer.

All of the Methodist educators could quote with conviction Wesley's famous saying about joining together "learning and vital piety," but vital piety looked more and more like religion in general serving a God in general advancing the cause of democracy, freedom, and the good life in general. Society would be enlightened and Christianized, but "Christianized" took on a different meaning. It began to refer to a society that reflected such values as freedom of inquiry and moral responsibility and industrial and social progress, all of which would lead to a different kind of millennium, the kingdom of God.

What were the obstacles on the way to this Christianized society? There was, first of all, the ignorance of the uneducated. This ignorance could be found within Methodism itself. A good portion of common ordinary Methodists saw cold formal education not as a help but as a hindrance to the spread of the gospel. It was a religion of the head and not the heart. It was not "spiritual."

Methodist religious educators on every level set out on a campaign to combat this ignorance of the uneducated. Methodists were supporters of a common school (public) education that would offer to every child an opportunity for an expanded mind and spirit through learning. This common school education would also be a means by which traditional

(Protestant) values and the American way of life would be inculcated into every child's life.

In addition, Methodists were also emphasizing church school education (see chapter 3). But this education would be different from the rote learning, indoctrination, and conversion-directed education of previous decades. It was "progressive education," stressing God-consciousness and values.

And then, in addition to common school education and church school education, Methodism would offer the best of higher education. In 1870, less than 2 percent of the nation's eighteen- to twenty-one-year-olds attended college. Methodists were on a mission to increase this. Dogmatism and absolutism were obstacles on the way to this Christianized society. Enlightened Protestants viewed the Roman Catholic Church unfavorably, with its narrow, dictated view of truth and its parochial school system that restricted free inquiry. Nor were they pleased with Protestant confessionalism and fundamentalism, which also restricted free inquiry. These restrictive forms of Christianity were to be resisted.

Despite good intentions, these Methodist leaders evidently did not realize how quickly their vision would veer off in other directions. Intellectual challenges began to deconstruct the prevailing Protestant culture.

The growing acceptance of the scientific method and of Darwinism cast doubts on the biblical view of revelation. Eventually unbelief became as respectable as belief among the country's intellectual elite. Then, within a few years, belief would be seen as prejudice, doctrine as sectarianism, confessionalism as restricting, and religious tests as the denial of academic freedom.

In addition, many wealthy benefactors of universities had little interest in protecting, or even furthering, a uniquely Christian perspective in the institutions they were funding. They seemed inspired more by the vision of the good life, free choice, and the pleasures of personal consumption than the moral uplift of the nation. Businessmen began to replace clergy as trustees in "Christian" institutions.

The earliest supporters of Methodist higher education seemed unalarmed by these developments. Protestant ethos was alive and well. There was no conflict between Christian faith and the secular academic vision. Methodist institutions were highly visible and highly influential in the life of the Church. DePauw University in Indiana sought leading

Methodist clergymen as presidents or chancellors. Six of those church-men—Matthew Simpson, Thomas Bowman, Francis McConnell, George Richmond Grose, Edwin Hughes, and G. Bromley Oxnam—used the DePauw presidency as a stepping stone to the episcopacy. The university trained the leading clergy of the Indiana Area. The college church was a leading pulpit in the conference and often attracted individuals from outside the conference as pastors. The school was well funded and well regarded academically, even by the secular world.

Not all of the Methodist schools were as successful as DePauw. Some struggled financially. Some compromised academic standards in order to stay alive. The desire for high-quality education was the major motivating force behind the founding of the University Senate by The Methodist Episcopal Church in 1893. The University Senate was envisioned as an accrediting agency to standardize and set minimum requirements for institutions desiring to be recognized as Methodist institutions. As such, it became the first national standardizing agency in the United States, antedating the North Central Association by three years.

One of the first questions the Senate had to ask was, "What is a college?" since a number of institutions claiming to be colleges seemed little more than glorified high schools. Were there not minimum standards that were required for a school to call itself a college, especially a Methodist college?

But there was an even more serious question: "What is a *Methodist* college?" The Senate needed to sort out a wide variety of different ways, legal and otherwise, that colleges were relating to conferences and churches. The Senate also needed to ask whether there were religious or Christian expectations demanded of schools that claimed to be Methodist. Was a Methodist college an institution that saw itself as Christian, that is, as approaching learning from a Methodist and Christian perspective? Would a Methodist institution be committed to Methodist doctrines and values as those doctrines and values were historically understood?

The question was not easily answered. The Senate evidently wanted institutions that were religious yet independent of religious restraint at the same time. In 1912, nineteen years after the Senate was first organized, the minutes recorded this astonishing statement: "We do not think that the time has come to give any formal hard-and-fast definition of a Methodist Episcopal institution."[10] Still, the Senate would offer a "suggestion": "A Methodist Episcopal institution is one which, frankly declaring that it is under the auspices of the church and distinctly claiming that it aims to plan and conduct its work so as to serve the Kingdom of Christ as represented by the life of the Methodist Episcopal Church."[11]

That suggestion, with its mention of serving the kingdom of Christ, was as close as the Senate ever came in linking Methodist higher education with the mention of Jesus Christ. The forces behind forming the Senate were already committed to concepts of nonsectarian education free from church control and mention of Christ was an embarrassment. Loyalty to Jesus Christ was a "sectarian" perspective and not consistent with "open inquiry." Furthermore, the Senate would not be composed of common ordinary Methodists, or even bishops, who might have had interest in linking the institutions with historic Methodist teaching. The Senate was composed of college and university deans and presidents, most of whom, such as W. F. Warren and Borden Parker Bowne of Boston on the very first Senate, were committed to bringing the Church out of its authoritarian darkness into the clear light of reason and science.

This is not to say that religion was ignored in Methodist colleges. One early requirement asked that English Bible be included in the Course of Study of Methodist institutions. When Wesleyan University sought to meet this requirement by offering Sunday afternoon classes on the life of Christ in the local Methodist church, this was deemed an adequate substitution for the requirement. The requirement was soon dropped.[12]

If the Senate had some difficulty defining what was a "Methodist college," it seemed to have less of a problem in understanding what should not be considered a Methodist college, at least one listed with the University Senate. The first "investigation" of a school took place in 1900 when the Senate took upon itself the responsibility of investigating Taylor University in Indiana. Founded in 1846 as Fort Wayne Female College by the North Indiana Conference, the school had become coeducational and, in 1888, had come under the sponsorship of the National Association of Local Pastors and was renamed Taylor University in honor of Bishop William Taylor, the populist, Holiness missionary bishop.

More significant, the school was the first (and perhaps only) attempt on the part of populist evangelicals in The Methodist Church to claim a college of their own, committed to evangelism and missions and traditional Methodist doctrine, particularly the doctrine of Holiness. It had become endorsed by the Christian Holiness Association, the very group that had become one of the greatest critics of Methodist colleges.

The University Senate delisted Taylor. The school had strong religious tests for faculty and students, which seemed in conflict with the open searching for truth. The "Taylor issue" came up time and again for discussion before the Senate.[13] Unlike leaders from several other Holiness institutions such as Chicago Evangelistic Institute and Asbury College, which sought to be "Methodist" but unofficially so, Taylor University leaders believed their institution would be strengthened with an official relationship to the Church. In 1921, the school claimed that sixty-one of its graduates were serving as missionaries, 92 percent of its student body was preparing for Christian service, and sixty-nine of the pastors in the North Indiana Conference were Taylor graduates. But these were not findings that would endear an institution to be authentically Methodist to the University Senate. A school could be so Methodist as to be sectarian; and to the Senate, to be nonsectarian was a higher value than being classically Methodist.

Just as Taylor became the first school investigated under the Methodist Episcopal University Senate, it also became the first school investigated in 1940 when the Senate was reorganized and made a part of the newly formed "Methodist Church." In the early 1960s, it again sought to become officially affiliated with The Methodist Church but was considered "too Christian"—that is, it operated from a confessional stance, which violated the Senate's standard of academic freedom.[14]

The Methodist Episcopal Church, South, The Methodist Protestant Church, the Evangelical churches, and The United Brethren Church had no group that performed the same function as the Methodist Episcopal University Senate. The Methodist Episcopal Church, South created a Commission on Education in 1898, but other secular accrediting agencies had already been established and the Commission seemed to be at some loss as to its function. In 1926, it dissolved, only to be resurrected in 1934 under the name General Commission on College Policy, with its main concern the difficulties church schools were facing because of the Depression.

Theological conservatives expressed resistance to these trends at every turn, with little success. There were several instances in which professors accused of heterodoxy were dismissed from teaching. One well-known professor, Borden Parker Bowne, from Boston University, was accused of heresy in 1904 but was acquitted. Another professor from Boston Seminary, however, Hinckley G. Mitchell, was accused of violating Church teaching and in 1905, his contract was not renewed.

In the ensuing controversy, the General Conference of 1908 passed legislation removing the bishops (who were instructed by the *Discipline* to guard the faith) from the responsibility of needing to guard the faith in regard to university or seminary teaching, thus effectively removing the Church from intervening in university or seminary affairs. Seminaries and universities from this point on would be free from all constraints in making Methodist higher education Christian.

The colleges of The Methodist Episcopal Church, South were slower to absorb their view of education into the national academic culture, but ultimately, they too would join the trend. In 1901, Bishop Warren Candler, a trustee on the Vanderbilt board, introduced a resolution that the university should give preference to hiring Methodists, all else being equal. When Vanderbilt discovered that the Carnegie Foundation and other potential donors were not interested in supporting "sectarian" (that is, Methodist or "Christian") education, it sought to reduce the role of bishops and, consequently, the influence of the Church in the affairs of the university. The growing secularism of the academic world precluded religious tests or religious hiring preferences, and acceptance by the academic world was far more important to Vanderbilt than its church connections. The ensuing battle between the Church and the university was carried all the way to the Tennessee Supreme Court, where a ruling in 1914 declared on behalf of the university. As a result, Vanderbilt no longer considered itself a Methodist school.

Conservatives in the South established two new universities and seminaries in reaction, Southern Methodist University in Dallas and Emory University in Atlanta. These, too, after a few years, drifted into the secular academic mainstream. Schools supported by Methodist Protestants, the Evangelical Church, and the United Brethren Church maintained a Christian witness longer than the Methodist Episcopal schools; but by the mid-twentieth century, not a single school in any of the denominations now a part of United Methodism could claim it was a Christian school operating from a perspective of the Church's confessional faith.

Thus the transition from Christian education to religious education to church education to church-related education. Schools that once sought to offer a Methodist and Christian education became schools that sought to offer a nonsectarian but Christian education. These in turn became schools that sought to offer religious but not specifically Christian education. These then became schools that sought to offer a value-centered education. And these ultimately would become institutions that sought as a goal simply to offer "excellent" education, which meant that education reflected the high academic culture, was free from the encumbrances of sectarian (that is, Christian) bias, and was committed to academic freedom; that is, Christianity was never a preferred perspective, but only one point of view among several.

By the turn of the twenty-first century, the University Senate was still trying to define what was a Methodist College. For over one hundred years, some of the best minds in the nation had tried to come up with a definition that had any meaning. In 1928, the Senate crafted this amazing response: "Educational institutions now appearing on the approved list of the Board of Education shall be recognized under the auspices of the Methodist Episcopal Church. Such institutions are requested to file annually with the Board of Education a complete financial statement properly audited."[15]

To be Methodist, then, was simply to declare oneself as Methodist. It had little to do with whether Methodist teaching was expressed or believed or even recognized, or whether professors or presidents needed to be Methodist, or whether worship to the Christian God was or was not encouraged. One was Methodist by claiming to be Methodist, unless, of course, a school (such as Taylor University) would set forth religious requirements and take them seriously. In this case, it was to be rejected as Methodist because it prohibited "freedom of inquiry."

Later in the century, the Senate discovered it did have standards (beyond academic and financial standards, which were what originally had concerned the Senate). These would be diversity standards, requiring racial and gender inclusiveness. Faith would mean nothing, but skin color and gender would.

The seminaries differed from the colleges and universities in their approach to education only in the matter of degree. The seminaries, too, desired academic recognition from the increasingly secular world, but they were also in the business of training pastors for churches. The question facing the seminaries was how to avoid sectarianism and still claim to be Methodist, or how to teach the Christian faith while at the same time, in the name of academic freedom, not requiring professors to be Methodist or Christian or even believers of any kind.

Theological modernism offered the solution. Modernism sought to balance the claims of science and modern learning with a religious worldview. Since doctrine and truth claims were areas of tension, modernism did its balancing simply by redefining the essence of Christianity and Methodism. Christianity (and Methodism) had always understood that the core of the faith revolved around certain "essential" (John Wesley's word) doctrines or truths. These were rejected by modernists who claimed that they were saving Christianity from a skeptical world by finding more fundamental essentials behind the doctrines.

In 1925, O. E. Brown authored the article "Modernism: A Calm Survey" printed in *Methodist Quarterly Review*, in which special note was taken of the seminary "problem." He noted the report of a special commission to the 1922 General Conference of The Methodist Episcopal Church, South, which stated:

> It may be that some, using the liberty which Methodism has always allowed its representatives, have gone too far in questionable speculations. . . .
>
> We therefore call upon all Annual Conferences, Boards of Trustees of our institutions of learning, and other responsible officers of our Church, to take all necessary steps to banish and drive away all erroneous and strange doctrines contrary to God's word. . . .
>
> We do not disparage devout scholarship nor discourage efforts to reach sound learning in all departments of thought and promote investigation along all lines of useful research. From the first Methodism has fostered education and walked unafraid along all the paths of intellectual culture. . . .
>
> Modish rationalism must not be permitted to affect our devotion to the established tenets of ancient and abiding Christianity.[16]

There is no reason to believe the report was received with any seriousness. "Modish rationalism" was not to be dissuaded from the course it had taken. In defending the new thinking, Brown noted that modernism did not reject the creeds and historic documents, but rather understood them for "time value." The Church's doctrinal tradition told us where we had been, not where we were or where we were going. Historic statements were subject to revision, reinstatement, and reinterpretation. Brown did not make the point, but the implication was that those seminary professors with superior knowledge not available to the Church in all ages and in all other cultures would themselves do this reinterpreting and would share the new truth others were to follow. Methodism was moving toward religion by mediating elite.

In assessing where the Church was, Brown noted that in a recent survey of ninety-one seminaries by *The Minister's Monthly*, thirty-three seminaries had identified themselves as orthodox, forty as liberal, eleven as middle ground, and seven as noncommittal. However, of the seminaries of the Methodist Episcopal churches and The Methodist Protestant Church, nine were liberal, one middle ground, and two noncommittal. None was orthodox. United Brethren seminaries were orthodox, and in the Evangelical Church, two were orthodox and one was liberal. In the crusade for modernism, Methodism was blazing the trail.

In a companion article in the same issue of *Methodist Quarterly Review*, "Theological Seminaries: An Evaluation," C. G. Thompson sought to assess the seminary situation by noting that Methodism's schools were being criticized not only by conservatives who desired to protect the integrity of the faith, but also by those liberals who charged that the seminaries were much too practical, not truly academic, and scarcely educational institutions at all. The institutions, according to the more liberal criticism, were much too dogmatic and narrow in their theological teachings. Liberals wished the seminaries to be free to follow truth wherever it led them, which, interpreted, meant to replace older views of revelation with reason and the scientific method.

Thompson noted that what was going on would not sit well with folks "down the forks of the creeks," but there was no turning back from the Church's commitment to seminary education. Like many others who followed, Thompson wished to portray the seminaries as following a road neither too liberal nor too conservative. He then made this astonishing claim: "There are dangerous heretics in the Church, and a few of them occupy professorial chairs in theological seminaries, but the Church is suffering a thousand times more from poorly prepared ministers than from heresy."[17]

The articles in *Methodist Quarterly Review* were written at a time when revivalism was still a distinguishing mark of Methodism, when Methodism was still overwhelmingly rural (in 1926, only 36 percent of members of The Methodist Episcopal Church, South lived in cities over 25,000, the lowest of any other major denomination save the Southern Baptists), and when local preachers were in place and filling numerous pulpits throughout the North and the South.[18]

Indeed, during the 1920s, over 57 percent of the 11,275 pastors in the northern church had received their training through the Course of Study rather than through the seminary (and this does not include local preachers). In 1924, in the southern church, 2,500 pastors were enrolled in the Course of Study, compared with 1,000 students enrolled in the seminaries.[19]

Methodism was developing a ruling class of seminary-trained elitists. Pastors with seminary credentials could expect appointment to the larger churches in any conference. From the ranks of these pastors, college presidents would be selected, editors of church periodicals would be hired, and bishops would be elected. Ministerial candidates were urged to attend seminary not only to seek an academic training that would help them relate to the eminent leaders of their communities, but also because seminary, especially the right kind of seminary, would "advance their careers." Few persons were making an appeal to attend seminary because it would motivate them for evangelism or lead to deepened spiritual life.

Even at this point in the Church's life, however, the Church sought some direction over the seminaries. As late as 1924, the *Discipline* of The Methodist Episcopal Church could state: "The theological schools of the church shall be those whose professors are nominated or confirmed by the Bishops, and they shall exist for the benefit of the whole Church."[20]

This idea that the Church should have some control over the seminary would quickly change, however, with the seminaries' desire for academic recognition and growing conviction that freedom of academic inquiry could be pursued only with freedom from church control. The 1928 General Conference changed the paragraph to read: "The Theological Schools of the Church are established and maintained for the training of Ministers. They exist for the benefit of the whole church, and the church recognizes its obligations for their maintenance and support."[21]

William Henry Bernhardt, in a 1926 study on the influence of Borden Parker Bowne, observed that by the mid-1920s, three of the five books on doctrine in the Course of Study were written by Bowne.[22] In addition, three of the fifteen book editors appointed by bishops had studied with Bowne as well as nine of the forty-three active bishops. According to Bernhardt, through the influence of Bowne:

> The dogmatic method was replaced by the philosophical and empirical largely as a result of his work. The content of the theology of his associates and his students was turned from the traditional Biblicism of the Protestant Church of the past century toward a restatement more in terms of an idealistic philosophy. This restatement in terms of personal idealism has enabled the Methodist Episcopal Church to meet the problems encountered in the new thought-world of the twentieth century with considerable optimism.[23]

After every other effort had failed to restore a Course of Study that was faithful to Methodist standards of doctrine, or even offer any kind of balance to the proscribed modernism of the Course of Study, Harold Paul Sloan of New Jersey and the Methodist League for Faith and Life made an appeal to the 1928 General Conference of The Methodist Episcopal Church with petitions to "take such steps as will guarantee obedience to the order of the Church on the part of " the commission on the Course of Study.[24] Petitions signed by 10,000 persons from 41 states and 540 communities were submitted but they were promptly and decisively rejected.[25]

In the same year, 1928, G. Bromley Oxnam, later Bishop Oxnam, was elected president of DePauw University, which was gaining a reputation as one of the most prestigious and the most Methodist of the Methodist schools. Oxnam began his presidency by making an appeal that if DePauw was to prevail as a "definitely Christian institution," it would need to set policy to:

(1) Recruit a restricted carefully selected body of superior students.
(2) Offer superior instruction by a faculty composed of liberal-minded men and women.
(3) Maintain superior facilities.

If the University Senate was reluctant to define carefully what was a Methodist college, or a Christian education, Oxnam was not. For Oxnam, a Christian education was a superior and liberal-minded faculty teaching superior students in superior facilities. Oxnam's presidency was considered a great success before he was elected Bishop in 1936. Wealthy Republican supporters of the school sent their youth and their money, and the school weathered the Depression well. The school revivals, which once featured such speakers as Dwight L. Moody, were now called "Religious Evaluation" weeks, with leading liberals brought in to lecture.

Leaders of Methodism celebrated the high quality of Methodist higher education, although in keeping with the times, such education became identified not as "Methodist higher education" or "Christian higher education," but as "church education" and then, later, "church-related education."

The redesignations were significant. Though the schools valued their historical ties to Methodism, they wanted to make it clear that the schools were not restricted in any way by bishops, confessions of faith, commitments to doctrine, standards of piety, or religious perspectives. Such restrictions would be understood to restrict "freedom of academic inquiry," which by this time was taking on an almost-religious significance in the academic world.

The church at large did not seem overly troubled by these developments, in part because many of the schools still carried a religious, and Christian, flavor. Evangelical Methodist churches sent their evangelical students to Methodist schools where numbers of the faculty were active church members and reflected Methodist beliefs and values. The University Senate concerned itself with academic quality and fiscal responsibility.

The seminaries did not require major time from the Senate because ministerial candidates were credentialed for ordination by the Course of Study. When a seminary degree was accepted as a substitute for the Course of Study, the Senate had to ask, in addition to "What is a college?" the question "What is a seminary?" Evangelical schools would not qualify, because, among other reasons, they were seen as glorified Bible schools. The Senate welcomed the formation of the Association of Theological Schools (ATS), which became an accrediting agency and agreed that only accredited seminaries were qualified to train Methodist students.

Since almost no evangelical schools met the accrediting standards of ATS, evangelicals who wished a credentialing education were forced to attend liberal seminaries. Thus for a period of nearly fifty years, from 1920 until the 1970s, liberalism had a virtual monopoly over ministerial education and had opportunity to fashion the Church according to its own vision.

Otto Baab, longtime professor at Garrett Biblical Institute and acting president from 1953 to 1954, spoke of the new day in seminary education in this way: "At last we have been emancipated from the literalism and fundamentalism of our fathers, set free from bondage to bibliolatry and proof-text theology. Through this release the conflict between religion and science, Genesis and geology, ceased to have importance."[26]

Emancipated Methodist (and increasingly, United Brethren and Evangelical) seminary education could change and adapt and create and recreate. It could deconstruct and reconstruct. It could be relevant; it could let the world set the agenda. Dogmatism, literalism, revivalism, and confessionalism were things of the past; the kingdom of God could not be far off.

The results were, at least from an orthodox point of view, disastrous. Freed from any church or confessional constraints—and therefore subject to every cultural, political, and religious fad that posed itself as fresh new truth—the seminaries began to take on the character of the culture around them. In the 1960s, that culture was the radical student culture of the era. Seminaries, no less than colleges around them, became involved in demonstrations, boycotts, and causes. Anti-Vietnam and anti-establishment and anti-institutional fervor became the ethos of the times.

In June 1967, Louis Cassels in a syndicated column for United Press International laid out the problem:

> Should a man be ordained to the ministry if he rejects, or is agnostic about, some of the basic tenets of the historic Christian faith?
>
> That may strike you as a far-fetched hypothetical question. But it's a real and agonizing one for deans and professors at many Protestant seminaries.
>
> It's their responsibility to certify that a seminary graduate is ready for ordination. This is easy when the candidate is a committed Christian. . . . But there is a substantial minority—in some seminaries, teachers say it includes more than a third of the graduating class—who are not Christian believers in any traditional sense of the term. . . .
>
> [This] would raise no problem if the seminary graduate were going into the ministry of the Unitarian-Universalist Association. But a question of integrity arises if he intends to be ordained in a Protestant denomination which is supposed to be committed to the doctrines of the Apostles' Creed.
>
> Some candidates shrug off the question on the grounds that doctrines are unimportant. What really matters, they say, is for the Church to get dynamic young leadership that can make the most of their potential for social service. They do not feel they are being hypocritical if they use the "verbal symbols" of the Christian faith to reassure lay members of a congregation who are not quite ready for their theological views.
>
> A seminary faculty can also give reasons for granting the certifications which permit hundreds or thousands of agnostics to enter the Christian ministry each year. These are really very fine young men, the professors say, and their dedication to the service of humanity is completely genuine. The church desperately needs clergymen. Perhaps they will grow into faith after they're up against the hardships of the ministry.[27]

An even greater concern was expressed by Merlyn W. Northfelt, president of Garrett Biblical Institute: "'We have members of our student body who have not yet professed the Christian faith.' Many have had little or nothing to do with churches and are attending seminary simply out of idealism."[28]

Sexual freedom, free speech, experimentation with drugs, and political freedom generated more passion than prayer and biblical studies and evangelism among numbers of seminary students. Professors who had always seen themselves as liberal and on the forefront of social and academic change were accused of being conservative and irrelevant. Students were demanding curriculum changes.

Schools such as Garrett Biblical Institute became so embroiled in controversy that little education was taking place. In 1968, the seminary had become a staging area for the Weathermen, a radical wing of Students for a Democratic Society (SDS) that had come to Chicago for the express purpose of disrupting the Democratic Convention. The controversy around that and other events led to a disruption of campus life so extensive that chapels became occasions for demonstrations, or were boycotted. Students were boycotting classes, or professors, and numbers of caucuses were formed. Eventually the president resigned as did several faculty members. Campus life was paralyzed. In May 1970, the school, for a brief time, simply ceased to function. Only by some heroic efforts did the school even manage to hold a commencement.

It should not be seen as any coincidence that the membership decline in The United Methodist Church began in the late 1960s and has continued even into the twenty-first century.

This was the situation in the earliest days of Good News. Charles Keysor and the first Good News board had rather modest goals for their movement: to unite evangelicals in fellowship, to serve as a "forum for scriptural Christianity" so that issues ignored by the Church could have fair hearing, and to "articulate historic Methodism: forever relevant, forever vital."[29]

Good News was not articulating any grandiose ideas about reforming seminaries. The earliest Good News discussions about seminaries dealt mostly with how to survive in a hostile environment. Many of these discussions were taking place in newly formed conference renewal groups relating to Good News. Some of the laypersons, and particularly those who were responding to the "Silent Minority" article that launched the Good News movement, were agonizing over preachers who "didn't believe anything," who lacked spiritual disciplines, and who seemed more critical than supportive of the churches they were serving. Seminary training became an issue for these laypeople in response to what they considered poorly prepared pastors.

One voice of optimism in the midst of evangelical discontent was that of Charles Keysor—Mister Good News himself—who always articulated a bigger vision. Keysor could see hope in the larger religious scene. Keysor urged evangelicals to stay with the denomination because there was a brighter future ahead. He based this not on any encouraging signs in the seminaries or in other parts of the institutional church, but on such things as the Jesus People movement, Key 73, Expo 72 (in which over 100,000 college students gathered in Dallas under the sponsorship of Campus Crusade), and the renewed life in some evangelical seminaries.

Keysor argued that eventually the seminaries would have to come to a realistic assessment of the present church scene in America. Evangelical churches were growing; liberal churches were dying. Evangelical seminaries were vital and growing; liberal seminaries were racked with controversy.

In the October 9, 1972, issue of *Time* magazine, an article entitled "The State of Union" gave support to the Keysor observation. According to the article, there were problems brewing for the nation's prestigious liberal seminaries. Enrollment at Union Seminary in New York had decreased by 227 students in four years, and at the University of Chicago Divinity School, 200 students in four years. These and other liberal schools were running budget deficits. Meanwhile, evangelical schools such as Trinity Evangelical Seminary, Dallas Seminary, Fuller Seminary, Gordon-Conwell Seminary, and Asbury Seminary were flourishing, not only in number, but also in quality of students. According to the *Time* article, when a committee from one liberal seminary invited evangelical Carl F. H. Henry to the school to ask advice on attracting evangelical students, Henry replied, "Hire qualified conservative scholars." This suggestion was vetoed by the students on the committee.

The Methodist schools were also suffering decline. Garrett Biblical Institute, which had had the distinction of being the largest of the Methodist seminaries, declined in students enrolled in the B.D.-M.Div. program from 401 in 1961 to 216 in 1968. Part of the decline was because evangelical students, who previously had limited choices for alternative schools, were simply opting out of Methodist seminaries. Nor were they being recruited. In the 1950s, Taylor University and Asbury College were the schools with the highest number of their graduates at Garrett.[30] By 1970, the number of graduates from these schools was more than forty. In later years, it fell below twenty.

United Methodist seminaries were now facing financial crisis. It was the Good News contention that any Methodist (now United Methodist) seminary that wished to grow in enrollment had only to appeal to evangelicals by the hiring of evangelical scholars and the encouragement of an evangelical presence. Evangelical students were responding in large numbers to the call to the ministry—many out of local churches but more through the ministries of campus groups such as Inter-Varsity and Campus Crusade. Some of these students wished to attend United Methodist schools but were not attracted to the liberalism and radicalism found in the denominational schools.

To the seminaries, of course, any opening to evangelicals would be seen in the larger academic world as a step backward. The response of the seminaries in crisis was to appeal to the General Conference for more money. Thus was born out of the 1972 General Conference the Ministerial Education Fund (MEF), which was an additional apportionment to the churches. MEF was presented as a way of moving the Church toward excellence, but was known behind the scenes as a "bailout fund."

From the Good News perspective, the Ministerial Education Fund was a discouraging step backward, not because there was not a need to support ministerial training, but because the money came with no strings attached, no understanding of accountability, and no expectations for greater quality. Furthermore, the funds did not directly help students (except for some of the money directed through annual conferences), but were lump subsidies to seminaries to, as one person interpreted it, "further fund mediocrity."

In 1974, nearly $7 million was channeled to seminaries through the fund. Some schools, such as Garrett-ETS were given the equivalent of $5,000 for each basic degree student, even though a number of these students were not United Methodist. Students would still graduate with tremendous debts, but seminaries themselves were not forced to make changes to stay solvent.

Interestingly, it was not until after the 1972 General Conference and the newly adopted doctrinal statement (which, within months, Good News would see as a great travesty), with its mention of "pluralism," that Good News developed any kind of consistent argument on behalf of evangelical inclusion. The Church after 1972 had suddenly discovered diversity. The quota system was mandated and in place. Caucus groups were forming around gender and race and age matters and other causes. The newly formed Commission on the Status and Role of Women began to monitor the seminaries' gender inclusiveness. The newly formed Commission on Religion and Race began to monitor the seminaries' racial inclusiveness. The newly formed Division on Ecumenical and Interreligious Concerns began to monitor the seminaries' ecumenical inclusiveness.

The seminaries, which for years had resisted Church intrusion on its independence, suddenly seemed to have a change of heart on "inclusiveness" issues. Already in disarray because of student uprisings and always wanting to be "relevant," the seminaries could not instigate affirmative action changes in the name of diversity and pluralism fast enough.

The Good News strategy called for evangelical inclusion in the name of pluralism and diversity. Should "diversity" not also include theological diversity? The doctrinal statement asserted: "All claims to Christian truth deserve an open and fair hearing for their sifting and assessment. The viability of all doctrinal opinion demands that the processes of theological development must be kept open-ended, both on principle and in fact."[31]

The question to be put to seminaries was: If evangelical theology—as the word "evangelical" was understood by persons identifying with Good News—was a viable, functioning perspective in The United Methodist Church, then, if the *Discipline* was to be considered with any seriousness at all, should not evangelical theology be allowed in the seminaries? Should there not be evangelical professors on the faculty? Should books and journals from the evangelical perspective not be ordered and placed in seminary libraries with the same seriousness as the books and journals from other theological perspectives? And could not these books be assigned for reading in classes? Should not issues of interest to evangelicals be included in workshops and seminars with the same seriousness as the issues of interests to other groups, and particularly radical groups, are discussed and addressed? And, at the very least, could professors not acquaint themselves with the evangelical world so that world could be discussed intelligently?

Good News contended that with as many United Methodist seminaries as were operating, surely one seminary could be given over to the evangelical perspective.[32] Failing that, surely several seminaries could hire evangelical professors so that there might be an evangelical presence on the campus. Failing that, surely the seminaries could present the evangelical perspective with integrity. Failing that, the seminaries might at least acquaint themselves with what was happening in the evangelical world.

It was the hope of Good News that these concerns might be discussed with persons representing the seminaries. With that in mind, Good News began to inquire whether such conversations would be possible. The problem was that Good News had no official standing in the church, neither could it muster any political clout. It had exerted no influence on the General Conferences of 1970 and 1972. It had no presence on conference Boards of Ordained Ministry. Good News was imaged as a "self-appointed," "right-wing," and "troublemaking" group.

Other voices were expressing the same concerns as Good News. William Stringfellow, an Episcopalian layman, theologian, and social critic, had been invited to a number of mainline campuses because of his identification with the peace movement. He was not encouraged by the life he observed. Writing in the August 1977 issue of *Sojourners*, Stringfellow commented:

> The seminaries have generally been so covetous of academic recognition, and so anxious for locus within the ethos and hierarchy of the university, that they have not noticed how alien and hostile those premises are to the peculiar vocation of a seminary. Thus the seminaries succumb to disseminating ideological renditions of the faith which demean the vitality of the biblical witness by engaging in endless classifications and comparisons of ideas. All this eschews commitment and precludes a confessional study of theology.[33]

It was difficult to find anybody in the seminary community, or on the Board of Higher Education and Ministry, who agreed with this analysis. Good News was particularly dismissed, not only because it was judged as an unfortunate throwback to an outdated theology, but also because it simply had no political influence. The so-called evangelical renaissance was labeled a passing fad. Furthermore, Good News was a populist movement consisting almost entirely of people without denominational influence.

But slowly this would begin to change. In 1974, John Grenfell of the Detroit Conference became the first district superintendent to identify with Good News by becoming part of the Good News board. In 1973, Paul Mickey, professor of pastoral psychology at Duke Divinity School, became the first person identified with a United Methodist seminary to join the board. Mickey was immediately placed on the Seminary Task Force Committee and later would become the chair of the Good News board.

Under the leadership of such persons as Paul Mickey, Good News began to develop a strategy to influence the seminaries toward the concerns of evangelicals. In the summer of 1975, following the address "Crisis of Theological Education in the United Methodist Church" by Dr. Ed Robb at the summer convocation at Lake Junaluska (see chapter 8), Good News requested time before the Association of Deans and Presidents of United Methodist Seminaries to present its concerns in more detail. This request was denied. However, with some encouragement from Robert Thornburg of the Board of Higher Education and Ministry, the association did indicate receptivity to visits on individual campuses by representatives of Good News. Paul Mickey wrote each Methodist seminary, asking for the opportunity of a campus visit. Jim Waits, acting dean at Candler, turned down the request on the grounds that such a visit would serve no useful purpose since Good News concerns were adequately represented on campus and the evangelical perspective already an important part of the curriculum.[34] Joseph Quillian, dean at Perkins, was more forthright, denying the request on the grounds that "the school does not welcome persons lacking in reasonable openness, especially an outside body whose primary intention is not to really know the school."[35]

Other schools were more receptive. Over the next two years, the visits were made. For the most part, the visiting teams were well received. Members of the teams, in some cases, were invited to speak in chapel, in other cases, were offered a hearing with faculty, and, in almost every case, were offered time with presidents and deans. Following the visits, written reports were sent back to presidents or deans. A report to the Good News board mentioned the positive and negative responses.

On the positive side, several seminaries indicated they would update their libraries with evangelical journals and resource material they did not have. At least one seminary asked for suggestions for qualified evangelical scholars. Several expressed interest in recruiting evangelical students (almost all of the seminaries were in an enrollment crisis). Several others spoke of the need for classes in evangelism or other areas of interest to evangelicals. Meetings with evangelical students were affirming, with a number of students willing openly to identify themselves as evangelicals. These in turn were emboldened even in faculty presence to contradict the faculty insistence that all points of view were heard and respected on the campuses. More important, Good News gained some friends among a limited number of faculty who admitted to being "closeted evangelicals." Unfortunately, and as an indication of the true seminary situation, these faculty members did not feel they could be openly identified as such.[36]

On the negative side, there was appalling ignorance at what was going on in the larger evangelical world and how it related to them and to the future of The United Methodist Church. Almost as one, the schools believed that all points of view were represented and heard on campus and that the so-called discrimination and lack of openness was a misreading of what was really happening in their seminary communities. One professor who made this claim found no inconsistency with his claim of no discrimination and his later remark: "I personally would be against any United Methodist candidate for ministry being ordained who did not believe in the documentary hypothesis of the Pentateuch."[37] Polite but firm statements were made about how the seminaries would resist efforts to dictate how they should run their schools.

Several of the seminaries expressed an appreciation of the Good News visits, and some comments were made about future contacts. It was the Good News's hope that the seminaries themselves might invite Good News persons to the campuses for the purpose of contacts between the seminaries and evangelicals. This did not happen, and Good News was reluctant, at least initially, to initiate further conversations.

The seminaries in the mid-1980s were not nearly as defensive as the seminaries in the mid-1970s. The Ministerial Education Fund (MEF) had brought some semblance of financial security to the seminaries. Enrollments had stabilized and in some instances increased. Though the seminaries may not have been intentional about responding to evangelical concerns, a new wave of evangelical students—older students, second-career students, and students who had come out of parachurch ministries—was changing the complexion of the student bodies. Spiritual formation was being discovered, and evangelism was suddenly in style again. At least one seminary, Candler School of Theology, identified the influence of Good News with the seminary's health. When the president of Emory University met with Emory alumni in Coral Gables, Florida, in October 1979 and reported on Candler, the *Miami Herald* reported:

> Laney feels that the conservative organization known as the Good News movement within Methodism has had a good impact at Emory

where the administration pioneered in making the local church the setting for a number of courses.

"The Good News group has made us aware that an awful lot of people in the church have not been satisfied with some of the theological trends in our school," he said.

"We have responded with new courses, changed content in some courses, and [used] speakers from that group. The result has been a greater openness in dialogue."[38]

At the same time, seminaries made known their absolute commitment to "freedom of academic inquiry" and that this value precluded any kind of doctrinal tests or requirements on the part of faculty or students. They also continued their total commitment to "academic excellence" and, when pushed, implied that this value took precedence over making the gospel believable, understandable, and communicable to persons in local churches. One seminary president indicated his distaste to the idea that he had to relate to persons of "simpleminded faith" and indicated the seminary did not intend to scale down the complexities of the faith in order to appeal to such people.

There was also continuing consternation among a number of Boards of Ordained Ministry that United Methodist students were choosing to attend non-United Methodist, and specifically evangelical, seminaries. This concern had also been expressed on different occasions by some seminary deans and presidents, as well as by the General Board of Higher Education and Ministry. Good News had been able to track these trends with its circulation of *Catalyst*, the newsletter that Good News was sponsoring and that was being sent to United Methodist students in the various seminaries, United Methodist and non-United Methodist.[39] *Catalyst* was a quarterly, fairly low-keyed resource that attempted to keep students in touch with Good News and happenings in the evangelical world.

In 1978, Good News had the names of 1,539 United Methodist students who attended non-United Methodist seminaries (in addition to Oral Roberts University and other schools that received bulk shipments). Not all of these students were in evangelical seminaries, but many were. Asbury Seminary alone enrolled 435 of these United Methodist students; Fuller enrolled 61; Trinity Evangelical, 27; Ashland, 32; Melodyland, 42; Eastern Baptist, 29; Southeastern Baptist, 42; and Gorden-Conwell, 52.

By comparison, United Methodist seminaries had enrolled 2,497 in the basic M.Div. program, with fewer than 2,000 of these actually United Methodist (1981 figures). It was obvious that many students were choosing to attend non-United Methodist seminaries. In many instances the decisions were based on convenience, but a large number of evangelical students were indicating their choices were based on where they felt they could be best prepared for ministry. Others went on to explain they wanted to be United Methodist but wanted education in an environment in which evangelical convictions could be affirmed, not ridiculed, and where there were emphases in areas such as church growth, evangelism, youth ministry, and missions, topics noticeably weak in United Methodist seminaries.

These trends were noted with alarm, especially by seminary deans and presidents whose schools were, despite the influx of the Ministerial Education Fund, and despite a stabilizing enrollment, still struggling for students and funds. Suddenly there was more talk about how United Methodist students needed to be trained in United Methodist seminaries. Whatever the official reasons for this sudden concern, much of the unofficial talk centered around numbers of students being trained in Baptist and "fundamentalist" schools, where, presumably, they were not receiving training in the historical-critical approach to the Bible and in the values of other world religions. Nor were they being exposed to all the "justice" issues so dear to the heart of liberals.

Since many students evidently were not being convinced of the value of the liberal and "official" seminary education that supposedly was in their best interests, an appeal was made for more institutional control. Specifically, the mediating elite called upon the University Senate. At the urging of the General Board of Higher Education and Ministry, the 1980 General Conference spoke about additional standards for seminaries. This was interpreted to mean that the University Senate should "weed out" seminaries that did not support the prevailing philosophy and ideology of the institutional seminaries. Up to this time, the University Senate recognized the accrediting authority of the Association of Theological Schools (ATS). Since the ATS accrediting standards were high—with clear recognition of the importance of freedom of academic inquiry, faculty with advanced degrees, sound financial management, adequate library facilities, and other commonly agreed standards—the University Senate had not in its ninety-year history sought to question the ATS accrediting procedure or add its own different standards. A degree from an ATS-accredited institution met United Methodist standards for seminary training.

But a number of evangelical schools were becoming accredited, such as Oral Roberts University, which caused consternation among several of those associated with liberal seminary education.[40] With the new Senate in place following the 1980 General Conference, the Senate began the weeding-out process. Questionnaires (not on-site visits) would serve as the basis for the reviews.

As the result, what some described as the "evangelical purge" began in 1981. In the initial "review," thirty schools were removed from the "approved" list of seminaries, most because they were Roman Catholic or Lutheran or Episcopal or fundamentalist and did not care if they trained United Methodists. Some were dropped from the approved list because they, as one president put it, "did not wish to play the United Methodist game."[41] But others who had always been approved and were educating numbers of United Methodist students simply "failed the test."

Among those who failed were Ashland, Trinity Evangelical, Eastern Baptist, and Erskine. Asbury Seminary passed, but not before some anxious moments.[42] This first de-listing brought reaction. For Good News, there was no question that the whole effort to "not approve" was directed toward evangelicals. Were not these schools meeting academic standards?

The Senate clarified. Though it was true in the past that academic excellence was the basic requirement for accreditation and approval, the Senate had now decided that seminaries needed more than academics. Schools also needed such things as "opportunities for growth in the United Methodist tradition and ethos," freedom of academic inquiry, compatibility with the United Methodist social principles, and racial and gender inclusiveness in the faculty and in the student body. The schools were dropped for reasons that the Senate would not make public, but they did comment generally that schools were weak in opportunities for growth in United Methodist tradition and ethos, failed to meet inclusiveness criteria, especially in regard to women, and denied academic freedom when seminaries required faculty to "confess loyalty to a specific doctrinal statement or face losing their jobs."[43]

Given these requirements, it was obvious that almost all evangelicals were vulnerable to nonapproval. The de-listed seminaries, when approached, were in many cases mystified as to the review process (How could the Senate really know what a seminary was about without on-site review, which was an important component in the accrediting process of ATS?) and what was meant by "Methodist tradition and ethos."

When asked to clarify, the Senate admitted that United Methodist ethos had nothing to do with doctrine and beliefs or the historic understanding of what was a United Methodist. Methodists historically had upheld classical Christian doctrine. They historically believed in high moral standards (total abstinence, for example, and such things as faithfulness in marriage and celibacy in singleness). They held prayer meetings and preached revivals. But the University Senate understanding of ethos had nothing to do with this. "Ethos" was a subjectively applied criterion that had more to do with matters of freedom of inquiry and freedom from institutional and church restraints.[44] Those schools were de-listed not for the denial of Christian faith, but for holding it too firmly.

The University Senate had gone far beyond the Association of Theological Schools' understanding of academic freedom. ATS had come to a careful understanding of the balance between a confessional approach to Christianity and the freedom of academic inquiry. A school, to be true to its heritage, could operate out of a confessional heritage and could expect its teaching faculty to reflect that heritage, if it made that clear at the time of employment. It was an expectation and requirement of employment.

But evidently the ATS interpretation was too restrictive for the University Senate. United Methodist schools were proud that in the name of freedom of inquiry they allowed no religious tests. One needed to have the proper academic degree and be open and accepting, but one did not have to go to church or be a practicing Christian. One did not have to believe in Methodist doctrine, or any doctrine, or even believe in God, to teach in a United Methodist school.

But, of course, the Senate admitted no theological bias. Persons associated with the seminary reviews, it was explained, were concerned about "literalism" and "fundamentalism" and "narrowness of spirit" (as if these were major problems in United Methodist churches). This was not understood as "bias."

In 1987, a number of additional evangelical schools were dropped from the approved list: Oral Roberts, Central Baptist, Fuller Extension Center, North Park, Reformed, Talbot, and Westminster. By the end of the 1990s, only several smaller denominational evangelical schools and two major evangelical seminaries, Asbury and Fuller, were still left on the approved list. No Reformed schools or Southern Baptist schools, or Church of the Nazarene schools, or any Baptist schools except one remained. Yet almost all of the schools in the liberal denominations were untouched.

In 1998, Gordon-Conwell was de-listed. This was of special concern to evangelicals because Gordon-Conwell was a mainline evangelical school, highly regarded in the evangelical world and in the world beyond. Supposedly, the school's statement on the authority of Scripture and its confessional statement of faith was too rigid for those who, in the name of inclusiveness, sought to exclude those with a perspective not their own.

At the same time Gordon-Conwell was disapproved, Harvard University was added to the approved list. The contrast between the two schools could hardly have been greater. Harvard made no claims to be a Christian school or operate from a Christian frame of reference. Of thirty-six full-time faculty, only one person was identified as a United Methodist (and she taught Hindu spirituality). No faculty member was identified as evangelical. At least seventy-five different courses were offered on other religions, including Celtic paganism, African religions, religions of Mesoamerica, Manichaeanism, Zoroastrianism, Armenian folk religion, Hindu Dharma, the Bhagavad-Gita, Bodhisattvas and their cults, but no course on Christian evangelism. Gorden-Conwell was considered too rigid in its teaching of Christianity, but Harvard's openness of inquiry and tolerance supposedly fulfilled all that United Methodist ethos was all about.

In the case of colleges and universities, the Senate in 1990 made another attempt to define the criteria by which schools could be approved for listing as United Methodist-related. These were: institutional integrity, church relatedness, sound finances and administrative management, and sound academic programs. For a number of colleges and universities, "church relatedness" had now become a matter of indicating that the school was "historically related to the Methodist Church," which freed them from embarrassment by mention of any present relatedness.

For some schools, such as DePauw University, whose first president had stated nobly "the only school that is non-sectarian believes everything or believes nothing,"[45] this meant that one could search the university catalog or the student handbook and find no references to the Church. The school, which claimed that six of its presidents had advanced to the episcopacy, had claimed no new bishops since 1926. It no longer called United Methodists as presidents. No United Methodists taught religion courses; indeed, the school policy was that to honor nonsectarianism, no clergyperson of any Christian denomination could teach religion. No persons directly related to the school served in any leadership positions in the denomination or in the conferences. The college church, which once was a flagship pulpit of the South Indiana Conference, was averaging 125 by the late 1990s, and the number of active, participating college students numbered less than a dozen.

In addition, the college chaplain, once an appointment by the bishop, was now selected by the college. The chaplain was given a new title, "Dean of the Chapel," but there was no chapel of which to be dean. Crosses and Christian symbols had been removed from all campus buildings. The chaplain's mission trips, once seen as a form of Christian outreach, were moved to the office of student affairs, where any identification of the trips as "mission" or as "Christian" or that might involve prayer was erased, and called service projects. The "compassionate rose" replaced the Jerusalem cross as the symbol of projects.

When a group of United Methodist and other students wished to form an evangelical Christian group on campus, they did so apart from any university sponsorship or encouragement. They struggled to get even minimal funding from the student organizations budget though they became the most active group on campus, with up to three hundred gathering at their weekly meetings.

In the spring of 2002, Janice Price, a professor at DePauw, lost her teaching assignment and was reprimanded by the academic dean for violating the school's policy on inclusivity. This was because Dr. Price had made available for discussion copies of the Focus on Family's magazine *Teachers in Focus,* which included an article on homosexuality that supported the biblical (and United Methodist) view that the practice of homosexuality was incompatible with Christian teaching. For DePauw, a supposedly United Methodist institution, secular ideology trumped and excluded Christian moral teachings.

DePauw did report to the annual conferences, however. The president announced the school had raised $317 million in its drive to provide "a quality higher education for and to influence their development as responsible citizens and future leaders in their communities."[46]

Not all of the developments in higher education have been discouraging from the Good News perspective. As the Church moves into the twenty-first century, there are a number of hopeful signs. With the exception of such schools as Claremont School of Theology and Iliff School of Theology, many United Methodist seminaries have hired faculty members with evangelical persuasions. A number of these have been trained with the help of A Foundation for Theological Education (AFTE) (see chapter 8). In addition, almost all of the seminaries have added courses on evangelism. So in many ways the future seems brighter for United Methodist seminary education than at any time in the last one hundred years.

CHAPTER EIGHT

RECLAIMING THE WESLEYAN HERITAGE

The spirit at the fifth national Good News Convocation at Lake Junaluska in July 1975 was exhilarating. For a number of evangelicals in The United Methodist Church, the yearly Good News Convocation was becoming a spiritual highlight, a time of encouragement and inspiration. The singing was so exuberant that Glenn Draper, song leader for the convocation, announced that as a climax to the last service, the nearly two thousand worshipers should stand and sing as a congregational hymn Handel's "Hallelujah" chorus (helped along by the Junaluska Singers).

But the 1975 convocation was intended to be more than just an evangelical family reunion. Good News was in the business of renewal, and The United Methodist Church was experiencing very little renewal. From an evangelical perspective, The United Methodist Church, the new colossus formed from the merger of The Methodist Church and The Evangelical United Brethren Church (EUB), was in crisis. The reports were discouraging:

(1) In the Church's new structure, approved by the 1972 General Conference, the worst fears of evangelicals (and others) were being

realized. Power in the Church was concentrated in the new superboard, the General Board of Global Ministries, which, under domination of the Women's Division, had declared itself on behalf of liberation theology. The General Council on Ministries, a new agency that was a carryover from the EUB Program Council, was simply being ignored by the other boards and was ineffective in its task of coordinating and evaluation. The Commission on Social Concerns in the former Methodist structure, controlled by persons many considered social extremists, had been elevated to the status of a board, while evangelism and education had been diminished by being subsumed as divisions under the Board of Discipleship. Youth ministry was disintegrating; curriculum sales were plummeting.

All of this preoccupation with structure was complicated by power shifts and struggles within each of the agencies, which were trying to integrate EUB members and Methodists and trying to operate under a newly mandated quota system with age, gender, and race requirements.

(2) Evangelicals were beginning more and more to be aware that the Church's new doctrinal statement, also approved in 1972 as a consequence of the merger, was serving further to undermine the Church's historic doctrinal heritage.

(3) The seminaries were experiencing gender and ethnic and political pressures but were still not open to evangelical presence.

(4) The former Evangelical United Brethren were finding that the merger was not a marriage of equals, but a corporate takeover. Despite the fact that former EUB members were given guaranteed representation and that a number found themselves in places of responsible leadership, they lost a seminary, a publishing house, a number of camp and conference grounds, and, most of all, a sense of identity. Forced EUB-Methodist local mergers were generally failures. EUB practices and beliefs, such as freedom of conscience in matters of baptism and infant dedication, contrary to reassurances given before merger, were being scuttled by the new Church.

(5) These discouraging developments were being reflected in dramatic reversals in membership, worship attendance, and Sunday school enrollment. The church at large seemed unable or unwilling to identify the decline with merger problems, board and agency problems, seminary problems, and the general lack of focus in mission, faith, and spiritual formation.

Like the Good News Convocations before it, the 1975 Lake Junaluska convocation was not directed primarily toward denominational problems or church politics. The convocation, like those before it, were times of celebration and learning and meeting new friends. Jack Grey led the children's program with his well-known "Bible Bowl." Art Erickson, nationally known youth pastor from Park Avenue Church in Minneapolis, led the youth program.

But the Church's problems could not go entirely unaddressed, and so the 1975 convocation would be remembered for two things: Ed Robb's keynote address on the failure of the seminaries, and the presentation and signing of the Junaluska Affirmation.

(1) Robb and the Seminary Crisis

Ed Robb's keynote address at the convocation spoke to the evangelical discontent with the seminaries. The presentation, entitled "The Crisis of Theological Education in The United Methodist Church," linked the problems of the Church to leadership and the problem of leadership to the seminaries: "The question is, who or what is responsible for this weak leadership. I am convinced that our seminaries bear a major portion of the responsibility. *If we have a sick church it is largely because we have sick seminaries.*"[1] Among the litany of failings and shortcomings linked to the seminaries, Robb further charged: "I know of no UM seminary where the historic Wesleyan Biblical perspective is presented seriously, even as an option."[2]

Robb asked (1) that two seminaries be entrusted to evangelical boards of trustees and continue as United Methodist seminaries; (2) that in the spirit of inclusiveness, every United Methodist seminary invite competent evangelicals to join the faculties; and (3) that greater support be given to established evangelical seminaries, especially those in the Wesleyan-Arminian tradition.

The seminaries, and the Church's Board of Higher Education and Ministry, if they even were aware of the Good News critique, were not inclined to treat the Robb challenge with any seriousness. No established "leaders" in the Church would ever even consider allowing evangelicals to operate a United Methodist-related seminary, and no seminary would allow such a radical shift in focus. And, these "leaders" would argue, the seminaries were already inclusive and diverse. Furthermore, there was absolutely no interest in supporting non-United Methodist schools, especially evangelical schools.

From the perspective of the institutional church and the seminaries, Good News was a reactionary throwback to a dead past. The fundamentalist-modernist controversy was long since over; Good News was associated with fundamentalism, and fundamentalism had lost. "Self-styled evangelicals" (fundamentalists in disguise) and their theology were not the wave of the future.

Though the convocation and Robb's address were well reported, especially by *The United Methodist Reporter,* there was little denominational response to the events of the convocation—with the exception to that of Albert Outler, professor of Historical Theology at Perkins School of Theology. Dr. Outler did note the address and was offended by the Robb charges, especially the accusation that there was no seminary where the Wesleyan biblical perspective was treated seriously, even as an option.

Outler, too, was longing for United Methodist renewal. In many respects, Outler was Mister United Methodist of the 1970s. He had chaired the Study Commission on Doctrine and Doctrinal Standards for The United Methodist Church. He had lectured bishops and represented the Church in ecumenical councils. In his Denman lectures, *Evangelism in the Wesleyan Spirit,* given at the Congress on Evangelism in New Orleans in 1971, Outler recognized a growing evangelical renaissance, the sterility of liberalism, and sought to call the Church to an authentic Wesleyan theology.

But Outler, in the lectures, was not pleased with much of evangelicalism, especially with that offered by Good News:

> But these fine old words ["evangelical," "evangel"] have . . . generated many a distorted image in many modern minds—abrasive zealots flinging their Bibles about like missiles, men (and sometimes women!) with a flat-earth theology, a monophysite Christology, a montanist ecclesiology and a psychological profile suggestive of hysteria. Every Saturday night in the *Dallas Times-Herald* there are advertisements for these characters—eyes ablaze, bodies coiled for the leap of faith, or for pouncing on the hapless sinner. Occasionally, we have gatherings of self-styled "evangelicals" who have much needful truth to speak, alongside many uncharitable remarks about other Christians. Last summer, it was announced to a large and lively convocation that our United Methodist Church seminary faculties would bear watching because some of their members "profess no faith in God, doubt his existence, regard Jesus as only a good man—not a Savior—have no place for prayer, etc., etc." . . . For even if we allow for a tiny fraction of truth in this indiscriminate libel, it still fails to endear the evangelical cause to fair-minded men.[3]

It is no wonder Albert Outler reacted strongly to the Ed Robb address. In a letter to *United Methodist Reporter,* Outler expressed his unhappiness:

I was . . . downright shocked by one of the quotations. It is sad that a well-meaning man should lodge a blanket indictment against the entire lot of United Methodist theological schools in terms so unjust that they are bound to wreck incalculable damage to the cause of theological education in the UMC—which is, as we all know, in grave enough peril already. . . .

What shocked me, though, was Dr. Robb's reported declaration: "I know of no United Methodist seminary where the historic Wesleyan biblical perspective is presented seriously, even as an option." The point, of course, is that, since Dr. Robb knows of Perkins, he has said, by strict logical entail, that the historic Wesleyan biblical perspective is not presented **seriously** at Perkins, "**even as an option.**"

Now, either the phrase "historic Wesleyan biblical perspective" means something that neither I nor other Wesley scholars—here and elsewhere—understand or else this accusation is simply false. . . .

In my case, as you know, I've spent the better part of twenty years studying, teaching, editing and writing about Wesley and his "historic biblical perspective," here at Perkins and elsewhere. Until today I should have thought, with no shred of immodesty, that I know as much about Mr. Wesley's texts, and context, as Mr. Robb does. Now, however, I stand accused either of not having been "serious" in a task that has consumed much labor and love, or else of having got it all wrong and misled others by my errors.

Last semester, I taught a course in Wesleyan theology, elected by more than forty students. I'd be willing for any competent and impartial jury on earth to examine the documentation of the course, the tapes of the lectures, the students' papers and examinations—and then judge whether something like "the historic Wesleyan biblical perspective" was or was not presented **seriously** and was or was not taken so by a majority of the students at least **as an option.** If their verdict is "guilty as charged," I am prepared to resign my post on this faculty forthwith and to abandon my life's work on Wesley. . . .

I can think of many ways in which a much needed, candid debate about Methodist theological education could have been stimulated and helped ahead; Mr. Robb's way resembles none of them.[4]

Even Spurgeon Dunnam, editor of *United Methodist Reporter,* was taken aback by the forcefulness of the Outler letter and contacted Ed Robb for a response. Robb wrote a response but believed more was needed. It was not good for Ed Robb and his evangelistic association, neither for Good News, nor for the cause of evangelicals, to be the focus of Albert Outler's ire. Outler was not only a respected Wesleyan scholar, but also had on other occasions shared some of the same concerns Good News had expressed.

A letter or a phone call was not enough. Robb called Outler and asked if he might come to see him. Outler, according to Robb, had to think about that request for awhile before he gave grudging consent. And so it was that Ed Robb and Paul Morrell, Good News board member and pastor of Tyler Street Church in Dallas, made their call on Albert Outler at Perkins School of Theology.

Outler gave his version of the visit in an article printed in *The Christian Century:*

> It was . . . downright disconcerting to have Dr. Robb and some of his friends show up in my study one day with an openhearted challenge to help them do something more constructive than cry havoc. Needless to say, I've always believed in the surprises of the Spirit; it's just that they continue to surprise me whenever they occur!
>
> Here, obviously, was a heaven-sent opportunity not only for a reconciliation but also for a productive alliance in place of what had been an unproductive joust. Moreover, as we explored our problems, some unexpected items of agreement began to emerge.[5]

Outler mentioned three points of agreement: (1) too many evangelicals had not paid the going price for full academic respectability; (2) theology in the Wesley spirit must be ecumenical; and (3) true evangelism must also include justice, nurture, and discipline.

Robb's evaluation of the meeting with Outler was no less surprising: "Outler was more radical than we were," he would reflect later.[6] Outler spoke of disintegrating United Methodism characterized by Pelagianism. Wesley studies were in disarray; Church leaders lacked vision.

Thus began an unlikely friendship and alliance that would lead to the establishment of A Fund for Theological Education (AFTE), later renamed A Foundation for Theological Education. Outler recruited Bishop Earl Hunt as the first chair. Outler's friends in the academic world were willing to trust Robb because of Outler. Robb's friends in the evangelical world were willing to trust Outler because of Robb.

One of the first projects of the newly formed AFTE was to sponsor a colloquy at Notre Dame, at which fifty-eight scholars from eleven denominations—leading scholars from Catholic and Protestant communities, from liberal and evangelical perspectives—came together for a week to discuss the topic "Loss and Recovery of the Sacred." Persons from liberal seminaries sat down, many of them for the first time, with such evangelical scholars as Carl F. H. Henry and Richard Lovelace. The week was considered a huge success (at least from Albert Outler's perspective) and set the tone for what Ed Robb, Albert Outler, and Bishop Earl Hunt had proposed to do with AFTE.

Albert Outler would later comment that AFTE was the most satisfying achievement of his life.[7] The friendship between Outler and Robb deepened. Correspondence between the two was often personal (Outler would address his letters "Dear Eddie"). In his own affirmation of Outler, Robb and the AFTE board, and not Perkins or Southern Methodist University, initiated the campaign to raise $1 million to endow the Albert Outler Chair of Wesley Studies at the seminary. Robb promoted the idea through AFTE and enlisted Bishop Finis Crutchfield to chair the committee. The money was raised and the chair established.

By the turn of the twenty-first century, AFTE had helped fund one hundred "John Wesley fellows." Four of those persons were serving as seminary presidents or deans: Greg Jones of Duke, Ted Campbell of Garrett-Evangelical, Steve Harper of Asbury Orlando, and Joel Green of Asbury in Kentucky.

(2) The Junaluska Affirmation

Albert Outler, however, was not universally appreciated by Good News, primarily because of the 1972 doctrinal statement, which would eventually become known, at least in some circles, as the "Outler Statement." Good News had, from its inception, believed that the recovery of classical Wesleyan doctrine was the key to denominational renewal. Indeed, Charles Keysor's original article "Methodism's Silent Minority" in *The Christian Advocate*, which sparked the Good News movement, had defined that silent minority as those who held to the historic fundamentals of the faith, which included the inspiration of Scripture, the virgin birth of Christ, the substitutionary atonement, the physical resurrection, and the return of Christ.

In the minds of a number of people for whom the idea of "fundamentalism" was anathema, Keysor's listing of specific "fundamental" doctrine made him, and the movement he represented, a reactionary fundamentalist to be avoided at any cost. These persons, both friend and foe, were not able to distinguish between "fundamentalism" as an ideology and the kind of responsible neo-evangelicalism that Good News represented. Either way, there was no discounting the fact that doctrine was at the core of the movement.

There were many areas on which church "moderates" might agree with Good News: the need for balance in social action, the crisis of faith in the seminaries, the need for more missionaries to press the claims of Christ. Moderates also concurred with the need for spiritual depth in the Christian walk, and even the need for a reasoned faith. But the great Methodist middle was at best ambivalent, and in some cases downright hostile, to the suggestion that renewal in the Church was directly linked with a recommitment to historic doctrine.

The arguments depreciating doctrine took several forms:

- Methodism was never a confessional church;
- Wesley had said, "If your heart is as my heart, give me your hand," suggesting that Methodism was primarily a religion of experience;
- the way a Christian lives is more important than what a Christian believes;
- doctrine divides; and
- the emphasis on correct belief is judgmental and unloving.

There had been a fleeting renaissance of attention toward doctrine in the 1940s and 1950s, with interest in neo-orthodoxy, but even this was too much for many liberals. In the fall of 1958, the Council of Bishops, in one of the very few statements on doctrine ever made by the council, castigated the new interest in neo-orthodoxy, with its emphasis on doctrine and especially beliefs in depravity and "the second coming," and spoke of the need to be optimistic and hopeful about God's ability to change society. The bishops, mostly seminary-trained in the liberal 1920s and 1930s, were still holding out for God's kingdom to be established on earth through human efforts:

Now, however, a strange theology has been infiltrating our thought. It results in passive and patient acceptance of injustice and of exploitation and calls upon man to await God's good time, and thus becomes a tool of reaction and a suffocating miasma. Its proponents appear to forget that man is to be a co-worker with God and, together, bring peace to warring humanity, justice to exploited humanity, brotherhood to segregated humanity.

Neo-orthodoxy is neither new nor orthodox. Methodism needs a neo-Wesleyanism. "The personal knowledge of the love of God and of its transforming power in human life is the creative source of Methodism."[8]

But even the interest in neo-orthodoxy was short lived. The 1960s, a time of turmoil in politics, in moral traditions, and in social customs, also brought with it a time of theological confusion: existentialism, personalism, fundamentalism, Death of God theology, process theology, and liberation theologies.

With the merger of The Evangelical United Brethren Church and The Methodist Church in 1968, the matter of stated doctrine had to be faced. Whether or not anybody believed in them—or even knew they existed—doctrinal statements had been carried in every *Discipline* of all the predecessor denominations from the first Methodist conference in 1784. What was now to be done with these statements, specifically the Articles of Religion of The Methodist Church and the Confession of Faith of the EUB Church?

The task was handed to a task force headed by Albert Outler. Outler was a professor at Perkins School of Theology and the best-known denominational theologian. He knew Wesley forward and backward. He believed in doctrine. He was active in the World Methodist Council and in a number of ecumenical endeavors. He was a published author. He had lectured before bishops.

Joining him on the commission were board and agency representatives, several prominent pastors and laypersons, and a heavy preponderance of seminary professors, including outspoken liberals such as John Cobb of Claremont and Harvey Potthoff of Iliff.

Good News, though still a fledgling movement when the commission was established, asked in letters to Albert Outler and Robert Thornburg, staff person for the commission, to participate in the discussions. This was, after all, the matter most dear to the heart of evangelicals.

There is no reason to believe the request was ever considered seriously. There was not even a response to the letters that asked for Good News involvement.

For his part, Albert Outler was devoted to the commission and its task. He was also, perhaps more than any other person, aware of the problems the commission faced:

(1) Both churches, the Methodist and the EUB, had stated doctrinal standards, even though there was some discussion as to what precisely the standards were. For Methodists, the standards started with the Articles of Religion. But did they include Wesley's sermons and his *Notes Upon the New Testament?*

(2) The doctrinal standards had been widely ignored, and even scorned, for a number of years. They were almost never referred to in Methodist seminaries. For a number of persons, the merger offered opportunity to revise, if not completely scuttle, the standards.

(3) The Evangelical and the United Brethren churches, when they merged in 1946, had created the Confession of Faith of the EUB Church, which was a combination of the articles of the former denominations. Many persons, especially members of the EUB Church, were anticipating that the new United Methodist Church would merge the documents into a new United Methodist Confession that would be faithful to both traditions.

(4) The scuttling of the EUB and Methodist statements, or the combining of the two, even if desirable, would probably not be possible, because of the restrictive clause in the constitution of the Methodist *Discipline* that stated: "The General Conference shall not revoke, alter, or change our Articles of Religion or establish any new standards or rules of doctrine contrary to our present existing and established standards of doctrine."[9]

The Outler solution was ingenious. Do not tamper with the restrictive clause (this would be a long, complicated, unproductive, and probably unsuccessful constitutional engagement), but write an additional statement that would interpret the doctrinal standards, placing them in historical perspective, and letting them inform the present task of theologizing even as they did not inhibit that task. Then call the Church to a new challenge to theologize and, in the process, to restate the doctrinal tradition while all the time making doctrine relevant for the present time. The emphasis of the new statement would not be on content, that is, on the actual teachings of Methodism and Christian faith, but on process, that is, how the Church went about determining what it believed:

> In this task of reappraising and applying the gospel, theological plural-ism should be recognized as a principle. It is true that some would wish traditional doctrinal statements and standards recovered and enforced; others would demand that they be repealed; some would urge that they be perfected; others would insist that they be superseded. When doctri-nal standards are understood as legal or juridical instruments, it is easy to suppose that a doctrinal statement of some sort could be drawn up that would be normative and enforceable for an entire Christian body. Many persons with quite different views on doctrine insist that our inherited statements (e.g., the *Articles, Confession, Sermons, Notes,* and *General Rules*) ought either to be reaffirmed and enforced or superseded by new propositions. The effort to substitute new creeds for old has a long history of partisanship and schism.
>
> Our older traditions and our newer experiments in ecumenical theology provide a constructive alternative to this confessional tradition. . . . Our newer historical consciousness allows us to retain the various landmarks of our several heritages, interpreting them in historical perspective.[10]

Good News handled the report of the Commission on Doctrine poorly (see chapter 12). With no money, little political expertise, and no access into the decision-making structures of the Church, there was confusion, even within the board, about how to respond to the commission's report. Chuck Keysor, in the months before General Conference, tended to play down the importance of the statement. In a note to Robert Mayfield, who was directing the Good News political efforts, Keysor argued:

> For a long time, the denomination has good theology "on the book." Our Discipline has had good theology—but the denominational leaders have gutted it and made it meaningless by simply ignoring our doctrines and substituting their own. You can see this in all phases of the church. This has never been legally challenged, and so it appears that our offi-cial doctrines are a matter of relatively small importance. Some value, of course, results from being able to point to "our doctrines" in the Discipline. But nobody really cares—and so I feel that the report of this commission will make little real difference in the life of United Methodism, since everybody makes their own theology, without regard for what is "official." FOR THIS REASON I CONSIDER THE REPORT OF THIS COMMISSION OF SECONDARY IMPOR-TANCE. EVANGELICALS WAGING A FIGHT TO THE DEATH

HERE WOULD BE A WASTE OF ENERGY. MORE CONSTRUC-
TIVE CHANGE CAN BE ACCOMPLISHED BY PUSHING FOR
OUR RESOLUTIONS THAN BY WAGING WAR OVER A DOC-
UMENT WHICH WILL HAVE NO REAL INFLUENCE.[11]

Keysor's note also blessed the idea of pluralism:

On page 27, the report says, "Theological pluralism should be recognized as a principle." This is highly important, and we ought to work to
be sure that the principle of pluralism (i.e., our right to full representation and participation) be fully emphasized. An editorial on this subject
appears in our April issue. LET'S WORK FOR AN EVEN
STRONGER EMPHASIS ON PLURALISM AS A KEYSTONE IN
U.M. DOCTRINAL THINKING.

Many evangelicals either shared Keysor's view or—perhaps what is
more accurate—were simply uninformed about what was about to happen
at Atlanta. Not so Robert Coleman, member of the Good News board
and professor of evangelism at Asbury Seminary. At the Good News
board meeting in April of 1972, Coleman argued that the new doctrinal
statement cut the heart out of the gospel. If passed, it would signal the
Church's darkest hour. Coleman went so far as to offer a motion that
Good News move to a strategy of withholding apportionments as a witness against the doctrinal crisis in the Church. The motion did not pass,
but the fact that it was even made was a sign of the strong feelings within
the Good News board over the statement.

The General Conference approved the report of the Doctrinal
Commission 925-17 without amendment and without discussion. No
Good News voice, nor any evangelical voice for that matter, nor any
voice from any perspective, even raised a question about the report or the
ideas therein. After accepting the report that asserted that The United
Methodist Church was not a creedal or confessional church and that pluralism was the guiding principle that would inform future doctrinal discussions, the conference moved immediately to "the social creed," and
social principles in an extended floor debate that lasted six hours. During
that time, the thought that diversity or pluralism might also apply to the
Church's social stances was not expressed even once.

The Good News full board, meeting simultaneously with the General
Conference in Atlanta (which in itself reveals the political inexperience
of Good News), was devastated by the lopsided approval of the doctrinal

commission's report and the fact that it was received so nonchalantly. Suddenly—but much too late—Good News was concerned.

The summer 1972 issue of *Good News* carried a twelve-page report on General Conference written by Chuck Keysor. Five of the pages were devoted to the doctrinal statement. Keysor, who by now was totally opposed to the statement, charged that the feature of "doctrinal pluralism" meant that "anybody was free to believe anything—with no negative limits." Quoting reports in *Engage* magazine and the *Texas Methodist,* he also argued that the statement was a revocation and alteration of the present doctrinal standards and was thus in violation of the restrictive rule in the *Discipline*.

Albert Outler was scandalized by the Good News evaluation. In true Outler-style, he wrote Keysor:

> Your surprisingly harsh and reckless comments on the new UMC Doctrinal Statement . . . have left me utterly appalled. I had not, of course, ever hoped for your positive *approval*, but I really had thought you *might* have been willing to recognize our positive efforts to make room for *both* conservative *and* liberal theological perspectives in the United Methodist Church. These two tendencies *do* exist in the church and neither can eradicate the other (or even ought to try). And I had also hoped that you could see that our proposal about the Wesleyan quadrilateral [Scripture, tradition, experience, reason] as the criterion for Christian doctrine would give you a basis for your advocacy of your own theological position. Now I see that all such hopes were fatuous.
>
> If there was *any* indication in your remarks that you had merely misunderstood our text or that, somehow, you had overlooked our resolute and repeated rejections of "doctrinal indifferentism," there would then be room for still further discussion, at least about our *intentions*—and about the *constructive* possibilities for future development of doctrinal debate in the UMC. One of our clearest and most highly self-conscious intentions was to indicate the *negative limits* of allowable public teaching in the UMC. And yet you assert that no such limits are even *implied*. This, to put it bluntly, is a perverse and malicious misrepresentation, a sin against charity and truth.
>
> Over the years, I have kept on trying to believe that *Good News* really was concerned for fair play. . . . Now, finally, I see at first hand why so many other people (also "evangelical" in some sense or other, and almost as disturbed as you are over the parlous state into which the UMC has drifted) have simply written you off as partisan, intransigent, bigoted. There is, therefore, something tragic in your reckless and total rejection of us, since it forecloses any possibility of further meaningful

dialogue. This, in turn, can only result in mutual loss, to all of us and to the church as well.[12]

Keysor responded in true Keysor-style:

> We find it ironic to hear you saying that our editorial shuts the door to dialogue. As I have already noted, there was no dialogue from you until after the editorial, so it seems that publishing more editorials is the way to increase dialogue.
>
> The second paragraph of your letter indicates that you intended to make a clear delineation of negative limits. It is unfortunate that you failed to accomplish this objective. However, the extraordinary care and skill with which your document was reasoned and worded makes it doubtful whether a mere communications failure is involved. Is it not, rather, that you deliberately avoided being specific about negative limits? Theological eclecticism is evident throughout your report, and this would have been nullified if you had spelled out the negative limits, and made clear what the essential core of faith actually is.
>
> If it is true, as you say, that many people have "simply written you (Good News) off as partisan, intransigent, bigoted," we are sorry. Nobody enjoys being thus labeled. But if this is the price we must pay for clearly and honestly declaring what we believe, so be it. Our objective is not winning popularity nor engineering broad and unscriptural consensus. Instead, we are called to speak boldly and without compromise on matters which we understand to be crucial for the well-being of Christ's Church. As we speak, we expect that God will pronounce the final judgment upon us for truth and conformity to His Word. We hope that you will be content to leave our condemnation to the Lord and that you will exemplify true pluralism by extending the hand of friendship in spite of our disagreement.[13]

Good News was not opposed to pluralism or diversity as such, but insisted that pluralism needed to operate within carefully defined limits, or an essential core of truth. Otherwise, nothing would be unacceptable as United Methodist teaching. Outler and the commission insisted that there was an essential core but never defined what it was. To Good News and others, this was like the proverbial emperor's new clothes; one might claim to see them, but they weren't really there. Outside observers as diverse as *Christianity Today* and *Time* magazine understood this quite well. The *Time* magazine report of the General Conference noted:

The Outler commission's solution qualifies the traditional creeds—Wesley's Articles and the E.U.B. Confession of Faith—with explanatory statements warning that they should be interpreted within their historical context. The statements maintain that Wesley and the E.U.B. patriarchs made "doctrinal pluralism" a major tenet and held to only a basic core of Christian truth—but the statements stop short of specifying what that core was.[14]

The problem for Good News evangelicals was greater than pluralism, lack of focus, and willful ambiguity. A number of Good News leaders now faced a crisis of conscience.[15] The question was whether the Church was now in a state of apostasy. Despite a pervading theological liberalism on the part of Church leaders and the compromises of schools, of boards and agencies, and of bishops, as long as the stated doctrine of the Church was sound, the denomination could be supported. But what if the stated doctrine of the Church was so severely compromised as to no longer be even theoretically operative? Indeed, what if the idea of revealed truth was to include all religions?

> We recognize that the ecumenical process has expanded across the boundaries of Christian unity to include serious interfaith encounters and explorations between Christianity and other living religions of the world—including modern secular religions of humanism, communism, and utopian democracy. While we are increasingly aware of the larger whole of the Christian movement . . . we must also be conscious that God has been and is now working among all his people. There is a new sense in which we now must realize that we are given to one another on this fragile small planet, to work out with God the salvation, health, healing, and peace he intends for all his people. In these less familiar encounters, our aims are not to reduce doctrinal differences to some lowest common denominator of religious agreement, but to raise all such relationships to the highest possible level of human fellowship and understanding.[16]

In several different ways, the doctrinal statement represented a departure from traditional Wesleyanism. The seriousness of the matter was outlined in a letter to the board signed by Charles Keysor and C. Philip Hinerman, chair of the board in July 1972:

> Some U.M. evangelicals consider Atlanta a step forward, particularly in the concept of "pluralism," which they feel further establishes our right to exist.

However, the main mood seems to be one of sensing a further movement in the direction of humanistic, secular institutionalism—i.e. near total capitulation by the church to the standards and priorities of the unregenerate world. This represents a logical extension of the secularizing trend which has been running for many years. The newly-adopted policy of "doctrinal pluralism," is widely seen as a repudiation of historic Christianity, which follows the Scripture's advocacy of certain absolutes, which cannot be sacrificed without sacrificing the right to be considered Christian. Our new doctrinal position repudiates the idea that God has finally revealed truth, but makes the search for truth relative to prevalent thinking. This, in fact, repudiates the idea of Jesus Christ being the same yesterday, today and forever. Similarly, it rejects the possibility of Eternal unchanging absolutes concerning the nature of God and His plan for dealing with the world. Thus the new position acknowledges the authority of existential philosophy rather than Scripture. And it makes a mockery of the Biblical certainties upon which the whole Methodist movement has been based.

The church has been fed a monstrous lie: pluralism—true Methodism. That only 17 of the General Conference delegates recognized this and voted against the doctrinal statement shows the extent to which U.M. thinking and reasoning has gone askew from the New Testament, Wesleyan heritage that is rightfully ours.

The Executive Committee felt strongly opposed to temporizing in order to gain supposed political advantages through advocacy of "pluralism." Instead, it seems that God would have us condemn it for the abomination which it represents, and proclaim the judgment of God upon all the prevailing humanism. We feel that God calls us to this prophetic stance, regardless of what the cost may be in terms of our own popularity and personal security. If our true security—measured in the Eternal dimension—is to be found only in Christ, then we dare not compromise. If we take the stand which harmonizes with Scripture, in direct obedience to Christ, then we are prepared to trust Him for the future.

And so, like Luther, we declare in the face of the prevailing "pluralism"—here we stand. We can do no other. So help us God![17]

With its stand clearly taken, Good News was willing to stay the battle. As Keysor editorialized in the summer issue of *Good News* in 1972:

What are evangelicals to do, in the aftermath of Atlanta? Many are quitting, feeling that the United Methodist Church has abandoned and betrayed Christ, the Gospel and its members.

Good News feels deep sorrow and pain at the exodus of these brothers and sisters in Christ. We do not condemn any person for following
God's leading, but we feel strongly that God calls us to remain. This has
been our motive from the start. . . .

To separate or not to separate, that is the basic issue. And so we feel
it desirable to share with readers why we believe the most important
place for evangelicals is inside the United Methodist Church.[18]

Keysor's reasons for staying reflected a remnant kind of thinking:

In the past (God) has worked miracles through tiny remnant groups
which fear only displeasing the One who has called them—the One
whom they know as Father. Who cares if we are a small minority?
Numbers and success are pagan preoccupations. To gain control of the
denominations means nothing; to be faithful to Jesus Christ means
everything.[19]

While a number of evangelicals, including some even on the Good
News board, were willing to make their peace with "pluralism"—indeed,
to use it as an appeal for acceptance—an inner core grew increasingly strident in its opposition. In August of 1974, Good News sponsored a
National Conference on Evangelical Strategy in Louisville at which issues
of doctrine and the doctrinal statement became the focus of attention.
The news release from UMCom (United Methodist Communications)
was perceptive:

United Methodist evangelicals associated with the Good News movement have taken a hard line in opposition to the denomination's doctrine of theological pluralism and may challenge the constitutionality of
such a doctrine through the church's Judicial Council. . . .

The stance, a shift from the groups' more open attitude since the
1972 General Conference adopted the theological pluralism doctrine,
was evidenced here during the Good News National Conference on
Evangelical Strategy, Aug. 6-8, and was endorsed by the Good News
Board of Directors at its meeting Aug. 9.

Keynoting the attack on the church's theology was the Rev. Charles
W. Keysor of Wilmore, Ky., founder-editor of *Good News* magazine, who
charged that a "condition of total confusion—of theological anarchy—exists"
within United Methodism. He alleged the adoption of theological
pluralism, placing Methodism's Articles of Religion in an historical
context, has "circumvented" the Articles "in defiance of the Restrictive
Rule, which is supposed to protect Methodist doctrinal standards from
alteration."

Issuing a challenge to Good News, an unofficial caucus of evangelicals, the Rev. Mr. Keysor asked, "Is it time to appeal to United Methodism's Supreme Court, the Judicial Council? Has the time come to establish that the Restrictive Rules have, indeed, been violated, and that doctrinal pluralism is therefore unconstitutional?"[20]

Prior to the 1974 conference, Chuck Keysor had opportunity for an intensive two-hour conversation with Albert Outler, when Outler came to Asbury Seminary in March 1974 to deliver a series of lectures on Wesleyan theology at the fiftieth anniversary of the seminary. In a detailed account of the conversation shared with a few members of the board, Keysor offered his impressions of Outler reacting to Good News concerns: Though Outler strongly believed in a core of irreducible doctrinal truth, he also believed that attempts at doctrinal definition "always result in inadequate conceptions of ultimate realities" (propositional statements demanding allegiance smacked of fundamentalism). He admitted, basically, that he was not interested in a specific of "core" essential doctrine, even though he believed the Church could refer to such a core.

Outler, however, was at least pleased that someone was willing to discuss doctrine and offered his own suggestions as to the sorts of actions Good News might pursue.

(1) Good News could test the seminaries' resistance to pluralism by underwriting the education of several outstanding young scholars who would take degrees at such institutions as Yale, Chicago, or Oxford in such areas as patristics, historical theology, and New Testament and, then backed by impeccable credentials, go to the Board of Higher Education and ask if there is any discrimination because of their conservatism (this would soon become the strategy of A Fund for Theological Education [AFTE]).

(2) If the Church really wanted a descriptive statement of the "core" of essential United Methodist doctrine, it could do so by amending or altering the present statement with a 51 percent vote of the General Conference (this, in fact, would soon become the Good News legislative strategy in coming General Conferences).

(3) Outler's intent in the 1972 statement was to sketch broad theological generalities and encourage "theologizing," in which identifiable groups in the Church would delineate their own essential core—what they would be willing to die for.

It was this third suggestion that gave additional impetus to a Good News effort, already being discussed and planned, to offer a contemporary evangelical interpretation of the essential core of Wesleyan doctrine for United Methodism. To do this, Good News called upon Paul Mickey, Associate Professor of Pastoral Theology at the divinity school at Duke, to lead a committee to draft a statement to offer to the Church. Chuck Keysor would serve on the committee, as well as board members Jim Heidinger, pastor from East Ohio, Riley Case, a pastor from North Indiana, and Lawrence Souder, an articulate layperson originally from Collingswood, New Jersey. Two other persons, however, were key to the committee if the effort was to represent the wider evangelical community and not just Good News. Dennis Kinlaw, president of Asbury College, and Frank Stanger, president of Asbury Seminary, both agreed to be part of the group that would draw up the statement.[21]

The statement would:

(1) Be an evangelical response to the 1972 doctrinal statement's invitation for groups to engage in theological discussion and affirmation. The statement had declared "all members and groups are responsible for clarifying the theological premises on which they operate," and evangelicals intended to do just that.[22]

(2) Seek to identify the "core of doctrine" that the 1972 statement alluded to but never defined.

(3) Serve as a rallying point for evangelicals in the Church.

The task force did not see itself as creating new doctrine, but rather as restating the Articles of Religion and the Confession of Faith in contemporary language. It did understand that it needed to distinguish itself not only from the far left in theology, but also from the far right. It needed to avoid fundamentalist code language, such as "inerrancy," and "infallibility."

Before the final draft, the statement was shared with Albert Outler. Outler obviously was pleased that at least one group was taking the 1972 statement seriously enough to draw up a doctrinal statement.

In a letter dated March 31, 1975, Outler replied to Paul Morrell, pastor of Tyler Street Church and Good News board chair:

> Thanks for that copy of the "draft statement" of "Scriptural Christianity for United Methodists." I've read it with care and real appreciation. This is an important response to that invitation in the *Discipline* (Part II) for United Methodists to engage in thoughtful, responsible doctrinal formulations—not as a displacement for Part II but as an exposition of a given doctrinal position that belongs within the framework of our Wesleyan heritage and of "Scriptural Christianity." This statement, even in its present tentative form, most certainly falls within those limits—and I welcome the venture, even as I have found it interesting and edifying. Power to the project—especially in its tone and temper![23]

Outler continued with an eight-page critique of the statement. His critique perhaps said more about his own theology than the work of the committee. Outler argued that the approach of the statement, that is, the organizing of essential doctrines around themes of systematic theology (sin, God, atonement, Jesus Christ) was not Wesley's approach, who rather located the "essentials" in the proclaiming of the holy story.[24]

The statement was made available at the 1975 Good News Convocation at Lake Junaluska, where it was discussed in small groups, adopted by the assembly gathered, and became known as the Junaluska Affirmation. The affirmation, along with Ed Robb's address on the seminaries, made the 1975 Good News Convocation one of the movement's defining moments.

The United Methodist Reporter editorialized positively on the Junaluska Affirmation and printed it in full. UMCom, the official United Methodist news service, commented briefly that the "affirmation" had been adopted and added remarks from Paul Mickey about the need for "theological clarity in a time of theological confusion" and from Good News referring to the doctrinal standards and the ancient creeds as the foundation for historic faith.

There was some disappointment on the part of Good News that the affirmation failed to stir up either reaction or critique or comment from the larger Church. It was pointed out, however, that except for the bishops—given the charge in the *Discipline* "to guard . . . the apostolic faith"—no board or agency or group in the Church felt ownership or responsibility for doctrine. It was not so much that the general Church agreed or disagreed or affirmed or denied the Good News doctrinal effort. It was rather that it just did not care that much.

Later, the September 1975 issue of *Interpreter* magazine carried an editorial by Roger Burgess entitled "Has Good News Become Bad News?"

Burgess did not critique the Junaluska Affirmation but was uneasy that Good News should draw up a statement in the first place. Burgess asked, "Suppose I wanted to set up my own denomination." If he did he might start by (1) criticizing the established Church as weak and sick; (2) establish his own statement of doctrine; (3) prepare training material for confirmands; (4) seek to develop theological schools; (5) create his own missions program; (6) publish his own general periodical; and (7) conduct regional and national meetings to rally the loyal minority. Burgess concluded: "I find it hard to discover much that is constructive or loyal in these actions and proposals."[25]

As far as Good News was concerned, the Burgess comments were a misreading of the intent of the Junaluska Affirmation and of the purpose of Good News. But for once, Good News was secure enough it did not need to be defensive about the accusations of the editorial. It would direct its energies from this time forth not needing to define who it was, but in understanding and seeking to bring renewal to The United Methodist Church.

And the task, at least as it related to doctrine, was formidable. The general Church, already in a state of doctrinal confusion, seemed to be able to make no sense out of the 1972 statement. The attempts to clarify seemed only further to obfuscate. In 1976, the General Board of Discipleship through Discipleship Resources published the pamphlet "Essential Beliefs for United Methodists" authored by James Hares from Texas. It was to be an attempt to interpret to local churches and individuals the 1972 doctrinal statement.

The pamphlet managed to feature "essential beliefs" without the first mention of doctrinal standards or of the Articles of Religion or the Confession of Faith or of the sermons of Wesley. The one belief that seemed more essential than all others was the belief that "our strength comes through unity in diversity rather than through rigid uniformity." If there were "essential beliefs," they were what we were to formulate for ourselves (the opening sentence was, "Our beliefs grow out of our experiences"), based on the quadrilateral: Scripture, Tradition, Experience, and Reason. These core beliefs evidently had nothing to do with Christ's death on the cross for our sin or, for that matter, Christ's death on the cross for any reason. Nor did it refer to the Resurrection, to salvation, justification, sanctification, heaven or hell, or to the New Birth. At least none of these were even mentioned. The pamphlet was obsessed with the importance of the quadrilateral, and that discussion took twelve of the sixteen pages. It spent time with sacraments and mentioned creeds, but only with the discounting qualification that "the living God cannot be reduced to or contained in any creed."

191

But, according to the pamphlet, the Church was not without stated beliefs. United Methodists did have agreement, if not about doctrinal beliefs, then on the social principles. "Essential Beliefs for United Methodists" closed with the Social Creed prefaced with the words: "Our Social Creed provides a summary of our beliefs as United Methodists."

Another example of the confusion is revealed in the book *United Methodist Primer*, which was published by Discipleship Resources and then revised and circulated widely as an explanation of United Methodists.[26] The chapter "What We Believe" focuses not on historic United Methodist doctrine, but on beliefs as mystery:

> There are still many aspects of the Christian faith that are a mystery to me. I "see through a glass darkly." I am awaiting further light. I trust, realizing there is truth embodied in what I do not fully understand. But I rejoice in the fact that I can still grow in my understanding of the faith. I invite you to think seriously about what it is you believe, and to share your beliefs with others.[27]

The chapter then spoke of "fundamental truths at the heart of the gospel that can be identified" and then introduced the "Four Guidelines"—Scripture, tradition, Christian experience, and reason—as a way these truths might be identified. The book did introduce the idea of "essential beliefs," but the essential beliefs did not mention original sin, the Atonement, the Resurrection, the Trinity, or salvation by grace through faith; instead the author spoke of God, Jesus Christ, the Holy Spirit, forgiveness, Scripture (the Word of God is "contained" in the Bible; the Bible helps us live in terms of God's will; the Bible is the record of experiences), church, kingdom of God, and eternal life.

The subunit "Emphases of Special Importance for United Methodists" in *United Methodist Primer* mentioned human dignity, grace, conversion (without mention of sin), faith and works, inclusive church, connectional church, and sacraments. The chapter mentioned "doctrinal standards" only to qualify that neither the Articles of Religion nor the Confession of Faith were to be interpreted in a legalistic or dogmatic way.[28]

Good News had a long and laborious task ahead of it.

CHAPTER NINE

GOOD NEWS AS POLITICAL CAUCUS

Following the news briefing in Indianapolis in January 1980 that brought together agency heads, caucus groups, and other interested persons prior to the 1980 General Conference, United Methodist News Service issued a news release that included the following observations:

> Major division of opinion erupted over the proposal of "designated giving," by which local churches could give to or withhold from specific boards. The idea was opposed by all agency and caucus representatives *except Good News*. . . .
>
> All the caucuses, *except Good News*, and several boards are urging the elimination of Discipline Par. 906.13, which prohibits the use of church funds to support or promote homosexuality or gay groups. This rule was deplored as preventing dialogue for greater understanding of homosexuality and restricting the exploration of ministries to gays and their families. . . .
>
> The Social Principles language adopted in 1972 and reaffirmed in 1976 will be under attack again, as most agencies and caucuses, *except Good News*, seek to remove the clause that "we do not condone the

practice of homosexuality and consider this practice incompatible with Christian teaching."[1]

From a Good News perspective, the 1980 General Conference in Indianapolis was shaping up as a first-class disaster. The Good News proposal for designated giving was in deep trouble. Its stand on human sexuality, especially in regard to the practice of homosexuality, was being countered by boards and agencies and caucus groups in favor of the "open view," which would not prohibit funding to homosexual advocacy and would remove all negative language in the *Discipline* regarding homosexuality. Good News seemed a lone voice in the wilderness.

But Good News, perhaps for the first time, was being taken with some seriousness. Previously it was viewed more as a nuisance, a vocal minority with a "conservative" agenda, but with no significant influence. Now, suddenly, it was a threat.

A number of religious observers, both inside and outside the Church, commented on what they saw was the growing influence of Good News. Kenneth Briggs, religion editor of *The New York Times*, commented that Good News was credited with "shaping much of the legislation at the United Methodist General Conference last year [1976]."[2] He also spoke of "schismatic trends" in several mainline denominations that heralded "shifting ground" on the Christian landscape.

The *Times* followed this up in the article "Good News Evangelicals Worry Leaders of the Methodist Church," by George Vecsey, which was circulated widely across the country. Vecsey reported that Good News was "shaking the United Methodist Church," was "causing tremors in Methodist centers in New York, Nashville and Dayton," and had been attacked by several bishops.[3]

Within the Church, Methodist Federation for Social Action (MFSA) pealed bells of alarm. In an eight-page exposé entitled "Apostles of Reaction," which first ran in MFSA's *The Social Questions Bulletin* (*SQB*) in the November-December 1978 issue and the January-February 1979 issue and was then reprinted and widely circulated,[4] the theology of Good News was interpreted as neither "evangelical" nor "orthodox," but actually that of "a rigid, traditional fundamentalism." Its interpretation of the Bible was "literalism"; its approach to theology, "uncreative scholasticism"; and its view of pluralism, one that only accepts "biblical literalists, while excluding everyone else."[5]

But it was not the theology but the "Political Views" of Good News that really concerned MFSA:

> Though they [Good News] claim they are only concerned about "spiritual" matters rather than any social and political agenda, a close reading of their literature reveals that they have their own social-political agenda. They do not in fact oppose the church involvement in social-political matters; they only oppose it when it does not further their own positions.[6]

This political agenda, according to MFSA, was that of the "New Far Right." Before the "analysis" was completed, MFSA had connected Good News with witch-hunts, McCarthyism, a "South African connection," with an amazing income "heavily subsidized by large gifts from rich supporters." Furthermore, "Good News"[7] leadership allegedly "reflects the paranoic tendencies, the apocalyptic and aggressive worldview, the suspicion of conspiracy, and the felt need to unmask secret evil which characterize extremism."[8]

What was frightening, according to the articles, was that Good News was gearing up for the 1980 General Conference to seek to impose its right-wing agenda on the Church.

The analysis closed with a liberal call to arms:

> Religious fundamentalism, with its moral absoluteness, its otherworldliness, and its holy war mentality, also thrives in a climate of fear and uncertainty. The wedding between militant fundamentalism and reactionary politics is a natural and recurring one.
>
> The New Far Right presents a special challenge. What is "new" is its sophistication in political tactics, fund-raising, mass organization, and coalition building. It is these characteristics which also make the New Far Right presence in the UMC a special challenge, for "Good News" leaders have been demonstrating considerable sophistication in these areas. Thus they constitute a greater long-term threat to the church's mission and life than earlier far rightist groups in the church such as the Circuit Riders of the 1950s.[9]
>
> "Good News" leaders would prefer to conceal their reactionary politics under a camouflage of "evangelical" concerns. However, in pretending that their program is spiritual and not political, they are at their most hypocritical, for "Good News" leaders have a political agenda— and a very reactionary one, as we have shown. "Good News" leaders not only wish to neutralize the church's commitment to social justice and its threat to entrenched principalities and powers of privilege. In addition, their political ties and social views suggest an ultimate goal of

aligning the church with the reactionary politics of the privileged sectors and giving religious sanction to their policies of oppression. . . .

The emergence of fundamentalist extremism in the church calls for a two-fold response. The church must make clear that a divisive sectarianism which sets out militantly to "save" us all, which condemns non-fundamentalists as humanists, which employs distortions, confrontations, McCarthyism and witch hunts to get its way, and which would align the church with those who "rob the poor and crush the afflicted," simply is out of step with the spirit of Christ as United Methodists have come to understand it.[10]

Good News should have felt flattered that so much power and influence and wealth had been assigned to it. At the time the articles were written, Good News had almost no money and hardly any strategy for the 1980 General Conference (eventually $10,000 would be budgeted for political strategy). The persons associated with Good News were hardly persons of privilege. No bishops identified with Good News. There was a district superintendent and a seminary professor serving on the board, but no members or staff of any general agencies. There were no wealthy benefactors. There were no ties or coalitions with any right-wing or, for that matter, any political groups. Good News was still primarily a populist movement made up of "little people." Two of its board members, Robert Sprinkle and Randy Jones, were involved in inner-city ministries and tended to be liberal politically. Charles Keysor himself, and several of the Good News board, had voted for Jimmy Carter in the previous presidential election. Far from demonstrating "considerable sophistication in these areas" (political tactics, fund-raising, and coalition building), Good News, at least from a later perspective, was in primary school.

"Paranoiac tendencies, . . . the suspicion of conspiracy, and the felt need to unmask secret evil which characterize extremism" was a description that better described Good News's critics rather than Good News itself. In the November 10, 1978, issue of *United Methodist Reporter*, Ignacio Castuera wrote a "Here I Stand" article in which he argued that "Good News" was not good news to ethnics, to women, to The United Methodist Church, and to the missionary enterprise of the Church.[11] Good News was racist because it questioned the quota system. Good News was sexist because it questioned the quota system. Good News undermined The United Methodist Church by wanting to force persons to conform to their own "narrow bigotry." According to Castuera, Good News undermined the missionary enterprise by disrupting its sense of unity.

In addition to these criticisms, a new caucus, the Coalition for the Whole Gospel, had been formed by George McClain, executive secretary of MFSA, Gilbert Caldwell, past president of Black Methodists for Church Renewal (BMCR), and other well-placed and well-known liberal activists, many of whom were staff members relating to the Board of Global Ministries, the Board of Church and Society, and the National Council of Churches. Though reporters were barred from the organization meeting on February 25-26, 1979, it was widely understood that the purpose of the group was to combat conservative and reactionary influences in the denomination (read: the Good News movement) and push for a liberal agenda at the 1980 General Conference. The caucus hired the Reverend Michael McIntyre, the former director of Bishops' Call to Peace, who had "blasted" Good News as a "new form of 'know-nothingism' well outside the whole of Christian tradition."[12]

Was all of the furor justified? In just over ten years of existence, had Good News really become a major political force in the denomination?

Evangelicalism in Methodism, and especially populist-Holiness-revivalism evangelicalism, despite the fact that it commanded the loyalty of many followers and, in many respects, and had major influence on Methodist culture and ethos, had never been a factor in church politics. Bishops, agency heads, seminary and college presidents, and General Conference delegates had seldom been drawn from the ranks of populist evangelicals. These evangelicals did well at writing gospel hymns, preaching revivals, becoming missionaries, and leading prayer meetings but were incompetent and even disinterested when it came to leading and managing the institution.

The earliest Good News leaders did not see themselves as a political caucus. Chuck Keysor was an acute observer of the religious scene and a visionary. He was well aware that evangelical renewal was already taking place in the larger Protestant world. He believed that renewal could also come to Methodism and that evangelicals were the key in making that happen; but like many evangelicals, he saw renewal more in changed lives and matters of the spirit rather than in changed paragraphs in the *Discipline*. Though there was no articulated "strategy" for renewal, there were certain convictions that characterized Good News at the beginning.

(1) Evangelicals in The Methodist Church were a "silent minority," but they were a significant minority. Good News evangelicals were the kind of people who taught Sunday school classes, attended prayer meetings, and tithed their income. Many, however, were discouraged, not realizing how

significant their numbers were. In many respects, these evangelicals were strangers in their own country. In their coming together and in the expressions of their corporate faith, they could call the Church back to its theological and spiritual roots. This could be through the *Good News* magazine, through renewal groups, and through the convocations.

(2) The radicalism of the 1960s had alienated many conservatives,[13] and the exodus from Methodism was reaching alarming proportions. Denominational leaders, captive to the trends of the time and stumbling over themselves to be "relevant," were either unaware or unwilling to face this hemorrhaging. Many saw the future of Methodism not in evangelicalism, which they viewed as retreat to the past, but in the radical trends of the time: the Death of God, the Secular City, Marxist sociological analysis, and various ideologies of liberation. On one level, Good News sought to engage the church theologically.[14] On another level, an inordinate amount of time was spent seeking to keep evangelicals in the denomination.[15] A certain critical mass was necessary for evangelical renewal. Because of this, an important part of Chuck Keysor's time in the first two years of Good News was spent in correspondence and in phone conversation seeking to convince discouraged evangelicals that there was a hopeful future for Methodism.

(3) On the one hand, Good News leaders saw marvelous evidences of God's working in nontraditional ways to bring renewal: the Jesus People, new music and forms of worship, parachurch ministries such as Campus Crusade, and the charismatic movement—all of which were celebrated by Good News.[16] On the other hand, Good News leaders were committed to traditional evangelical expressions such as revivals, youth camps, prayer meetings, missions, and the Sunday school. Of all of the groups in the Church, populist evangelicals were the strongest supporters of the Sunday school, which at the same time was the greatest source of irritation to Good News.

Given these convictions, it is understandable that Good News had not, at least in its earliest years, focused on political activity. The earliest magazines and the earliest minutes of Good News board meetings make almost no mention of the crucial 1968 General Conference that was to be held in Dallas. There was, however, a list of topics and petitions that Good News hoped persons would submit to General Conference, but there was no strategy to see if they were submitted or were supported in any way.[17]

The list of topics and petitions tells a lot about Good News's thinking · in the late 1960s. In keeping with its populist nature, there was a call to stop discrimination against supply pastors, for the Church to narrow the gap between leaders and the people of the pews, and for the Church not to make ecumenical commitments without the involvement of the local church. Other petition suggestions opposed "one-sided ecumenical enthusiasm," the failure of the Church to uphold doctrine, unrealistic committee structures in the local church, insensitive seminaries, and a distorted emphasis on social issues.

There is no reason to believe that the 1968 General Conference paid any attention to the Good News petitions. Good News did not publicize its agenda, did not contact any delegates, and, in fact, was not even represented at the conference, with the exception of Chuck Keysor who attended part time as a member of the press.

The 1968 General Conference, the uniting conference for the Methodist and Evangelical United Brethren merger, belonged to the avant-garde liberals. The year 1968 was a year of social upheaval. It was the year of Woodstock, the assassination of Martin Luther King Jr., and student unrest in many places. The merger itself, with the understanding that a new church would require a new structure, a new social ethic, even a new doctrinal statement, gave impetus to ideas of change, progress, and interacting with a brave new world.

In addition, there was a recognition that despite all the liberal platitudes about racial integration and justice, the Church had never really addressed racism within its own structures and institutions. It was dramatically reminded of this by two newly formed groups, Black Methodists for Church Renewal (BMCR) and Methodists for Church Renewal. Leaders in these groups included James Lawson, founder of the Student Nonviolent Coordinating Committee of Memphis (the person who had asked Martin Luther King Jr., to come to Memphis at the time of the assassination); Cecil Williams, whose politics were considered by some to be radical; and J. Robert Nelson, professor at Boston University's School of Theology. With tactics in keeping with the 1960s, the groups seized the General Conference floor, marched, sang, demonstrated, made demands, and were given just about everything they asked for.

That the conference capitulated to the demands so easily and so decisively surprised everyone, even the demonstrators themselves. A General Conference news release written by Raymond Wilson on May 2, 1968, commented in this way:

But what neither renewal group anticipated at Dallas was the built-in liberal mood of a majority of the delegates. The renewal-minded delegates found others making their motions for them, and in most cases the Conference voted with them without the cajoling, pressuring and pleading that marked their generally unsuccessful efforts at a special session of the Methodist General conference in Chicago 17 months earlier.[18]

The 1968 General Conference established the Commission on Religion and Race (with funding to be supplied by percentage reductions in the budgets of other agencies), went on record to support Project Equality, set up the $20 million Fund for Reconciliation, supported the Board of Missions in its withdrawal of funds from a bank pledging loans to the apartheid government of South Africa, and established a new social concerns magazine, later called *Engage*. In an action even more controversial, the conference supported the "right of non-violent civil disobedience in extreme cases." In the 1960s, this was considered a radical stance.

The conference also removed from ministerial qualifications the specific prohibitions on the use of tobacco and alcohol. If the actions of General Conference were any indicator, the momentum of the Church was clearly not with political and social conservatives.

In a confidential report to the Good News board, Chuck Keysor assessed the damage:

> Over and over, I met liberals in Dallas beaming with joy. More than one said radiantly to me, "This is far better than I had dared to expect." The non-conservative orientation of the church hierarchy (bishops, boards and agencies, superintendents and elected delegates) was well established, and comes [as] no surprise. What happened was that the experimental, left-moving social current was running swifter and deeper than anyone expected. So the General Conference represents simply a logical extension of the political, social and theological direction in which the church leadership has been traveling for a long, long time. The E.U.B. influence seemed to have little, if any, mitigating influence. . . .
>
> I was impressed by the blatant anti-theological pragmatism of Methodism, as reflected by people on the conference floor. I heard several openly scorn theological considerations as "impractical." And theological considerations, as such, seemed absent from most of the discussions. In place of theology the dominant theme was sociology. The death of Martin Luther King, Jr. commanded all attention; the

death of Christ none—as our President, Dale Bittinger, later expressed it. The conference underwent a flagellation of white guilt for unfair dealing with Negroes. This theme wove itself like a litany through speeches, entertainment, and worship. The Kerner Report's conclusion became Gospel.[19]

Some observers have suggested that the radical social stands of the 1968 General Conference triggered a conservative reaction and thus fueled the rise of Good News.[20] There may have been some conservative reaction in the larger church, but the inner core of Good News was dealing with different issues. Keysor's confidential report discussed at length the lifting of the ban against alcohol and tobacco:

Interestingly, some of the most powerful arguments for the ban being continued came from Negro delegates. They were almost the only speakers I heard mentioning things like the Bible, God, and Christ on the Conference floor.

Also, I was impressed by the archaic temperance arguments voiced by some white speakers in opposition to lifting the ban. These were voices from a far-gone era, and I sensed they were not even comprehending the present mood or issues.

The formal reasoning behind removal of the ban had logical appeal. The truth is, however, that the real driving force behind removal of the ban was desire to "get with the world." It was obvious, as the saying goes, that the church is taking its cues and orders from the unbelieving world. It is considered "bad form" to insist on anything that makes a distinguishing difference between believers and unbelievers. . . .

I found it significant that the question of removing this ban generated the most heat at the Conference. Apparently, people were willing to argue to the death against ministers smoking or drinking—but nobody cared, much, what heresy ministers broadcast from thousands of pulpits. Passionate debate over no smoking—but none over the heresy in official Methodist publications.

I would have been happier to see the heat generated on the basic theological issues which are destroying the church. But these never got into the agenda.[21]

Keysor found one bright spot in the conference:

A very significant fact, to me, was the militant spirit of "freedom" which hung over the conference. The far left has promoted this for all it's worth. And the significance lies in this freedom of the left, lessening the absolute grip of the hierarchy. For make no mistake about it, the far left hates everything about the institutional church—except its name and its money. There is no question in my mind that the New Freedom can redound to our benefit too.[22]

It was not because of anything Good News had done, but because of the "far left" that the conference removed the restrictions from the *Discipline* on the use of anything but "official" curriculum materials in the church school. If the conference would limit the institutional restraints and free evangelicals to follow their own visions for ministry, then the conference represented good.

In a telling insight into Good News populist thinking at the time, Chuck Keysor would later reflect:

> When the merger came in 1968, the new church plan of union emphasized greater freedom for the local church to be in mission—"to do its own thing" for Jesus Christ. Long experience had proved the sterility and futility of a bureaucratic structure where people in church agency offices, remote from the reality of the local church, hand down wisdom from on high . . . wisdom often given *ex cathedra*. This system has proved its futility. And so the 1968 merger wisely set the local church free from subservience to bureaucrats in faraway places. I thank God for the wisdom of General Conference, at this point.
>
> I have heard two top officials from the curriculum-producing portion of our Board of Education say the United Methodist Discipline does not compel United Methodist Churches to use Nashville's literature. . . .   .
>
> Brothers and sisters, we have been set free! Liberated from bondage![23]

In 1970, the Church held a specially called General Conference in St. Louis to deal with merger issues. The conference delegates were basically the same delegates who had gathered in Dallas in 1968. There was little to encourage Good News. Good News supporters had submitted 249 petitions asking for Sunday school material that could be used by evangelicals, but the petitions fell on deaf ears. In one revealing vote, the conference voted 465-431 against a petition that would have denied church funds to organizations advocating the overthrow of governments. At this conference, a group of radical "youth" (many were older than the *Discipline*'s definition of youth) demonstrated, seeking independence from any adult control or supervision from the Board of Education. In the spirit of the times, this was granted.

By late 1971, Good News leaders began to talk about making their next (or perhaps it was their first) serious run at influencing the General Conference. The board was encouraged by several developments. The 1970 Good News Convocation had been successful beyond imagination, renewal groups had been formed in a number of conferences, and the circulation of the magazine was growing (to over twelve thousand). It was time for political activity.

In another confidential report distributed in late 1971, Keysor gave the rationale:

> The increasing evangelical current, of which Good News has been a primary generating force, has resulted in the election of a considerable number of new delegates known to be openly evangelical or leaning strongly in this direction. If it can be organized, and if we can overcome the powerful counter-pressures of other "caucuses" we stand a good chance of making some significant changes through the legislative process at General Conference.[24]

The Good News plan called for a three-fold approach: (1) work through renewal groups to flood the conference with petitions, and then follow these petitions through the legislative process; (2) bring five hundred evangelical youth to Atlanta to counteract the control the "new left" holds over the "denominational youth apparatus"; and (3) draw together the evangelically minded delegates for strategy, discussions, and prayer.

The key figure in the 1972 strategy was Robert Mayfield, Good News board member and Director of Development at Asbury Seminary. Mayfield was an attorney and had served for sixteen years as General Secretary of the Board of Lay Activities. He had chaired the 1970 and 1971 Good News Convocations. He was experienced and connected in ways other Good News leaders were not. Mayfield counted among his friends a number of bishops and church leaders. He was knowledgeable of church politics and had been a delegate to General Conference on several occasions. Mayfield agreed to head Good News's political strategy for 1972.

Identifying issues, writing suggested petitions, and generating interest from the constituency to write petitions was the easy part. Once again, Good News's concerns were primarily populist in nature: allow lay members to vote on ordained clergy issues in the annual conferences, limit tenure of general agency staff, allow churches to use non-United

Methodist Sunday school material, allow local churches to follow some form of designated giving, place Jesus Christ at the center of United Methodist programs, and withdraw from COCU (Consultation on Church Union). *Good News* magazine pitched these causes.

It must be noted that however Good News might have assessed its own importance, it was still not being viewed very seriously, if at all, by the larger Church. In a revealing article that appeared in the March 1972 issue of *Engage*, an analysis was done on the major "caucuses" that would be seeking to influence the 1972 General Conference.[25] Black Methodists for Church Renewal was mentioned, as was the Woman's Caucus, the Youth Caucus, the Young Adult Caucus, and (possibly) the Gay Caucus, but not Good News. Good News was not even a blip on the radar screen.

With or without influence, petitions were written and flowed in. Official boards, individuals, Sunday school classes, took to heart the idea that ordinary people could have a say in the direction of the Church. Between fifteen thousand and sixteen thousand out of a total of twenty thousand petitions were generated by the Good News effort. It was, if anything, a true populist effort.

Unfortunately, it was in large part an effort wasted. An unprepared General Conference staff was not able to process the stacks of petitions. Petitions submitted by general boards and agencies and by special task forces were printed and distributed among the delegates ahead of time. Petitions from individuals and from annual conferences were printed with only a title and the name of the submitter. The petitions generated by Good News were simply lumped together into "representative" petitions. Three hundred petitions could be treated as one with no special consideration. Most of the petitions were summarily dismissed.

In addition, other parts of the Good News strategy did not go well. Good News had set a goal of $2,000 for General Conference efforts. It raised less than half of that amount. The plan to bring evangelical youth to the conference never materialized. The plan to draw together evangelical delegates for discussion, prayer, and strategy had very limited success. Of course, it did not help that the Good News board was physically present at the conference but otherwise occupied. The board had decided to hold its regular board meeting at the site of the conference at the very time the conference was taking place. This meant that the board itself was not able to track or follow its own legislative efforts. Good News still had a lot to learn about political strategy.

Good News did manage to publish several issues of a news sheet at the site of the conference. Indeed, one positive note from an evangelical point of view in an otherwise dismal General Conference was the arrival on the scene of two articulate and committed young adults drawn to the Good News cause. Robert Sprinkle was on the staff of Urban Ministries in the North Georgia Conference. He had some training from Saul Alinksy and an innate sense of politics. Helen Rhea Coppedge would eventually fill several key roles in the cause of evangelical renewal, as a board member and then chair of the Good News board, as a cofounder of the Women's Task Force of Good News (later RENEW), and then, following her marriage to John Stumbo, as a key figure in the Bristol Books spin-off and in the founding of IRD (Institute of Religion and Democracy) and its United Methodist component of IRD, UMAction.

Sprinkle and Coppedge, both from the Atlanta Area, and without any other special contact with Good News apart from the magazine, in a "dear sir" letter to the editor, volunteered to give full time to the Good News effort in Atlanta and, armed with typewriter and mimeograph machine, to put out a newssheet, "Word to the Wise."

Coppedge and Sprinkle also, unlike almost everyone else connected with Good News, made contact with their own North Georgia delegation, even as the General Conference was taking place. In a letter to all delegates from North Georgia, they let their convictions be known:

> As young adult members of Grace United Methodist Church, Atlanta, Georgia, we are deeply concerned at what we see happening to United Methodism. At this General Conference, we have heard the Bishops' Call to Peace and Self-determination; we have heard statements from the Commission on Religion and Race; we have heard condemnation of the nation's military-industrial complex; we have heard the Social Principles Commission Report; etc. Nowhere in the course of Conference business have we heard a Call to Commitment to the Person of Jesus Christ.
>
> We have heard the report from the Commission on Doctrine and Doctrinal Standards. We are distressed. Our vital Wesleyan heritage has been compromised—in the name of pluralism and relevance to a new day. We feel the basic tenets of our faith have been treated as historical landmarks, which one visits rather curiously, and then relegates to the past as being irrelevant and unnecessary for daily living.[26]

On the whole, the Atlanta General Conference was a crushing defeat for Good News and for evangelicals. The doctrinal statement was approved without debate, introducing the idea of pluralism as a guiding doctrinal principle. The new denominational structure centralized tremendous power in the hands of a few boards, and especially the Board of Global Ministries. Evangelism and church school education were diminished and made subunits of larger boards, while social action was promoted to board status in the new General Board of Church and Society. Two new commissions were established, Status and Role of Women and Religion and Race, the purposes of which were primarily to monitor internal Church experience.

In addition, a resolution was passed that basically placed the Church on record as supporting abortion on demand. The Ministerial Education Fund would apportion churches to the tune of $11 million to subsidize ailing United Methodist seminaries, but without any additional account-ability. An independent youth ministry organization was established and controlled by youth who were, by age, actually young adults. A Social Principles statement, which in its original form would have rendered homosexual practice acceptable, was passed. Only a last minute motion from the floor that added the words (which would be the center of much debate in conferences to come) "We do not condone the practice of homosexuality and consider it incompatible with Christian teaching" saved the Church from the approval of homosexual practice.

Good News went back to the drawing board after the 1972 General Conference. When Robert Mayfield asked that someone else handle political strategy for 1976, the board selected Robert Sprinkle to take his place. Sprinkle called for a strategy conference for Good News board members and other interested evangelicals in St. Petersburg, Florida, in April 1974.[27] The conference would be held in conjunction with the Good News board meeting. There, perhaps for the first time in the short Good News history, evangelicals associated with Good News seriously analyzed issues, reassessed its political strategy, and laid a course for future action.

Chuck Keysor set the tone for the meeting in his report to the board:

> Lots of things have changed since Good News began. Today I hear some people talking about a new day for evangelicals . . . about chronic problems such as those of curriculum, missions and even the seminaries taking a turn for the better. I heard some optimistic evangelicals saying, "There is no need for Good News now—we have a bishop who believes in evangelism; he is going to save the church."
>
> Others report a stepped-up moving of the Holy Spirit, and receptiv-ity to things spiritual, unknown in mainline Methodism's recent history.

These things may be true. I hope so. But brothers and sisters, we must be realistic. *There has been no change in the basic attitudes and precepts which have caused Methodism's gradual decline into spiritual ignorance and secularism.* In fact, the church now operates under a doctrinal pluralism which is closer to Hindu syncretism than to Biblical Christianity! As long as the root problems remain it seems unlikely that significant changes can or will occur.

There are indeed some signs of official church openness toward evangelicals. But how deeply has the ice really thawed? Let us not be deceived by a few inches of water on top; underneath remains several feet of solid, unveiled hostility and opposition to Biblical truth.

There is one central issue facing many, if not most, of our Good News people: *Shall they stay in the United Methodist Church, or has the time come to quit?* That is the real gut issue. Large numbers of laymen and pastors are "fed up" with the official church. They hang on only by an eyelash, so to speak. Every month more are giving up. "Leave the dead to bury the dead," they say, going off to join churches where an evangelical is not regarded as a trouble maker or a three-sided freak. And so the evangelical constituency of United Methodism seeps away, almost unnoticed. This attrition is a major factor in our thoughts about the future.

In spite of any optimism we may feel, *we must deal with the fact that many, perhaps most, of our constituency feels little if any optimism.* If we fail to deal with this hard reality we shall be dealing with non-reality. And we shall have failed God significantly.[28]

The spring 1974 board meeting was one of the most significant board meetings in the story of Good News. The board recommitted itself to the cause of renewal, to spiritual encouragement, and set a course that would include greater political involvement. The board realized that up to this point Good News had been reactive, rather than proactive at the General Conference. Good News had brought no significant issues before the conferences and, indeed, had been wholly lacking in discernment on the significance and implications of such actions as the doctrinal statement, or how restructuring had concentrated power even more in the hands of the mediating elite. The board also realized, perhaps for the first time, that the issue of homosexuality would be a point of controversy in the months (and years) to come.

In regard to the issue of pluralism, after a two-hour debate, the board passed this resolution: "While Good News welcomes all opportunities extended by the United Methodist Church to proclaim the truths of

Scriptural Christianity, Good News will refuse to demand or ask for the legitimacy of Scriptural Christianity in the United Methodist Church and related boards on the Basis of the existing pluralistic ideology."[29]

The action was significant. "Pluralism" had been touted as the principle by which evangelicals were allowed some legitimacy in the Church, but "pluralism" was not working. The seminaries, in particular, saw no need to include evangelical teaching as "pluralistic," neither did boards and agencies.[30] At the same time, "pluralism" was an excuse under which all sorts of deviant ideologies sought legitimacy.

The board also planned a different kind of summer gathering. Instead of a rally-type convocation featuring inspiration, the 1974 gathering was called Evangelical Action Conference. It was an open-invitation conference at which grassroots evangelicals were encouraged to share in their vision for a renewed Church. The conference met in Louisville in July (during the same period of time that national politics was following the resignation of Richard Nixon from the presidency). Workshops were planned around issues such as curriculum, evangelism, missions, and doctrine.

Good News was capable of dreaming big dreams but was still operating on a shoestring budget and with a staff that was almost entirely volunteer. It was time for a leap of faith. The opportunity came when Asbury College offered Chuck Keysor a part-time position in journalism. The rest of Keysor's time could be underwritten by Good News. In the summer of 1972, Chuck Keysor moved to Wilmore, Kentucky, and began working one-third time for Good News. An office was opened on Wilmore's Main Street. As part of the new leap of faith, Good News also began publishing its magazine six times a year (instead of quarterly).

By this time, the 1976 General Conference was attracting more attention, particularly because of the homosexual issue. Several boards and caucuses, and especially the National Council on Youth Ministry, had declared themselves in support of an effort to reverse the 1972 statement in the Social Principles that spoke of homosexuality as being incompatible with Christian teaching. No group, or at least so it seemed, had declared itself in support of the existing statement. The Board of Global Ministries, in fact, had given a $300 grant to a pro-gay advocacy. Good News suddenly found itself in an unusual position, that of seeking to defend the *Discipline*'s statement against a broad coalition of Church caucus groups and leaders who opposed the statement. In the spring 1976 issue of *Good News* magazine, Chuck Keysor wrote an editorial under the heading "The Gathering Storm": "Should the church abandon its present Biblical stance against homosexual practice [enslaved sin], it will precipitate the most divisive climate since the slavery controversy split American Methodism back in 1847."[31]

Critics of Good News did not respond positively to any references of division. *The Michigan Christian Advocate* editorialized:

> I am . . . concerned about threats and counter-threats, the confrontational mentality, "be-like-us-or-I'll-take-my-marbles-and-go-home syndrome." . . .
>
> There is no good purpose being served in groups, whether left or right, that threaten schism. The genius of Methodism is and has been its oneness without sameness, its unity amid diversity. . . .
>
> The Good News movement is challenging the theological pluralism of United Methodism as inscribed in the Doctrinal Statement of 1972. It is time for those of us who have had sympathy for its cause to say, "That's going too far!"[32]

Whether going too far or not far enough, Good News really believed the future of the Church was at stake and was willing to extend whatever meager resources it had in the cause to uphold the Church's historic stand on sexual morality. No other group, no other board or agency, went on record as seeking to support the existing 1972 statement in regard to homosexuality.

In the fall of 1975, Good News once again put out the call for grass-roots United Methodists to send petitions to the General Conference. A Good News packet of sample petitions addressed its favorite issues: designated giving, withdraw from COCU, and accountability from boards and agencies. But this time added were petition samples that opposed a general human sexuality study and any changes in the Social Principles that dealt with homosexuality.

Once again the petitions flooded in. During one period, they were arriving at the secretary of the General Conference's office at the rate of several hundred a day. By General Conference time, a total of eleven thousand Good News-generated petitions had been received on issues of human sexuality alone, opposing the Church study and supporting the Social Principles statement.

This time under the guidance of Robert Sprinkle, Good News did make some effort to contact delegates. Referring to Sprinkle and the Good News effort, *United Methodist Reporter* observed: "'This is the first organized "evangelical" presence at the General Conference since 1939' he [Sprinkle] said, and 'it's a learning experience for us.' The strategist said 'evangelicals' have finally 'bothered to sit down and figure out how the system works.'"[33]

The 1976 General Conference not only turned back the efforts to change the Social Principles statement regarding homosexuality, it also added a paragraph denying the use of church funds to any group advocating the acceptance of homosexuality. The petition for a church-wide study on human sexuality, which would have focused on the practice of homosexuality, lost to a vague substitute that encouraged local churches to conduct studies on their own. The substitute was the work of John Grenfell, a district superintendent from the Detroit conference and a Good News board member. Whether the conference might have taken this action without the influence of Grenfell and eleven thousand petitions remains to be seen. At any rate, for the first time in twenty-five years, the agenda set by liberals did not prevail.

That was enough for some commentators to declare an evangelical victory. In its June 1976 issue, *Christianity Today* gave its assessment:

> Conservatives in the 9.9-million-member United Methodist Church are still pinching themselves to make sure that the UMC's sudden shift to the right is not just a dream.
>
> For years the church had been drifting leftward and downward, suffering a loss of one million members over the past decade. Delegates to the denomination's quadrennial conferences seemed to plow eagerly into controversial issues, adopt unpopular—and often unrepresentative—positions with a let-the-chips-fall attitude, then return home and try to sell their fellow church members on what had transpired.
>
> Last month, when the 1976 General Conference concluded, it was as if the fed-up folks back home at last had had their say—and way.[34]

Christian Century weighed in with a not dissimilar observation:

> After the smoke cleared, it was evident that the conservative, southern-based[35] "Good News" movement, which had worked for two years to affect decisions made here, could take satisfaction in its success in moving the church to respond to its concerns. Liberals, shaking their heads in dismay, could only recognize that progressive forces, having failed to heed the temper of the times, had not done their homework.[36]

Other observers added their voices. In commenting on the major religious news stories of 1976, James M. Johnston of the *Milwaukee Sentinel* spoke of Jimmy Carter, the year of the evangelical, and then added:

> The United Methodist General Convention swung to the right under the influence of delegates known as the "Good News" group, who planned their moves and did their homework before the convention. They buried the homosexuality issue, revolted against the "New York bureaucracy," took pokes at ecumenism and gave evangelism top priority for the next four years.[37]

Good News itself was much more cautious in its assessment. Bob Sprinkle indicated that if Good News had done anything, it had only helped "put out a few fires." Keysor would comment that pluralism was still a plague on the Church, liberal ideology dominated all the boards and agencies, the episcopacy was still dominated by institutionalists, the Church's curriculum material was still inadequate, the seminaries were still hostile to the evangelical cause, designated giving in all forms had been rejected, and all of the Good News petitions had gone down to defeat.

All the same, Good News was, after the 1976 General Conference, now visible. Liberal and institutional forces began suddenly to consider Good News a threat. It was in this context that Good News was portrayed as "reactionary," "highly subsidized," "fundamentalist," "out-of-step," "seeking to undermine the Church's social witness," and "not serving the best interests of the Church" in the quadrennial leading up to 1980 and the General Conference in Indianapolis (see the beginning of this chapter).

"Planning their moves," "doing their homework," and "well subsidized" hardly characterized Good News's political efforts in the months before 1980. Bob Sprinkle, who had been Good News's political strategist, suddenly left the denomination, and Good News efforts for General Conference were stalled.[38] In desperation, the board turned to Virginia Law Shell to coordinate Good News's political strategy.

Virginia Shell understood the general church. She was a staff person from 1969 to 1975 in Family Life and in the Board of Discipleship. Still, Virginia was hesitant to involve herself in politics. She had no political expertise and had never attended a General Conference, even as an observer. She sensed no special gifts for this task but was willing, in her words, to seek God's guidance. After prayer, Virginia became convinced that it might be possible if her husband, Don Shell (to whom she had been married in 1975), helped. Before she could say a word to Don, he spoke to her about a conviction that maybe they needed to become more involved in the causes of Good News. It was a confirmation of her prayers, and the Shells agreed to work together on political strategy.

But how? It was January and General Conference was in April. The supposedly "well-oiled machinery" was not oiled at all. The supposedly "well-funded and heavily subsidized" effort was scratching for dollars. A friend finally gave $5,000, and this at a time when all of the major caucuses and most of the boards and agencies were organized and funded and together had declared themselves in support of a more permissive stand on homosexuality and against any form of designated giving. Good News stood alone in the effort to continue the Church's stand on sexual morality.

Good News positions had already been prepared. First and foremost, Good News decided to petition General Conference to establish a committee to define "pluralism" and the "core of doctrine" in the doctrinal statement. It sought to introduce the concept of "designated giving" as a part of church funding. Good News sought to retain the present statements on homosexuality and to make plain that practicing homosexuals were not to be ordained or appointed. It sought to make Family Life a missional priority. A Good News petition would replace the Church's quota system with an intentional effort toward affirmative action without quotas. And, as always, there was a petition on COCU (Consultation on Church Union). Populist evangelicals were suspicious of church mergers or church councils that tended to create more bureaucracy and further de-emphasize the importance of the local church. The Good News petition called for any agreements of COCU to be based on the historic faith.

Good News also endorsed a "full disclosure" petition for boards and agencies. Almost immediately upon assuming responsibility for political action, Don and Virginia Shell had become caught up in the Jessup Report (see chapter 6). David Jessup, a layman who worked with the AFL-CIO, had—on his own—discovered and researched a number of controversial Church grants given to secular and political (and mostly far-left and Communist-related) causes.

The Jessup Report was shared with General Conference delegates without any proposed legislation or resolutions, except one. Jessup, with the help of the Shells and Good News, proposed Full Disclosure legislation. Jessup had encountered tremendous opposition from staff people in

Church and Society and Global Ministries in researching the grants, pro-grams, and gifts given to controversial groups. Jessup was repeatedly told the information he sought was privileged or was unavailable. If the boards had nothing to hide, why the resistance?

Jessup personally came to Indianapolis to lobby for the Full Disclosure legislation. If nothing else, Good News workers received training from David Jessup on how to work the legislative system. Jessup was present in the legislative group and sublegislative group. He spoke to delegates about the importance of the legislation and to committee chairs when the petition would have been quickly passed over and defeated. He was given opportunity to address the legislative group. Staff persons from Global Ministries fought the petition strenuously. They claimed Full Disclosure would take staff time and dollars that might be better spent elsewhere. Full Disclosure implied a lack of trust, they argued.

The legislation requiring Full Disclosure passed. From the Good News perspective, it was about the only bright spot to come out of the 1980 Good News efforts. Good News petitions on doctrine never made it out of subcommittee. Designated giving failed miserably. Not only that, but in a "stealth maneuver," the last bit of freedom local churches had over their own finances was removed when World Service giving was moved from a "goal" to an "apportionment" (see chapter 10). Family Life as a missional priority had no chance of passing. Nor did the petitions addressed to COCU. Good News attracted only a few persons to its breakfasts in Indianapolis. Again, the 1980 General Conference handled the Good News petitions poorly. Petitions from the Coalition for the Whole Gospel and other caucus groups received numbers. Good News petitions were once again grouped and not given individual numbers. Three thousand petitions from Good News on homosexuality received less consideration than one petition from Church and Society. Despite the united efforts of the other caucus groups and most of the boards and agencies to move toward a more permissive stance on homosexuality, the General Conference retained the existing language in the *Discipline*. However, it seemed a hollow victory. The Good News petition that would bar practicing homosexuals from ordination and appointment was rejected. The "existing language" was vague enough that in numbers of conferences, it was believed ordination of practicing homosexuals could proceed.

Adon Taft, religion writer for *Miami Herald*, offered an interpretation that was typical of the non-Church press. In the article that appeared

April 23, 1980, under the heading "Methodists Refuse to Bar Homosexuals from Ministry," Taft observed:

> The United Methodist Church refused Monday to bar homosexuals from the ministry and an evangelical leader called the vote a tragedy that could cause a mass exodus of church members.
>
> The 1,000 delegates to the every-four-years General Conference of the nation's second largest Protestant church voted overwhelmingly to retain present vague guidelines on who can be ordained. The decision will be left to the regional conferences. . . . [39]

Taft then quoted Paul Hardin, chair of the Committee on Higher Education and Ministry, and Bishop Roy Nichols, incoming president of the Council of Bishops, both of whom agreed that the legislation passed was not strong enough to prohibit the ordination of practicing homosexuals.

Taft also made reference to Chuck Keysor's remark that the unwillingness of the General Conference to take a strong stand on homosexuality would increase the tempo of exodus from the Church. The Church had already lost 1.5 million members in the last fifteen years, and Keysor was quoted as saying, "Multitudes of people are barely hanging on as members."

It was not an encouraging time for Good News.

CHAPTER TEN

GROWING EVANGELICAL PRESENCE

The old warrior was tired. And sick. And discouraged. The news came in a letter to Good News board members in the fall of 1980. Charles Keysor, Mister Good News himself, was considering resigning as president of Good News and editor of *Good News* magazine. A special board meeting was being called for October 29-31, 1980, to discuss the situation.

The news took most of the Good News board members by surprise. Good News without Chuck Keysor seemed unthinkable. Thirty-five members, almost the entire board, attended the meeting. Perhaps no other Good News board meeting was ever characterized by such agonizing soul-searching as this one. What was happening?

First, Chuck Keysor had been diagnosed with cancer. The doctor had advised a cutback in schedule. Keysor, still employed primarily by Asbury College to teach journalism, admitted he was having difficulty keeping up with the rigorous pace. Second, Keysor confessed to pessimism over the future of The United Methodist Church. He who had always been upbeat and hopeful was now questioning the effectiveness of the cause to which he had given himself so completely. Third, internal staff problems had created tension between Keysor and the executive committee of the board.

Good News had always been blessed with the quality of its staff. Associate editors such as Ed Robb III and Diane Knippers had been trained and recruited by Keysor himself from his Asbury College connections. Virgil Maybray, in addition to his position as a fund-raiser and advocate for missions through the Evangelical Missions Council, was also a well-respected pastor and a cooperative colleague. Maybray also had an excellent feel for the denomination through his many local church contacts. The office staff was drawn in large part from the Asbury community and was generally committed to the Good News cause. Ann Coker, office manager, was the wife of an Asbury College professor. In addition, in 1978, Good News had brought on staff Robert Wood, a United Methodist pastor from Kansas.

It had proved difficult for Wood, who was hired full time to work under Keysor but was still only part-time with Good News. Things had not gone well, and Wood felt it was best to leave. There was a question about vacation pay. Keysor felt, under the circumstances, that Wood had forfeited his vacation pay. Wood appealed to the executive committee of the board, which also served as the personnel committee, and the committee sided with Wood.

Keysor felt betrayed. The committee decision had come on top of his diagnosis with cancer and his growing discouragement about the Church. He expressed the thought that perhaps it was time for him to move on. He spoke of his love for teaching and for Asbury College. The offer was there for him to teach full time.

The board needed to sort matters out. The Good News board by this time was a broad-based and diverse group of individuals. Among its forty members were two seminary professors, Paul Mickey from Duke and Robert Tuttle from Oral Roberts University. John Grenfell from the Detroit Conference was the board's first district superintendent. Paul Morrell of Tyler Street Church in Dallas and Bill Mason of Asbury Church in Tulsa pastored significant churches. Randy Jones, who pastored in the inner city of Philadelphia, was a strong voice from the African American community. The lay members of the board included Virginia Law Shell, Helen Rhea Coppedge, Charles Shuman of Illinois (formerly head of Farm Bureau), Harvey Phelps of Colorado, Robert Mayfield, Flo Martin (an effective young adult who had been a delegate to General Conference), David Miller of North Dakota, and Dottie

Chase of Ohio. Dale Bittinger of Tennessee and Mike Walker of Texas from the original Good News board were still active. Ed Robb, Robert Neely of Pennsylvania, and Bob Snyder of East Ohio were Good News veterans.

The meeting was chaired by Jim Heidinger. The discussion quickly moved to the future of The United Methodist Church and the role and purpose of Good News. Keysor gave a pessimistic assessment: Despite a growing evangelical renaissance in the wider Church and despite the efforts of Good News, the Church bureaucracy was operating with a foreign theology that was a corruption of historic Methodism. For Keysor, the 1980 General Conference had signified how resistant the institutional establishment was to renewal, or to any kind of change. It was difficult to see any signs of hope for the denomination in a system that was hostile to evangelicals and conservatives and insensitive to the needs and convictions of the local church.

Then came a hard word: Good News had spoken of wanting to turn the ship called United Methodism around. Perhaps it would be better if Good News were to let the ship self-destruct and then seek to build something out of the wreckage.

Keysor's new plan: Stop raising money for the General Board of Global Ministries (Good News was raising considerable amounts of money for Advance Specials through Virgil Maybray); develop evangelical curriculum materials and go head-to-head with the denomination; publicize just how many United Methodists were actually leaving the denomination and make public their many grievances; and offer a ministry to persons, especially to pastors, who have left.

Perhaps there was reason for despondency. The 1980 General Conference Keysor had referred to had not been kind to evangelicals (see p. 213).

Not only that, but the one small piece of freedom local churches had in determining how funds would be used in the general Church was taken away when, in a "stealth" (a secret procedure or action) maneuver, World Service was made a required apportionment instead of a church asking. Charles Keysor believed there would be an effort to change the paragraph and editorialize in the spring 1976 issue of the magazine: "Powerful pressures will soon be exerted to have General Conference take out of the *Discipline* the important right of the local church [to set its own World Service goal]. . . . [This] would be the 'last straw that broke the camel's back' for many of our finest people who are already disillusioned. Let us pray that this ill-advised proposal will be voted down by the General Conference." Up until this time, at least in the former Methodist Church, World Service was considered a goal set by the charge conference in the local church. Even though almost every church treated the fund as an apportionment, theoretically, the option was there for a local church to set its own World Service goal.

As it so happened, the General Conference never had a chance to vote the proposal down. It simply mysteriously disappeared when the 1980 *Discipline* was printed and World Service was declared an apportionment. How could this have happened without Good News's, or anyone else's, knowledge at the time of the conference? When and where was the legislation presented, debated, and passed? It turned out there was no legislation and no discussion. There had obviously been a great deal of confusion (deceit?) in assembling the material for the *Discipline*, and the change had been made "accidentally." But no one wanted to assume responsibility for the "accident."

Good News asked whether material in the *Discipline* could be binding if, in fact, it was placed there without action by the General Conference.[1] Could appeal be made to the Council of Bishops or the Judicial Council? It was difficult for Good News to believe there had not been a conspiracy. If, as Good News suspected, this was not really an "accident," then no institutional appeal could be successful. Not only had the Church not yielded an inch on "designated giving" in 1980, but also one little freedom it had in designated giving had been taken away.

Good News was, in 1980, successful in helping maintain the traditional stand on homosexuality. Despite the fact that all of the major boards and caucus groups petitioned for a more lenient position, the wording of the 1976 *Discipline* was retained. Even this was a hollow victory, for legislation proposed by Good News that explicitly sought to deny ordination or appointment to self-avowed practicing homosexuals was defeated.

Keysor was convinced—correctly, as it turned out later—that the wording of the *Discipline* as it stood was not strong enough to prohibit conferences from ordaining and appointing homosexuals if they so desired.

Keysor offered his assessment of the conference in the magazine: "In spite of a lot of comments about 'the conservative mood of the conference,' essentially what we have done is to slow the rate of shift; the direction of the shift is still away from us rather than toward us."[2]

There were other reasons for discouragement. Despite the careful research that went into the Jessup Report on the use of church funds to controversial causes, the response of bishops and boards and agencies was, instead of dealing with the report, attacking Jessup and Good News and calling the report "divisive." Conversations between the Evangelical Missions Council and the Board of Global Ministries were becoming increasingly frustrating.

Most of all, the battle against "pluralism" seemed hopelessly lost. Pluralism not only had not opened any doors in boards and agencies or in the seminaries to include an evangelical, but also was being used to justify everything on the far left from liberation theologies to witchcraft.

All of this discouraging news, on top of cancer and a difference with the board on a staff problem, led Keysor to believe it was time for someone else to lead Good News.

The board needed to respond. And it did, with personal testimony and theological reflection. Several agreed with Keysor and indicated that if Keysor left the board they would probably leave also. A greater majority, however, believed that though the signs for renewal were not everywhere evident, there was increasing appreciation of evangelical presence and influence in the Church, and the future looked hopeful. On the national church scene, statistics from Gallup surveys had indicated that 19 percent of Americans could be identified as evangelicals.[3] They also reported that 39 percent of Americans held a literal view of the Bible, and 38 percent indicated they had been "born again."

Within The United Methodist Church, there was an increasing number of persons and churches who were willing to be identified as "evangelical" and who were indicating that they were looking to Good News for reliable information about the denomination. They also longed for assurance and hope. The magazine was printing twenty-one thousand copies of each issue. It had become highly regarded, if not within United Methodism, at least by journalists outside United Methodism. In 1979, it received the award Journal of the Year by the Evangelical Press Association. Good News had by this time become the only United Methodist-related magazine with general readership. *Candle*, the newsletter for evangelical women, was printing twenty thousand copies per issue; *Catalyst*, the newsletter for seminary students, five thousand; and the missions newsletter, thirty-eight hundred.

Good News veteran Dale Bittinger gave an analogy from the story of Gideon and Jericho: Good News had walked around the walls six times.

He for one was now preparing to blow the trumpet and walk the seventh time.

At the end of the three-day meeting, Keysor resigned. It was, in his words, the hardest thing he had ever done. The board and the Good News constituency were like family. But it was time for someone else to lead the movement.

United Methodist Reporter, which had been much more open to the concerns of Good News than any of the institution-related media, was chosen to break the story. Keysor was made a life-time member of the board and would commit himself to Asbury College and journalism full time.[4]

Paul Morrell was made head of a seven-person search team to replace Keysor. The team felt that Good News was at a place financially where a full-time person should be hired to lead Good News. The ideal person would be a nationally known leader committed to the cause of Good News who was willing to make the move to Wilmore and commit to a long-term ministry.

The logical person seemed to be Ed Robb. Robb knew a number of bishops. He was also acquainted with grassroots United Methodism. As a well-known evangelist, he had perhaps preached to as many different United Methodists as anyone in the denomination. Robb prayed, ago-nized, and sought the advice of friends. One friend who responded was Albert Outler. In a personal letter, which reveals a great deal about both Outler and Robb and the relationship between them, Outler wrote:

> Dear Ed:
>
> I have been thinking about you over these last days and remember-ing you and your decision in my prayers. The key post in *Good News* is bound to have a strong attraction and to offer many strategic advan-tages. But there are some disadvantages and I am sure that you are aware of them: a past history of embattlements and a constituency that would, at least from time to time, fence you in more narrowly than your open-hearted spirit would find wholly compatible. If you succeed (as I would expect you to) it would take you out of the work of active evangelism and might identify you more completely with "the Methodist right" and less with a "right-and-center coalition" (that I believe holds more prom-ise in the long run). On the other hand, if, for any reason it did not work out, the way back into your mission as an evangelist might not be as open as it seems now to be. With Billy Graham fading and with Oral Roberts lurching off to the right (apparently), the number of true-blue evangelists with a vital balance and a "catholic spirit" seems to me to be

dwindling. We (especially we *Methodists!*) must not be left to the uncertain mercies of the likes of Robison, Bakker and Falwell.

For all of this, if you have looked deep within and listened closely for the still, small voice (beyond ambition and utility) and have a clear leading to take up this new role, you can count on my sincere acknowledgment of it as a responsible vocational decision—and on my hearty hopes for true fulfillment in it.[5]

Robb declined the Good News position. He felt he could make his contribution to the evangelical cause more effectively in other ways. One of those contributions was even then in the process of formation. If the leadership of The United Methodist Church had sought to downplay and discount the Jessup Report, which had laid bare the use of church grants to controversial and mostly leftist revolutionary movements and causes, others in wider Christian community had not. Jessup's findings had implications for more than just The United Methodist Church. Other mainline denominations and groups such as the National Council of Churches had been involved in the same leftist political activity. At the same time, the mainline churches had ignored important matters such as the persecution of Christians, especially under communism, and advocacy of religious rights. Persons with these concerns would soon form themselves into the organization known as the Institute of Religion and Democracy (IRD). Robb was key in making this happen. He was also heavily involved with Albert Outler in A Fund for Theological Education (AFTE), the effort to fund evangelicals seeking advanced degrees who might eventually assume leadership in the Church.

With Robb's refusal, the search committee turned to James Heidinger. Heidinger was the chair of the Good News board and was himself on the search committee. A pastor from the East Ohio Conference, Heidinger had Asbury College and Seminary credentials. He also held a Doctor of Ministry degree from Wesley Seminary in Washington, D.C. He understood Good News. He had worked with Charles Keysor. He was young, just thirty-nine years old, and could give a number of years to Good News. His election to the position took place at the January 1981 board meeting.

At the same board meeting, a list of recommendations were made to give Good News direction under a new executive director. Good News would continue to seek renewal in the Church, primarily through an emphasis on doctrinal integrity and through greater accountability of boards and agencies. It would seek to fill needs in areas of discipleship and training that were not being met by the official channels of the denomination. There was also a recognition that renewal was a long-term commitment.

Despite Chuck Keysor's negative assessment of the future of evangelicals in The United Methodist Church, a strong argument could be made that the transition from Keysor to Heidinger was coming at a time when there was a growing acceptance and appreciation of Good News. Bishop Roy Nichols, when he was president of the World Division of the Board of Global Ministries, had indicated a willingness to meet with as many of the Good News board as could be assembled. The meeting, a three-hour no-holds-barred session, took place in March of 1979 with twenty board members present. Bishop Nichols's private message was one of encouragement, especially as it related to the Board of Global Ministries.[6] The Church needed Good News. It was the first time in its fourteen years of the existence that Good News had a bishop willing to spend so much time with Good News and had been so forthrightly positive.

Bishop Nichols followed that with a public expression of support in an analysis that appeared in *The United Methodist Reporter* in its January 30, 1981, issue.[7] In a three-column feature written by Roy Beck, *UMReporter* sought to assess the place of Good News in the Church. Though a number of remarks were negative ("Good News never has anything good to say about the Church"), Nichols made an observation that few others outside the movement had been willing to recognize:

> Look at what happened in other denominations. . . . The same theologically conservative groundswell that created Good News . . . also created similar organizations in most major denominations. There was much financial disruption—even splits. Groups similar to Good News led people to succession. But Good News carried on the struggle within the house of faith. That's a legitimate witness.[8]

The Good News movement was in good shape financially. Averaging a growth rate of nearly 30 percent each year, Good News had reported an increase of yearly income from $9,813 in 1967 to $524,553 in 1980. This had come primarily from donations, the magazine, and convocations.

Heidinger gave a new face to Good News. His writing style was not nearly as abrasive as Keysor's. Gone were the references to "humanist," "corruption," "abomination," and "unregenerate." In his first editorial in the May-June 1981 issue of the *Good News* magazine, Heidinger laid out his assessment of the Church and his challenge to evangelicals:

(1) Spiritual and evangelical renewal is taking place in the main-line denominations to a greater degree than any of us could have imagined.

(2) The key to lasting church renewal is in doctrinal and theological faithfulness.

(3) Good New has prevented untold thousands from leaving the denomination.

(4) Evangelicals have enjoyed the luxury of neutrality and non-involvement for too long.[9]

This was not to say that Heidinger would be compromised and tamed by the institutional church. Heidinger had no sooner moved to Wilmore than a new cause presented itself. In March 1981, Alex Ufema and John Finkbeiner, two young pastors from the West Pennsylvania Conference, had indicated that because of findings in the Jessup Report and for other reasons, their churches would be withholding World Service funds. Unfortunately, their bishop, Bishop James Ault, was one of the most outspoken critics of the Jessup Report and of Good News and was not known for his openness to evangelical concerns. Ault, working with the Board of Ordained Ministry, made use of the "stealth" legislation of the 1980 General Conference that made World Service an apportionment instead of a goal. In a display of institutional power, the bishop arbitrarily and summarily relieved the two young pastors of their pulpits for disobedience to the order and discipline of the Church and placed them on involuntary leaves of absence.

For Good News, it was just another example of prejudice against evangelicals and heavy-handed institutionalism. Ultimately the two young pastors were denied even a trial. Good News ran several stories on the case throughout 1981. Though Good News was not successful in helping Ufema and Finkbeiner be restored to their pulpits, it was the beginning of another role for Good News: advocacy on the part of those misused by the system.[10]

Heidinger was also soon involved in another role for Good News, that of encouraging, enabling, and ultimately blessing a number of emerging ministries. The Institute of Religion and Democracy (IRD) was launched in 1981 as a result of the Jessup Report at the 1980 General Conference and the work of Ed Robb (see chapter 6). The Mission Society for United Methodists (MSUM) opened its doors in February 1984, out of concerns about United Methodism's declining overseas missionary force and an apparent lack of a theology of missions. The Transforming Congregations movement, which had started with a group of pastors in the California-Nevada Conference in 1988, was given encouragement and was made, first, a task force of Good News and, then, a separate ministry group in 1996. The group included a number of former homosexuals and was committed to healing the sexually broken through the power of the gospel. Good News formed Bristol Books in 1989 and sold the publishing venture in 1991, when it became a for-profit corporation. The RENEW ministry, the women's program arm of Good News, was launched fully in 1989, with Faye Short giving leadership as executive director.

Jim Heidinger's first challenge in the political arena came when the General Conference met in Baltimore in 1984. Don and Virginia Shell would once again lead the political effort for Good News. One of the Shells' immediate concerns was to find a way for Good News legislation to get a fair hearing at the conference. The populist approach of bombarding the conference with petitions had not been successful.

However, the Good News approach had forced the General Conference to take a new look at how petitions were handled. Alan Waltz, staff researcher with the General Council on Ministries, had written a report detailing the problems of petitions and the legislative process. One of his conclusions was that a better way to handle petitions needed to be found.

Another analysis was done by Jean Caffey Lyles, associate editor of *The Christian Century* and well-known journalist. Writing in the winter 1983 issue of *Quarterly Review*, Lyles accused Good News of clogging and disrupting the petition process with a glut of petitions that were intended not to get new ideas considered, but to act as a kind of "all-church referendum on select issues."[11] According to Lyles, Good News had subverted a useful process of the Church and made it unworkable.

The Good News answer, for once, was not to stand outside the process and cry foul, but to make thoughtful response. Through Don Shell, Good News offered five pages of recommendations for the handling of General Conference legislation. Included in the recommendations: prohibiting general agency staff members from serving on legislative committees that handle matters affecting the agency by which they are employed; banning unofficial groups such as Good News from submitting petitions; and encouraging and upgrading the importance of petitions from annual conferences and district conferences.

Perhaps more important was a promise on the part of Good News to pull back from the multiple-petitions approach if there was some assurance that individual petitions would be treated fairly. The General Conference eventually—in large part because of Good News—made provision for having a printed volume containing every petition put in the hands of the delegates.

There were few surprises in the Good News agenda for the 1984 General Conference. Good News petitioned to retain the Church's stand on homosexuality and add a paragraph that would prohibit the ordination and appointment of self-avowed practicing homosexuals. Following the populist position that it had advocated from the beginning, Good News wanted associate members of annual conferences and local pastors to be eligible for election to General Conference. It again advocated designated giving and wanted to add a statement in the responsibilities of the General Board of Global Ministries that called for a specific reference to winning persons to Christ. Good News also called for a stronger statement against abortion.

A major Good News emphasis was directed toward the doctrinal statement (see chapter 11). Officially, Good News wanted a new statement on tradition and a statement that would define the limits of "pluralism." Unofficially, Good News urged individuals and churches to write petitions that would address sentences and paragraphs in the statement instead of large blocks of material (which were less likely to be approved). The 1984 conference responded to the flood of petitions by authorizing the new Task Force on Doctrine to rewrite the 1972 statement.

For those seeking to uphold doctrinal integrity, a new challenge was facing the Church in the matter of "inclusive language." Feminist influences had for some time been seeking to deconstruct the language (and consequently the doctrine) of the Church with the imposition of language "guidelines." Masculine pronouns were to be considered unacceptable not only in referring to human beings, but also in referring to God. The guidelines de-emphasized the use of the word "Father" in referring to God, even to the extent that alternate language was proposed in the trinitarian formula ("Father, Son, and Holy Spirit") in benedictions, in the Doxology, and even in the "Gloria Patri." These guidelines were rapidly becoming policy for curriculum writers, in worship materials, and in "official" Church communication. Words of hymns were frequently changed in worship settings.

The language issue in seminaries became cause for language wars.[12] Imposed guidelines were introduced in classroom speaking and writing. Students who neglected to follow the guidelines were graded lower. That such guidelines were in violation of the seminaries' own stated positions on academic freedom and freedom of expression seemed to make no difference at all. At the same time, the Boards of Ordained Ministry were strongly urging "inclusive language" in spoken and written responses by ordinands. Boards were known to delay or deny candidates for using male pronouns for God while at the same time approving candidates who were unitarian in their beliefs about God. Language revision became most serious when injected into the liturgy of the Church. Substitute phrases such as "Creator, Redeemer, and Sustainer" were being used in ordination and baptism, replacing the trinitarian formula, "Father, Son, and Holy Spirit."

"Correct" language usage was rapidly becoming the new orthodoxy; and failure to comply, the new "heresy." Good News was not the only group in the Church that saw serious theological compromise in the capitulation to what soon would be known as "politically correct" language, but Good News was the only voice organized to resist the change. Language became not only a theological, but also a populist issue. Numbers of common ordinary church people resisted the idea that a mediating elite, whether seminaries, boards and agencies, or the General Conference, should dictate to them what kind of faith language was appropriate for use in church settings. Perhaps no other issue as "inclusive language" pitted an "enlightened" few against the masses.

This issue came into focus at the 1984 General Conference in the report of the Task Force on Language Guidelines formed by the General Council on Ministries. The task force, chaired by Carolyn Oehler of the Commission on the Status and Role of Women, was, like typical General Conference task forces, dominated by liberals and by board and agency members. Its report to the conference, "Words That Hurt, Words That Heal," addressed not only language about humans, but also language about God. The radical recommendations discouraged use of words such as "Lord" and "King" and "Father" for God as well as gender-specific pronouns in general.

Originally the report called for another monitoring agency (such as the commissions on Religion and Race and the Status and Role of Women) whose task would be to enforce and ensure language policies were being followed. For populist evangelicals, this would have been the ultimate insult, to have the Church acting like Big Brother (or Sister) continually correcting the language of its siblings.

The 1984 General Conference heard the report on language guidelines and then, in a response of compromise (or perhaps ambiguity and confusion), neither adopted nor rejected the report, but simply "received" it. The Good News interpretation of this action was that though the Church needed to be aware of the issues raised by feminists, it was not ready to impose these guidelines as policy. Good News agreed that the Church needed to be sensitized in its language about persons. It objected, however, to changing biblical images and language in favor of feminist-inspired language guidelines.

Others in the Church, however, interpreted the action of the General Conference in "receiving" the report as support for imposed language changes. The confusion was reflected in a question directed to the presiding bishop after the vote. Edwinna Johnson, a delegate from Liberia, asked, "I would like to know what we will refer to God and—because we can't use Lord and we can't use Father, what will we use?"

Within a few months, the Rocky Mountain Conference sought to put teeth in the report by declaring a policy that candidates for the ministry would "be expected to use inclusive language both in reference to deity and to persons" in order to be approved for ministry. The action stirred such an outcry that it was eventually rescinded (at least officially).

The language issue took on added urgency with discussions about the possibility of a new United Methodist hymnal. Several agencies, and especially the Commission on the Status and Role of Women, had argued for a new hymnal primarily on the basis of need for inclusive language. Good News, other evangelicals, and a great many common ordinary United Methodists also believed it was time for a new hymnal but were wary of an elitist, "politically correct" hymnal that would change the language of traditional hymns and might reduce the number of populist gospel hymns.

The General Board of Discipleship had done preliminary work on the need for the hymnal. One of the findings revealed that only 13 percent of United Methodists believed that "more inclusive language" was a factor in the need for a new hymnal, while 48 percent believed that more traditional gospel hymns (a basic populist evangelical conviction) was a factor in the need for a new hymnal.

In large part because of Good News publicity about the possibility of a "butchered" hymnal, nearly one thousand petitions flowed into the 1984

General Conference, asking that the traditional language of hymns be maintained if a new hymnal was to be made available to the Church. None of these was from any general board or agency, but a number had been channelled through annual conferences. For once the number of petitions impressed the legislative committee, and representative petitions on behalf of traditional language were forwarded to the General Conference floor. The General Conference approved the development of the new hymnal accompanied by the petitions on traditional language.

The homosexual issue again faced the 1984 conference. Liberal voices wanted all negative references to homosexual practice removed from the *Discipline*. Good News, by contrast, and other evangelical voices favored a strong statement that would prohibit the ordination of self-avowed, practicing homosexuals. A group of moderates favored a statement that spoke of "celibacy in singleness and faithfulness in marriage." The conservative argument was that that language was not specific enough to prohibit the ordination and appointment of self-avowed, practicing homosexuals.

The "moderate" statement passed and was immediately referred to the Judicial Council for a ruling as to whether the language was specific enough to prohibit the ordination and practice of self-avowed, practicing homosexuals. When the response came back that it was not, there was a motion for reconsideration. Leading in this endeavor was David Seamands, who had headed up Good News's Evangelical Missions Council and was a former missionary to India, an effective pastor of the Wilmore United Methodist Church, and a counselor who had worked with numerous homosexuals.[13] A key speech was made by William Morris (later Bishop Morris) of Mississippi. The homosexual issue was reconsidered, and legislation similar to that proposed by Good News was passed by a vote of 568 to 404.

For the first time in its existence, Good News came away from a General Conference with some encouragement. The conference had received thirteen thousand petitions, many of which, perhaps even a majority, had been generated by Good News. Thirteen hundred petitions had been received urging a statement prohibiting the ordination and appointment of self-avowed, practicing homosexuals. Nearly one thousand petitions asked for the retaining of traditional language in hymns. Nearly five hundred petitions addressed the doctrinal statement.

The 1984 conference also passed legislation advocated by Good News that called for the listing of all of the petitions in the *Daily Christian*

Advocate. For a populist movement such as Good News, this meant that petitions from local churches, or from ordinary United Methodists, would be guaranteed a place on the agenda.

The organization of two key task forces—the Hymnal Revision Committee and the Theological Task Force—promised even more hope. Though Good News would not be allowed representation on the Theological Task Force, several other evangelicals would be, and Good News would be allowed a hearing before the committee (see chapter 11).[14] In addition, the chair of the committee, Bishop Earl Hunt, was about as close a friend as Good News could expect among the bishops. Furthermore, the committee was willing to solicit input from common ordinary United Methodists.[15]

But the work of the Hymnal Revision Committee was even more encouraging. A substitute proposal at the General Conference had placed responsibility for the hymnal not with the Board of Discipleship, but with the denominational publishing house. This was significant because the publishing house was far more market driven and much likelier to present a hymnal that would sell rather than one ideologically driven.

There was widespread recognition that decisions made about the hymnal would help determine the future direction of the Church. The hymnal was for United Methodism what the *Book of Common Prayer* was for Anglicans. And, as important as the doctrinal statement was, the hymnal in many respects not only proclaimed, but also informed, what United Methodists really believed. In a denomination of diverse theology, geography, and racial and cultural makeup, the hymnal was supposed to be one symbol of unity. But the committee would have to work through a number of issues: liberal versus evangelical theology, tradition of the EUBs as well as that of former Methodists, social issues (racism, militarism, nationalism), culture ("good" music versus popular music), and inclusive language versus traditional language.

The desire of many evangelicals was for a hymnal that would reflect the authentic part of Methodism that was related to revivalism, gospel music, Wesley, and evangelical theology. Gospel music, including black gospel music, had important historical roots in Methodism, particularly in populist, Holiness, and revivalistic Methodism. But previous "official" hymnals, though "evangelical" in many respects, were not always friendly to that expression of Methodism. As a result, many churches opted for hymnals from other publishers.[16]

The United Methodist Publishing House did extensive research on hymn usage. The committee made use of "consultants," including evangelicals and charismatics and Wesley scholars. Four hundred and eighty grassroots advisors were recruited to provide input into crucial issues. In addition, six hundred reader consultants agreed to make suggestions on the committee's work. Even better, the committee worked in the open. When it became known (and publicized) that the committee was prepared to drop two hymns—"Battle Hymn of the Republic" and "Onward, Christian Soldiers"—because of militaristic images, twelve thousand letters objecting to the decision were received, and the committee reinstated the hymns. More gospel hymns, African American spirituals, and Wesley hymns were added. A compromise was worked out for the use of traditional language. Hymns reflecting images that were meaningful to women were selected. Ethnic hymns were introduced.

The 1988 General Conference was held in St. Louis. The evangelical cause had gained new supporters as the result of the Houston Declaration (see chapter 11). Don and Virginia Shell coordinated the Good News efforts at the conference. Some special donations had been given to the political strategy effort, which allowed Good News to offer a breakfast briefing to all delegates. The breakfasts—especially during the first week when legislative groups were meeting—were low-key and largely informational and for the first time were able to attract numbers of delegates—the average attendance was about one hundred—including many who were not necessarily committed to the Good News agenda.

Once again Good News could speak positively about a General Conference. The 1988 conference adopted both the hymnal report and the doctrinal task force report.[17] The Church again turned back efforts to compromise the Church's stand on sexual morality, especially as it related to homosexuality. The conference added a new and significant phrase to the Social Principles on abortion: "We cannot affirm abortion as an acceptable means of birth control, and we unconditionally reject it as a means of gender selection."

Since 98 percent of all abortions were performed for purposes of birth control, this newly added statement that did "not affirm abortion as an acceptable means of birth control" effectively and officially moved The United Methodist Church from a basic pro-choice to a pro-life position. Curiously, liberals in the Church did not interpret the *Discipline*'s language in that way and continued to present the Church's stand as pro-choice. However one interpreted the newly added statement, the

Church's position on abortion was now much more nuanced and complex.

Jim Heidinger evaluated the conference in an editorial entitled "United Methodism Moves Toward Center" in the May-June 1988 issue of *Good News* magazine. After affirming words about the doctrinal statement and the new hymnal, Heidinger concluded: "We believe historians will view the 1988 General Conference as a change of direction for United Methodism. By any measure it was unlike previous conferences."[18]

Later, in the November-December 1988 issue, Heidinger would editorialize on the topic in his article "A New United Methodism in the Making?"[19] Good News did extensive coverage of the 1988 conference in *Good News* magazine and received a number of commendations. Bishop William Cannon in a letter to Jim Heidinger, expressed appreciation: "You have given the best coverage of General Conference yet. . . . You have made more of the Episcopal Address than our own publications have. Your assessment of the conference is fair in every way."[20]

But there was a calm after the storm. A few months after the 1988 General Conference, Good News found itself facing difficult times. The country was experiencing economic slowdown, and Good News found itself in an economic crisis. In late 1989 and early 1990, revenues were down, Bristol Books was experiencing slow book sales, and the organization was facing a $185,000 debt. Jim Heidinger began his report to the summer board of Good News in this way:

> The months of May and June have been difficult ones at Good News, probably the most difficult I have experienced in my nine years at Good News. . . . As you have read in our board reports, the Executive Committee saw the need early in May to take drastic action in light of our financial situation, which included heavy indebtedness, slow contribution revenue and slow book sales.[21]

Some suggested that things had gone too well for Good News. The doctrinal statement had been accepted in 1988, the hymnal had been accepted, and statements in support of high moral standards, including statements regarding the appointment of practicing homosexuals, had been inserted in the *Discipline*. Perhaps the Good News constituency had been lulled into complacency. Outrageous news generated income, and for a period of time there was no outrageous news.

The better explanation was that Bristol Books had not been as financially successful as had been hoped. Though it was performing valuable service to the Church, it had become a financial drain. The board moved to find a solution for Bristol Books (it was sold to friends of Good News), to cut costs by reducing the staff by three and a half positions, and to make a major appeal to its supporters.

By the January 1991 board meeting, the financial picture had brightened considerably, and Good News began to make plans for the 1992 General Conference. Don and Virginia Shell would again lead the Good News effort.

The 1992 conference was held at Louisville. For the first time, as the result of legislation passed in 1988, all petitions were printed in full in the *Daily Christian Advocate*. Good News, true to its word, did not ask its constituency to flood the conference with petitions. As a result "only" 2,433 petitions were submitted to the conference.

Several important task forces or studies that were of interest to Good News were to report to the 1992 General Conference. These included the Homosexual Task Force Report, a study on the feasibility of moving the Board of Global Ministries from New York City, the Book of Worship Report, the Baptism Report, and the Ministry Study.

The Homosexual Task Force Report had been of special concern for Good News. The 1984 General Conference, sensing that its votes on homosexuality would be interpreted as harsh, had responded positively to a petition for a special task force study on homosexuality. Good News had not supported such a task force. A myriad of studies had already been conducted, and there was little chance that enough new material would be unearthed to change positions already strongly held. Good News believed that a study conducted by a general agency of the Church (the General Council on Ministries) would in the end be ideologically driven. Despite the good feelings about the Doctrinal Task Force (appointed by bishops) and the Hymnal Revision Committee (the responsibility of the publishing house) in 1984, there was still suspicion that a general agency task force would never be fully inclusive of the Church's evangelical constituency.

The fears were justified. Though several well-known evangelicals were placed on the committee—David Seamands of Asbury Seminary and Jim Holsinger, for example—the committee was dominated by a number who were already on record for support of the homosexual agenda. Relying on its vast network of evangelical contacts, Good News would comment before the committee ever met that only eight to ten of twenty-six members were on record as supporting the present stance of the Church. The rest, including two representatives from the gay caucuses, were on record as opposing the Church's stance. The "study" would hardly be an objective study.

After spending $200,000 of the Church's money, the Committee to Study Homosexuality came to the 1992 General Conference, as expected, with a recommendation (17-4 support within the committee) to remove the restrictive language in the *Discipline*. After a long and draining debate, this recommendation was not supported by a conference vote of 710 to 238. However, the study would be made available to the general church.

The Book of Worship was approved, but not before evangelicals and others were able to delete a Native American Service of Thanksgiving with what many considered to include non-Christian symbols and elements. Traditional trinitarian language ("Father, Son, and Holy Spirit") was restored to several services that had been compromised in favor of feminist substitutes in the original report on the *Book of Worship*. The Baptism study was referred back to the committee for another four years of study. In a close vote, the 1988 General Conference voted to relocate the General Board of Global Ministries.

The 1996 General Conference was held in Denver. In 1994, the Good News board made a decision to start sending complementary copies of *Good News* magazine to General Conference delegates and selected others. As a result, the magazine's circulation increased from eighteen thousand to sixty-five thousand.

Steve Beard was the managing editor of the magazine. The son of a United Methodist pastor from California, Steve had a degree in journalism and had worked in Washington D.C. at the Ethics and Public Policy Center and at the Institute of Religion and Democracy before coming to Good News in 1991. Since the official Church media seldom covered Good News concerns, the magazine was the most effective way of communicating evangelical perspectives to United Methodism's growing evangelical constituency. Under Beard's editorship, the magazine combined news and inspiration (about 80 percent of each issue's content) with evangelical commentary. The decision to enlarge the mailing list (with increased costs) was an effort to expand not only the ministry, but also the evangelical presence in the denomination. The magazine presented position papers by Good News leaders on issues before the 1996 General Conference.

Scott Field, pastor of the Wheatland-Salem United Methodist Church in Northern Illinois, coordinated the political strategy efforts of Good News. More than two hundred delegates were now attending Good News's morning briefings, and many, including a number who did not agree with Good News, expressed gratitude for the fair way the information was shared.

The issue of a "leadership crisis" was a concern for a number of evangelicals. Before the 1996 conference, the Church had spent more than two years embroiled in controversy over the RE-Imagining Conference held in Minneapolis in November 1993 (see chapter 11). The RE-Imagining Conference advocated a deconstruction of historic faith in the name of feminist ideology. What was so disturbing to evangelicals and others was not so much what went on at the conference, but the unwillingness of bishops and leaders in the Church to defend United Methodist doctrine in response to the conference. The Women's Division supported the conference and was most critical of those who found the conference offensive. Bishops tended neither to defend nor to criticize the conference, but to speak vaguely about "understanding," "dialogue," and "freedom of expression."

Then, at the opening of the 1996 General Conference, fifteen active bishops, soon known as "the Denver fifteen," made a statement expressing their opposition to the Church's stand on sexual morality in regard to homosexuality. To many in the Church, it was an act of defiance. Bishops were denying publicly the very *Discipline* they had sworn to uphold. The Council of Bishops, meeting behind closed doors, could make no public statement as to whether the action of the fifteen was in any way inappropriate. Five of the first six early morning worship services conducted by bishops stressed unity, but unity was in short supply.

The fifteen bishops were quickly lifted up as courageous prophets by liberal forces in the denomination. Evangelicals, on the other hand, pointed out the connection between the "courageous stands" and membership decline. The areas served by the fifteen bishops had declined in membership an average of 4.4 percent in the years 1990 to 1994, while the areas served by all the other bishops had declined by only 2.6 percent.[22] The California-Pacific Conference, one of the fastest growing population areas of the nation, had decreased in membership by 8.12 percent over those four years.[23]

Despite the efforts of the fifteen bishops, the 1996 General Conference maintained the standards on the practice of homosexuality and added, by a vote of 553 to 321, the following statement to the Social Principles: "Ceremonies that celebrate homosexual unions shall not be conducted by our ministers and shall not be conducted in our churches."[24]

The 2000 General Conference met in Cleveland. Scott Field again directed evangelical efforts at the conference. The coalition of evangelical groups included Good News, the Confessing Movement, the Mission Society for United Methodists, Aldersgate Renewal Fellowship, LifeWatch, RENEW, Transforming Congregations movement, and United Methodist Action.

The conference affirmed the Church's stand on sexual morality, particularly in regard to homosexuality, condemned partial birth abortions, supported the Day of Prayer for Persecuted Christians,[25] and made a course in evangelism a requirement for persons desiring ordination in The United Methodist Church. Evangelicals also nominated three persons from the floor for election to the Judicial Council—Keith Boyette, James Holsinger, and Mary Daffin—and all three were elected.

Good News magazine offered extensive coverage of the Cleveland General Conference. That many persons were now depending on *Good News* as much for its objective reporting as for its commentary was exemplified by the following letter from Neil Sweet Jr., which appeared in the September-October issue of *Circuit Rider*, the journal for United Methodist pastors:

> I find it striking that the July/August 2000 issue of *Good News* . . . devoted 46 pages to reports of General Conference . . . while *Circuit Rider* devoted 16 pages. . . . More subjectively, it seems that a larger percentage of the *Good News* issue focused on direct reports of the decisions, while the *Daily Christian Advocate* included more "human interest" articles, . . . or articles that focused on the reporting rather than the reports.[26]

An evangelical interpretation of the conference was given by Tom Oden in his article "Mainstreaming the Mainline: Methodist Evangelicals Pull a Once 'Incurably Liberal' Denomination Back Toward the Orthodox Center" for *Christianity Today:*

> Growing evidence suggests that evangelicals are exercising increasing influence within denominations previously written off as incurably liberal, and the latest evidence comes from the recent United Methodist Church General Conference in Cleveland. . . .

> The [evangelical] shift has not happened overnight but is the result of decades of work by renewal groups. The Good News movement was founded 33 years ago to bring a more distinctly evangelical emphasis to the denomination.[27]

Not all of the interpretations of the 2000 General Conference were as positive. *Christian Social Action*, the "official" journal of the General Board of Church and Society, devoted 80 percent of its November-December 2000 issue to the actions of the 2000 General Conference in regard to the conference actions on homosexuality. In the article "The Conservative Shift in The United Methodist Church," Harry C. Kiely offered a sinister interpretation of the future of The United Methodist Church based on the evangelical influence at the conference:

> A coalition of United Methodist-related organizations that identify themselves as evangelical and conservative have claimed credit for several recent actions by General Conference. Debates were moot because the coalition had already worked out pre-decided votes on the controversial issues.

Kiely then listed the "controversial issues" and "predecided votes":
(1) Exclusion of homosexual persons from ordination.
(2) Election of three consecutive members to the Judicial Council.
(3) Passing of a revised formula for representation to the General Conference in which the southern jurisdictions would have more delegates.
(4) Increasing of the conservative representation on the University Senate, the body that oversees the accreditation and approval of colleges and seminaries.

For evangelicals, the formula for representation and the elections were a matter of balance. The overseas converences and the southern conferences had been underrepresented by the old formula. In the case of the University Senate, the "increasing representation" was the increase of the number of evangelicals from zero to a token one person on the senate.

But the one person was a cause for alarm. Kiely identified Good News and Confessing Movement as the main culprits.[28]

Kiely described the three groups as follows:

> *Good News* . . . has no official connection to The United Methodist Church. . . . It has carried on an adversarial relationship to the denom-

ination since its creation more than 30 years ago, regularly attacking the General Boards of Global Ministries and Church and Society. . . .

As part of its resistance movement to the official UMC, *Good News* has its own missionaries and mission board, publishing house and church school literature.[29]

Kiely charged that the Confessing Movement would make church members "confess" a specific theology that would claim "Jesus Christ as the Son of God, the Savior of the world, and the Lord of history and the church." According to Kiely, the Confessing Movement interpreted this to mean that other world religions were not means of salvation. Kiely continued: "This statement contradicts a tradition extending back to John Wesley, which not only affirms a variety of Christian theologies within the denomination, but also respects and celebrates the diversity of world religions through which God continues to speak."[30] IRD, according to Kiely, has a long history of attacking mainline denominations and ecumenical groups. It has received funding through foundations that support right-wing political causes.

Kiely then stated that homosexuality was the galvanizing subject for conservatives. Good News had warned that full acceptance of gays and lesbians would result in a schism or at least a mass exodus of conservatives from the denomination: "Whatever the motivation for the consistent two-thirds votes against inclusiveness, it is questionable whether the conservatives could have made the advances they did at this Conference without the energizing effect of feelings and fears about homosexuality."[31] Kiely concluded: "The conservative wing of the UMC probably is not large enough to bring about a coup like the one witnessed by the Southern Baptists, however it has already demonstrated its capacity and willingness to create havoc and to undermine the ongoing ministry of our denomination."[32]

Kiely's article reflected the perception of a number of institutional leaders toward evangelical renewal groups, and especially toward Good News. These institutionalists were now willing to state openly that Good News, the fast-growing Confessing Movement, and other evangelical renewal groups were a major influence in the life of the denomination. However, this influence was viewed not as renewal, but as "havoc" and as the "undermining of the ongoing ministry of the denomination."

For its part, Good News graded the 2000 General Conference with a B. There was no question that the evangelical groups working together had had an influence on the conference. More important, these groups had been joined by numbers of moderate delegates who were convinced by evangelical arguments on a number of issues.

Still, a large portion of the Church was untouched by evangelical renewal. Conferences and local churches seemed unable or unwilling to deal with the erosion of faith taking place in their midst. Church leaders, including bishops, as well as boards and agencies and seminaries, were denominated theologically by a dead liberalism. Numbers of local churches, the Church at its leadership level, in its bishops and its institutions and its boards and agencies, seemed mostly untouched by the wider evangelical renewal in The United Methodist Church and in worldwide Christianity.

The United Methodist Church was entering the twenty-first century, still struggling to find its soul.

CHAPTER ELEVEN

THE STRUGGLE FOR DOCTRINAL INTEGRITY

Every ten years, *Christian Century*, one of the best-known and most influential magazines of Protestant opinion, identifies what it considers the leading theologians and thinkers of the Protestant world and asks each of them to contribute an article with the theme "How My Mind Has Changed." The series was significant not only because it sought to single out the most influential thinkers, but also because it traced the changing theological scene in America.

Of the group selected for the 1980 publication, four either were United Methodist or taught in United Methodist seminaries: Shubert Ogden of Perkins, John Hick of Claremont, Rosemary Reuther of Garrett-Evangelical, and John B. Cobb of Claremont. Ogden was known for his interest in Rudolf Bultmann and the task of "demythologizing" the gospel, Hick for his position that Christianity was just one voice among a number of valid world religions, Reuther because of her commitment to radical feminist liberation theology, and Cobb because of his advocacy of process theology and a finite God.

None of these nor, for that matter, anyone picked by *Christian Century* could be considered a scholar committed to Wesleyan theology. Of the four, only John Cobb had even shown an interest in the Methodist heritage. None of the four could be considered "mainstream" or even "moderate" in their approach to Christianity.

The fact that these four were identified as the best of United Methodism, that their messages were lifted up as an indicator of where the Church was and where it was going, and that all of them were identified with the extreme left theologically lent credibility to the argument that United Methodism had lost its theological footing in the decades before 1980 and that seminary education had lost contact with ordinary United Methodists. If renewal was taking place at all, it had not touched the leadership of The United Methodist Church. The Church seemed to operate in the context of theological anarchy.

Evangelicals were not encouraged when they assessed the state of doctrine in The United Methodist Church. Thirteen years of Good News's effort had borne no noticeable fruit. Good News leaders were questioning whether renewal was a lost cause. Pessimism over lack of hopeful signs in the area of doctrinal integrity was the main reason that Charles Keysor stepped down as the head of the Good News movement. The growing evangelical renaissance in the wider world seemed to have bypassed United Methodism.

For Good News evangelicals, the theological confusion in the Church was epitomized by the doctrinal statement of 1972 and by the official embracing of the idea of "pluralism," the principle that, at least in its extreme form, bestowed validity on any and all theological expressions in the Church.

Through *Good News* magazine, in editorial and in other commentary, through discussion with boards and agencies, and through numberless conversations, Good News supporters pressed the issue of theological integrity, focusing especially on the doctrinal statement and the matter of "pluralism." Critics of Good News pointed out, with some justification, that Good News was inconsistent in its arguments. On the one hand, Good News argued that pluralism had undermined the integrity of United Methodist teaching and needed to be rejected. On the other hand, Good News used pluralism in its discussions with curriculum makers, with seminaries, and in regard to annual conference appointments, arguing that since pluralism was now a guiding principle in the Church, the evangelical perspective had the right to be represented and heard.

In 1976, *United Methodist Reporter* ran an article by Bud Herron on reactions to Good News's charges that "conservative evangelicals" were not heard or accepted in seminaries or church councils.[1] The general response was that Good News's accusations were "not supported by the facts."

In an editorial in the August 10, 1979, issue of UM *Reporter,* however, there was an expression of appreciation for remarks by the Good News board chair, Paul Mickey, on his analysis of the denomination's "theological and spiritual crisis." Mickey called for a clearer spelling out of the denomination's basic theology and for episcopal leadership in doctrinal matters. The editorial then defended the concept of "pluralism." Pluralism, according to the editorial, was not as bankrupt a principle as Mickey had suggested. At the same time, the editorial admitted the Church needed a clearer focus on what the principles and doctrines were that all United Methodists were supposed to hold in common.

By this time, Good News was already setting its legislative agenda for the 1980 General Conference. One of its major proposals was to ask the General Conference to form a task force to clarify the "essential core" that was so often referred to in the doctrinal statement but never defined. As the General Conference approached, several hundred proposals, some with Good News wording and others with variations on that wording, were submitted to the General Conference. Some of the petitions were approved and forwarded through annual conferences.

The petitions were never seriously considered. The 1980 General Conference was still operating under a procedure by which only petitions submitted by boards and agencies would be printed in *Daily Christian Advocate, Advance Edition.* Other petitions were in the hands of only the legislative and sublegislative chairs, to be introduced in a manner that was at the discretion of those chairs. This allowed chairpersons of legislative and sublegislative groups to control and manipulate how and when petitions would be considered. The chair of the doctrine sublegislative group was Harvey Pothoff, a seminary professor from Iliff, who was able to divert serious consideration of the petitions with arguments that the present statement, if correctly understood, already covered the concerns of the submitted petitions. Furthermore, he, and the committee with him, argued that the Church needed no more task forces that would cost money and increase apportionments to local churches.[2] Most of the Good News petitions were not even read, and none came with positive approval to the floor of the General Conference. The Good News strategy on doctrine at the 1980 General Conference produced no positive results.

Because of the debacle of 1980, Good News adopted a different strategy for dealing with the doctrinal statement as the Church began looking forward to the 1984 General Conference in Baltimore. The new strategy was to write and encourage petitions that would seek change by increments, by addressing not the whole statement, but words, lines, sentences, and paragraphs. A sublegislative group would be much more likely to accept revision in small pieces rather than to accept rewritten sections or to respond to a call for a new task force.

When the 1984 General Conference met in Baltimore, the sublegislative group related to discipleship that dealt with doctrinal petitions suddenly found itself in a difficult position. There were approximately five hundred petitions—the majority from Good News–minded persons or churches or groups—addressing the doctrinal statement and doctrinal issues. Because of the way General Conference functioned—with petitions from general agencies in printed form only—the group was having to deal with the petitions without prior preparation. Furthermore, a number in the sublegislative group admitted openly that they were not qualified to deal with complex doctrinal matters.

The legislative group, unlike its counterpart in 1980, agreed that the Church's doctrine was important and needed attention. Furthermore, since there seemed to be so much dissatisfaction with the 1972 doctrinal statement, perhaps the time had come for a special task force to deal with doctrinal matters, and not just to define the "core of doctrine" (as Good News's petitions had requested in 1980), but to rewrite the whole statement!

This was more than Good News had ever even hoped for. What had been summarily rejected in 1980 was accepted in 1984, and more so. To perfect a petition originally written by Paul Stallsworth, an evangelical who would later become identified with the Confessing Movement and LifeWatch (the organized pro-life witness within The United Methodist Church), the proposal for a doctrinal task force was carried from the legislative group by the Reverend Mark Trotter from California to the floor of the conference where it was adopted.

But who would serve on the task force? Would Good News be able to have a representative? If the committee was to be made up by the same kind of people as the group that drew up the original statement in 1972, was it not possible that the Church's stated doctrine would be even more unacceptable to evangelicals? The truth was that the general church had not distinguished itself on prior occasions by forming theologically balanced task forces.

This time it seemed different. The bishops, not the boards and agencies, would select the task force. Bishop Earl Hunt, who was sympathetic to Good News's concerns and had expressed interest in the committee, was picked as chair. Good News, of course, would not be represented (despite the fact that it was Good News that had raised concern over the doctrinal statement).[3] However, Kenneth Kinghorn of Asbury Seminary would be made a committee member. Though primarily a historian, Kinghorn was theologically astute. He was also a writer and eventually would make a crucial contribution as a member of the writing team.

In addition, persons in the Church through *Interpreter* magazine and other official Church channels would be invited to make suggestions to the committee. And Good News would be given time to speak to the committee from an evangelical perspective. Those presentations were made by Paul Mickey and Riley Case.

By spoken presentation and written recommendation, Good News addressed the major points of concern in regard to the 1972 statement:

(1) "The doctrinal standards not to be construed literally and juridically."

The 1972 statement had redefined the whole idea of "standards" so that they were not "standard," in any meaningful sense of the word:

> The aim [of the Wesleyan doctrinal standards] was not to impose an inflexible system of doctrine or to inhibit responsible intellectual freedom, but rather to provide a broad and flexible framework of doctrine which would define the outside limits for public teaching in the societies.[4]

"Intellectual freedom" or "academic freedom," code words imported from the secular, academic, and intellectual worlds, meant that no doctrines or beliefs were required or necessary for an individual or an institution to be United Methodist. Thus, according to this imported ideology, there could be no "heresy." One did not have to believe or confess anything. Though the statement made reference to a "framework that would define the outside limits for public teaching," the idea of legitimate and enforceable boundaries was rendered invalid by the continual references that the standards were not to be construed legally or juridically. In other words, doctrinal standards were not really doctrinal standards and, for all practical purposes, were useless.

(2) The "quadrilateral"—Scripture, tradition, reason, experience.

> Since "our present existing and established standards of doctrine" cited in the first two Restrictive Rules of the Constitution of the United Methodist Church are not to be construed literally and juridically, then by what methods can our doctrinal reflection and construction be most fruitful and fulfilling? The answer comes in terms of our free inquiry within the boundaries defined by four main sources and guidelines for Christian theology: Scripture, tradition, experience, reason.[5]

By the wonder of liberal eisegesis, the framers of the 1972 statement had discovered that the "quadrilateral" had been a part of Methodist tradition since the days of John Wesley. Furthermore, each of the ideas was being defined not by Wesleyan use, but by liberal revisionists:

- Scripture was not really the written Word of God, but "the deposit of a unique testimony to God's self-disclosure,"[6] thus making Scripture a human response rather than a divine disclosure.

- Tradition was not the early ecumenical councils, the classic creeds, the consensus of Christian truth gathered from all churches, or even United Methodism's own doctrinal standards, but, along with other things, "the history of that environment of grace in and by which all Christians live, which is the continuance through time and space of God's self-giving love in Jesus Christ," a definition which placed the whole idea of tradition beyond rational comprehension.[7]

- Experience was not, as in Wesley, the confirming presence of the Holy Spirit that gives witness to the truth of the gospel, but "the personal appropriation of God's unmeasured mercy in life and interpersonal relations." It was "to the individual as tradition is to the Church." Whatever the intent of the commission, "experience" was soon widely interpreted as "whatever I feel is right in my heart."[8]

- Reason was defined as doctrines "submitted to critical analysis so that they may commend themselves to thoughtful persons as valid."[9] While the comment was made that revelation and "experience" may transcend the scope of reason, "reason" was soon interpreted, at least by some, as secular rationalism, with authority to declare that supernaturalist claims often made by evangelicals and other Christians were to be rendered invalid by modern thought.

Instead of providing United Methodists with a common court of appeal by which doctrinal claims could be tested, the quadrilateral only added to United Methodism's growing confusion over doctrine. There was no common understanding of how the quadrilateral could practically function. Could the practice of homosexuality be blessed by God? The argument was given that "reason" and "experience" could be claimed in support of homosexual practice and these two trumped "Scripture" and "tradition."

(3) "Pluralism."

Pluralism was at the heart of the Good News concern. Pluralism was a legitimate concept only if it operated within well-defined boundaries, usually understood as a commonly accepted "core of doctrine." The Good News effort was either to delete the word "pluralism" or to define the "core of doctrine."

(4) The conciliar principle.

The 1972 statement spoke of the "conciliar principle" in contrast to the "confessional principle." But in the hands of liberals, the conciliar principle was perhaps the most dangerous of all the ideas in the doctrinal statement. It was being interpreted to mean not that the earliest ecumenical councils of the Church provided an authoritative interpretation of Scripture and doctrine for succeeding generations, but that present-day councils—The World Council of Churches, the National Council of Churches, or the General Conference—could revise and change doctrine pretty much at will. The last thing spoken was authoritative.[10]

The final report of Hunt's task force, either intentionally or incidentally, addressed all of the Good News concerns. The references to "doctrinal standards not construed legally or juridically" were eliminated. The quadrilateral was redefined with a strong statement on the primacy of Scripture. "Pluralism" was no longer a guiding principle. Indeed, the word "pluralism" was not used at all in the statement. Gone also was the reference to the conciliar principle.

But could the report make it through the 1988 General Conference at St. Louis? For the first time in its short history, Good News found itself supporting and lobbying for a General Conference Task Force report. In contrast to previous General Conferences, a special legislative group called Faith and Order was added to the legislative groups of the General Conference. Persons seemed genuinely interested in theological discussion. Was there a real—not just imagined—theological shift taking place in the Church?

As 1988 approached, the whole evangelical agenda was given a tremendous boost by the Houston Declaration. The Houston Declaration grew out of the concern of a number of large church pastors who were not—at least officially—a part of the Good News movement but who nevertheless agreed with Good News that The United Methodist Church needed renewal. These pastors were also convinced that under the then-existing leadership of the Church, absorbed as it was with institutional protectionism, with its overemphasis on inclusivity and quotas and the politicizing of the gospel, renewal would never come.

One night in early 1987, as he lay sleepless pondering these things, Ira Gallaway, pastor of First Church, Peoria, Illinois, was impressed by the vision of gathering a group of these pastors and others for the purpose of affirming and giving witness to the historic faith of the Church. He contacted a number of persons he knew. The response was overwhelmingly positive. Bill Hinson, pastor of First Church, Houston, agreed to host a gathering, and so, in November of 1987, a letter of invitation was sent to a selected list of moderate and evangelical church leaders to gather in December to frame a statement that would deal with major theological and moral issues facing the denomination. Signing the letter of invitation were pastors of seven of the most significant churches in the denomination: Bill Hinson of First Church, Houston; John Ed Mathison of Frazer Church, Montgomery, Alabama; Ira Gallaway of First Church, Peoria; O. Gerald Trigg of First Church, Colorado Springs; Maxie Dunnam of Christ Church, Memphis; Ellsworth Kalas of Church of the Saviour, Cleveland; and James Buskirk of First Church, Tulsa.

Eighty-seven key pastors and laypersons met in Houston. While a number of Good News–related individuals were present, support in Houston came from a whole new segment of the Church. There was, of course, no support from board and agency staff persons. But there were other key leaders, both lay and clergy. Geoffrey Wainwright of Duke Divinity School gave major leadership and was the main author for the statement. Forty-eight pastors from eighteen states signed the final document including such persons as Barbara Brokhoff, evangelist; Kirbyjon Caldwell of Windsor Village, Houston; William Morris, district superintendent from Tennessee; and Cornelius Henderson, district superintendent from Atlanta. The latter two would eventually be elected to the episcopacy.

The statement affirmed the primacy of Scripture (the same wording that would appear in the new doctrinal statement), the importance of the Trinity and traditional language in the liturgy of the Church, and the necessity for sexual purity in the clergy (referring to homosexual practice) as sin. The Houston Declaration was mailed to fifty-five thousand United Methodist clergy and lay leaders. Ninety-five hundred clergy and seven thousand lay leaders responded. Ninety-four percent of the respondents marked their agreement with the declaration. A paid ad was placed in *The United Methodist Reporter*. This received fifty-eight thousand responses of which only eighty-seven were negative.

The interest in the Houston Declaration was the clearest sign to that point that a seismic shift was taking place in the Church. Good News might be dismissed by bishops, boards and agencies, and seminaries as a small, vocal, angry, negative minority, but the Houston Declaration revealed that an evangelical presence and a concern for doctrine was far greater than just Good News.

The Houston Declaration and the response it generated was also a sign of a new reality facing The United Methodist Church. What evangelicals called "doctrinal integrity," a call that for a number of years was ignored, would now be a matter of discussion in the Church and would itself inform other issues, including matters of church unity, social and economic issues, and authority. It would also lie at the core of differences around homosexuality.

Richard John Neuhaus noted the new reality in United Methodism in the April 1988 *Religion & Society Report*. Under the title "A New Methodism Afoot?" Neuhaus commented about Methodism as the "most American of America's churches," which in recent years had been noted for changing its "solid, Wesleyan heritage for both silly and serious elements of American culture."[11] But its wandering in the theological wilderness might be coming to an end. Neuhaus then spoke of the two most important signs of change: the proposed doctrinal statement and the Houston Declaration.

Obviously, not all in the Church were pleased with the Houston Declaration. Some pastors in California, with some additional signatures

from other parts of the country, prepared and circulated a document entitled "Perfect Love Casts Out Fear," which sounded an alarm about the
persons meeting in Houston: "They . . . present truths as Wesleyan which
are anathema to the spirit of Wesley and Methodism. . . .They do not
speak for us. They do not speak for women. They do not speak for persons
of color. They do not speak for Wesley. We pray that they do not speak
for the General Conference."

The "Perfect Love" statement was issued with a great deal of passion.
The signers referred to the Houston group as those "whose power is
threatened," "whose prejudices are challenged," and "whose preoccupations blind them to truth." The statement went on to charge that the
Houston people were operating from "anxiety," "fear," and "egocentri-
cism," accompanied by "theological repression," "repressive stances," and
"narrow sectarianism." "Perfect Love" opposed the proposed doctrinal
statement and called for flexibility in language in regard to the Trinity
and for openness on the issue of homosexuality.

Though they were not organized and issued no public statement,
another group that tended to oppose the doctrinal statement was liberal
seminary professors. Writing in *The United Methodist Reporter* in the
weeks before General Conference, Donald Messer of Iliff Seminary gave
his response after reading the task force report:

> Frankly, I was shocked that my judgment would be that we're better off
> with the current statement with its flaws than with the radical surgery
> being proposed by the new document.
> The new document is more doctrinaire than doctrine.
> For example, it fails to substantiate its claims. It not only wants to
> state the primacy of Scripture but wants everything to flow to that con-
> clusion even if it's not appropriate. It tries to claim clarity where none
> exists. It's not ready for adoption.[12]

Everett Tilson, acting dean at METHESCO, the United Methodist
Seminary in Delaware, Ohio, weighed in with sharp criticism of the new
statement at a gathering of delegates in the North Central Jurisdiction
meeting at METHESCO in March 1988.[13] According to Tilson, the
statement substitutes one source of authority (Scripture) for four sources
(Scripture, tradition, reason, and experience) and suggests a Christian
arrogance that there is only one way to God. As such, according to
Tilson, the document was not helpful in dialogue with those from other
religions. Furthermore, the task force report emphasized the normative

rather than the originative character of authority. It assumed the proposition that those who subscribe to the document had the truth and others didn't. Its stance was inward and backward, rather than outward and forward. Tilson expressed the conviction that the statement would be divisive because it sought unity in doctrinal statements rather than in other important aspects of church life.[14]

One of the more interesting responses to the new doctrinal statement came from Albert Outler, author of the 1972 statement, onetime critic of Good News, but now, through his friendship with Ed Robb, an encourager of Good News. In an eleven-page letter to Bishop Earl Hunt,[15] chair of the task force, Outler at first praised the report and then expressed his misgivings. Outler admitted the 1972 statement needed drastic revision but he was not expecting such *radical* drastic revision. The 1988 statement was couched in assertive propositions ("we believe," "we understand," "we assert," "we hold," "we stress," "our distinctive belief"), which implied a unity of United Methodist belief, which, in fact, Outler believed probably did not reflect the actual situation. Outler did not object to this more confessional way of dealing with doctrine if the Church would support it. But he had questions. The new statement left very little open to question; the old statement stressed inquiry and development.

Outler also jumped into the unresolved problem of what exactly constitutes United Methodism's doctrinal standards. The new statement dropped the traditional Wesleyan *Sermons* and *Notes* as part of the standards. Thus United Methodist doctrine would stand without appeal to the Wesley material. Just as John and Charles Wesley were beginning to acquire theological status in the wider world, according to Outler, they were being demoted in The United Methodist Church.

Outler also argued that "tradition" in the new statement was "backward" looking instead of "forward" looking. Referring to the Roman Catholics and Vatican II, Outler argued for a "conciliar" understanding of tradition rather than a "confessional" understanding. Outler was enough of a liberal to believe that new truth could be revealed through the studied efforts of councils and conferences.

Outler recognized that the statement was a radical shift and wondered if that was what the Church really wanted:

> If these fundamental doctrinal re-orientations mark out the pathway United Methodists really want to follow, for a long future, they are autonomous and free to do so. They wanted a new statement and now

they have gotten one. But it would be a comfort to those of us who had hoped for a more continuous development of doctrine in the United Methodist Church, if we could see the whole denomination caught up and involved in this crucial shift, and a responsible party to it.[16]

Albert Outler's points were well made, but it is possible that he had the academic and ecumenical community in mind when he made his remarks. Many others in the Church, ordinary pastors and laypeople, wanted a more sure word and were ready to welcome a new statement. The Houston Declaration, though it did not directly mention the doctrinal statement (the task force's final report was not available at the time the Houston Declaration was being circulated), resonated with many moderates in the Church and generated interest in and support for the statement.

Even the bishops were finally beginning to agree. In the episcopal address opening the 1988 General Conference, Bishop Jack Tuell explained it was time to lay "pluralism" aside: "There is no evangelistic appeal to join a group whose principal identifying point is that everyone disagrees with everyone else."

Since the proposed doctrinal statement did not directly relate to the work of any of the boards and agencies, there was no direct opposition from any of the major boards. Opposition at the General Conference came from theological liberals. A number of amendments were added to the statement from the General Conference legislative group. One rather serious challenge came in the form of an amendment offered by Phil Wogaman, professor at Wesley Seminary, who wanted to add these words: "We recognize that Scripture contains both authoritative witness to the word of God as well as human fallibility and cultural limitations."

The amendment, which would have made official the idea of scriptural fallibility, would have cut the heart out of scriptural authority. In the end, the amendment was defeated and the doctrinal statement was accepted. For Good News and other evangelicals this was a major breakthrough.

The significance of the revision of the doctrinal statement and Good News's role was noted by James Wall. Writing an editorial addressed to "Aunt Florence" in the May 18-25 issue of *Christian Century*, Wall reflected:

> I thought you might like to hear something of the dynamics of the delegates' decisions regarding doctrine, a somewhat strange emphasis for Methodists, since, as you well know, John Wesley centered on mission—

doing the faith—rather than on doctrine. The General Conference is a political gathering, and this one was responding doctrinally to pressure from the newest political bloc in the UMC, the "Good News" folk who resonate with the country's conservative mood.

This whole doctrine thing actually started in 1972 when the General Conference voted to adopt a belief statement designed to pull together the various branches of the newly formed United Methodist Church. Much to the chagrin of the church's theologians, the conference was more concerned with the restructuring of the denomination than with doctrine. The participants were acting in the Wesleyan tradition, eager to organize themselves for maximum efficiency to fight the next battle. They gave little attention—about 17 minutes—to what proved to be a most thoughtful statement, written, for the most part, by Albert Outler. . . . This cursory treatment proved to be a disappointment to Outler, who had looked forward to teaching theology to the delegates, most of whom were relieved that the statement eased through without rancor.

The statement was largely ignored until 1984 when the "Good News" people decided it was too "pluralistic"—by which they meant it was so open to a variety of doctrinal options that it gave informal approval to John Wesley's statement that it didn't matter what one believes. As he was supposed to have put it, "If your heart is right, give me your hand." The "Good News" folk, I should remind you, are those among the United Methodists who have a greater affinity for piety than for praxis. They are not fundamentalists, but they do have a fondness for the language of the spirit and scripturally based preaching. They say "Jesus" [frequently]. . . .

Among the United Methodists conservatives were strong enough by 1984 to call for a new doctrinal statement, hoping in 1988 to shift to the right the way we express our faith. As they wished, the document, which came before the General Conference's legislative body this month, strongly propounded the conservative viewpoint, so much so that the theologian John Cobb, of the Claremont School of Theology, warned that if the church moved entirely away from "pluralism," it would be in danger of becoming so scripturally focused that its only source of truth would be the Bible.[17]

Wall argued that the new statement did not give conservatives a clear victory. Amendments to the original report and approved by the conference softened the emphasis on the primacy of Scripture by mentioning that experience and reason could still be considered as sources and criteria for theology.

Wall then went on to link that amendment with the debate over homosexuality. If the Church were open to the idea of experience as a source of truth, then it could affirm that God was continually working to introduce new levels of wisdom. This meant that there was still something to learn from persons who follow a lifestyle different from the traditional lifestyle. Wall expressed some hopeful optimism regarding what the four-year study of homosexuality might recommend to the 1992 General Conference.

> So you see, Aunt Florence, the doctrinal statement keeps us open to experience as well as to Scripture. If the church is mistaken in its ban on ordination of gay or lesbian persons—and it must acknowledge that all church bodies are fallible—then experience will speak, and we will have to measure what we hear against Scripture, reason and tradition.[18]

The official *Good News* response to the passing of the new doctrinal statement was given by Jim Heidinger in the July-August 1988 issue:

> United Methodism has an excellent new theological statement. The prominent theme ringing through it with bell-like clarity is the primacy of Scripture. This theme has replaced the controversial and problematic phrase, "theological pluralism," which the Hunt Commission purposefully omitted.
>
> United Methodists will welcome the new statement and be encouraged by it. We all need to study the new document carefully. We need to discover just how pointedly the theme of "primacy" has been enunciated by the Hunt task force. Moreover, we need to be prepared to resist those who would cling to "theological pluralism," claiming little has changed for the church theologically.[19]

Good News realized that statements on paper do not themselves bring theological and spiritual renewal. But it was a start. In the struggle for doctrinal integrity, the *Discipline* was now an important ally.

The task facing Good News and other evangelicals was to interpret the significance of the newly discovered doctrinal standards and the 1988 doctrinal statement. Statements on paper did not in themselves mean renewal. Gospel truths must be understood, preached, and defended. And even if a majority of General Conference delegates could reaffirm the importance of doctrine, there was little reason to believe that the vast United Methodist constituency, which had suffered under years of neglect, if not under outright denial of the importance of doctrine, would so quickly be renewed. Beset by mushy theological thinking in the general church, on the one hand, and by an aggressive fundamentalist and charismatic teaching in the wider culture, on the other, ordinary United Methodists were not easily united by a doctrinal core they did not understand.

But Good News would no longer be alone in the effort. The Houston Declaration group reassembled in Memphis in January 1992 and issued a statement preceding the 1992 General Conference. Though doctrine per se was not the motivating factor that drew participants to Memphis—at least for some, issues around homosexuality were a motivating force behind such meetings—there was an increasing realization that issues of authority were behind many church differences and that these issues needed to be addressed. The Memphis group affirmed that Jesus Christ is the only way of divine salvation, that holy living is the way for Christians to live out the mandate of discipleship given by Jesus Christ, and that the local congregation is the center of mission and ministry to the world.

Again, the Declaration was circulated to the larger church and again there was tremendous response. A total of 171,169 persons signed in support by the time of General Conference. Later the number of signers would approach 200,000.

But the Memphis Declaration—perhaps unwisely—then went on to make specific recommendations on a number of legislative issues facing the 1992 General Conference: reaffirm the use of biblical language and images; abolish the General Council on Ministries; reduce the number, size, and staff of general church boards and agencies; establish a new General Board of Evangelism; move the Board of Global Ministries from New York; reaffirm Christian sexual morality, especially in regard to homosexuality; and clarify that baptism is a means of grace but does not replace the necessity of a decision to accept Jesus Christ as Savior and Lord.

Though a number of moderates agreed with the general principles espoused by the Memphis Declaration, not all were willing to support its specific General Conference agenda. As Good News had discovered, public statements in themselves do not necessarily translate into votes or reform. With the exception of the homosexual legislation, the Memphis Declaration agenda was widely ignored or rejected in 1992. The Memphis Declaration did not have the dramatic effect that the 1988 Houston Declaration had had.

Was it time for something more? While at the 1992 General Conference, Good News board member Budd Sprague, a pastor in East Ohio, had a conversation with Tom Oden, professor at Drew, about church renewal. Out of that conversation, Budd Sprague presented a paper at the 1992 summer board meeting of Good News, proposing another approach to renewal.

What the Houston Declaration of 1988 and Memphis Declaration of 1992 had revealed clearly was that there was a large group of persons in the Church who more and more was sharing Good News concerns but had not, and probably would not, become publicly identified with Good News. For some, Good News carried the image of shrillness and negativism. Primarily because of its populist history, Good News was still considered a group of outsiders. And for some pastors in some conferences, it simply was not good for one's "career" to be associated with Good News.

In addition, though there were a number of respected church leaders associated with Good News, it was apparent that no bishops had done so, nor had any general agency staff and few persons associated with seminaries, nor, for that matter, had there been many pastors of the large and leading churches of the denomination. Could Good News work with these people for the larger cause of renewal?

In March 1993, a group of Good News board members—Ed Robb, Wesley Putnam, Donald Shell, Scott Field, James Heidinger, and Budd Sprague—met with three others: Tom Oden of Drew University School of Theology, retired Bishop William Cannon, and Maxie Dunnam, pastor of Christ Church, Memphis. The purpose of this gathering was to discuss the theological crisis in the Church and explore the possibility of a different approach to renewal.

Out of this meeting came another meeting called by Bishop Cannon. Cannon knew the kind of people who could take the vision to another level. At Cannon's urging, Bill Hinson, pastor of First Church, Houston, and a key figure in the Houston Declaration, and John Ed Mathison, pastor of Frazer Memorial Church, Montgomery, joined Cannon and Dunnam and Oden at a gathering in Atlanta. Out of that meeting came plans for an ongoing movement to advance the cause of doctrinal renewal. The key idea was a "Consultation on the Future of the Church," which would be held in Atlanta in April 1994.

The "consultation" took on new urgency after the RE-Imagining Conference was held in Minneapolis on November 4-7, 1993. The conference was sponsored by local and state ecumenical councils to mark the midpoint of the World Council of Churches' "Decade in Solidarity with Women." The conference was given a major grant from the Presbyterian Church (U.S.A.) but was also funded and supported by a number of different groups, including The United Methodist Church, the Evangelical

Lutheran Church, and the American Baptist Churches in the U.S.A. Twenty-two hundred participants from forty-nine states and twenty-seven countries attended. The Women's Division of The United Methodist Church encouraged and funded the expenses of thirty-six directors, nine staff members, and eleven conference vice presidents.

The conference heralded a new development, the dawn of a "second Reformation," which, in the eyes of its sponsors, was more valuable and important to the health of humankind than the first Reformation. The preface of the conference program justified the need for radical theological surgery. There were grand calls to rid the church of sexism, racism, and classism, with the underlying assumption that these were tied with Christian doctrinal orthodoxy. The conference celebrated the goddess Sophia, the gift of lesbianism, and the spiritual experiences of persons who found the god within themselves.

The RE-Imagining Conference was nothing if not a coming-out of radical theological feminism. Every Christian truth at the core of the faith— the Trinity, the Incarnation, the Atonement, the primacy of Scripture, the supremacy of Christ—was either denied outright or at least undercut by one or more of the speakers at the conference.

The conference might not have drawn so much public attention without the efforts of Faye Short, the president of RENEW, the women's task force of Good News, and several other women who were part of mainline renewal efforts. Faye Short was well aware of the ideology of radical feminism. She had been active and had held district and conference offices in the North Georgia United Methodist Women. She had also attended the national assembly of United Methodist Women and had written an article expressing concern, which she shared with Good News.[20] As a result of her interests and insight, she was elected to the Good News board in 1988, was part of the founding of RENEW in 1989, and then was made president of RENEW and a Good News staff person. She realized the significance of the RE-Imagining Conference in the summer of 1993 and was soon in touch with other renewal leaders. Dottie Chase, long-time Good News board member, attended the conference on behalf of RENEW.

Good News duly published Dottie Chase's report as well as the remarks of other observers. By late November 1993, a number of other journals and papers—*Christianity Today, Focus on the Family, Presbyterian Layman, United Methodist Reporter, First Things, Faith and Freedom, Challenge, Minneapolis Star Tribune,* and *Christian Century*—had also published articles on the conference. A complete analysis of the conference and a discussion of the issues the conference raised were laid out in a nine-page paper done in March of 1994 by the Evangelical Council for United Methodist Women/RENEW (ECUM/RENEW), the women's task force of Good News:

> The [RE-Imagining Conference] . . . is categorically different from anything we have faced. We have observed the Church dabbling in heresy and drifting toward apostasy. Quite frankly, the soul of the Church is at stake. We have witnessed the public dismantling of Christology—the nature, person and work of Jesus Christ—under the very banner of the mainline Christian denominations.[21]

In large part because of the efforts of RENEW, but also because of the wide publicity in other publications, large numbers of people began contacting bishops and United Methodist Women leaders to oppose the conference and the theology behind it or to ask questions. Bishops generally either expressed ignorance of the conference and downplayed its importance, or deflected the criticism with ambiguous references to "dialogue" and "understanding."

Meanwhile, United Methodist Communications (UMCom) rushed in to try to do damage control. UMCom admitted it had been caught off-guard by the controversy surrounding the conference and that it should have been present from the beginning to interpret the conference's significance. However, it offered no serious analysis of the conference. Instead, UMCom and Methodist News Service simply reported on the controversy and then offered space for those who defended the idea of RE-Imagining.

Women bishops and a number of feminist leaders made no pretense of neutrality in regard to the ideas of RE-Imagining. Bishop Susan Morrison joined eight other United Methodist Women leaders (almost all general staff persons or persons related to seminaries), including such persons as J. Ann Craig and Jeanne Audrey Powers, in issuing a paper, "A Time of Hope—a Time of Threat." The paper was endorsed by bishops Leontine Kelly, Sharon Radar, Judith Craig, Sharon Brown Christopher, and Mary Ann Swenson, and 830 other United Methodist Women.

The paper spoke of the present "threat" facing the Church:

> Hostility toward outspoken, creative, and courageous women of faith is not new, but it is now more sharply focused. Public attacks on the

leadership, theology and funding of a recent conference call us to speak out. We are convinced that people frightened by fresh theological insights and by challenges to narrow orthodoxy are attempting to discredit and malign women. Constructive dialogue is welcome, but irrational and distorted attacks increase an environment of violence against women.

For years the United Methodist Church has been divided by controversy over the leadership of women, reproductive rights, inclusive language, and homosexuality. As women have addressed these issues, the clash of theological perspectives has intensified. At the heart of the conflict are diverse images of God, the meaning of a multi-racial, multicultural church, ecumenical commitment, equal participation of women, and the dynamics of control and power. What is at stake is who will name these issues, how the issues will be described, and who will set the agenda for the future of the church.[22]

Meanwhile the evangelical and general church reporting of the conference itself was becoming an issue. Along with the feminists, other institutional leaders now took up the argument that Good News, and much of the other Church press (including *Christian Century*) had overreacted, misreported, or misunderstood what really happened at the RE-Imagining Conference. As with a number of earlier controversies, the issue became not the theology of the event, nor the event itself, but what were motives and agendas behind the reporting. According to a number of liberal interpreters, the deeper problem was hostility against women:

There's a chill wind blowing in United Methodism. A fringe group of radicals have launched a concerted assault against the heart of faith, pounding out alarm, hatred and controversy. Yes, I am speaking about the current uproar over the so-called Goddess Sophia and the RE-Imagining Conference as laid out in the recent issue of Good News sent gratis to all UMC pastors and lay leaders. But the extremists I refer to are not members of the Women's Division of the Board of Global Ministries, feminist pastors, or liberal seminaries. They are the new heresy-hunters of Methodism.

Charging "apostasy," pronouncing "heresy," demanding purges, writing inflammatory denunciations of everything but their own brand of Christianity, they put themselves forward with unflinching arrogance as the true believers. In a traditionally nondoctrinaire denomination, they would have faith tested for D.C.—doctrinal correctness![23]

In the midst of the RE-Imagining controversy, the Bishop Cannon group that met in Atlanta the summer before finalized its plans for its program "Consultation on the Future of The United Methodist Church." Letters were sent to one hundred selected church leaders to meet in Atlanta in April 1994. The RE-Imagining Conference was never the issue that drove the consultation, but there is no doubt that the Minneapolis conference was a powerful reminder that there were serious doctrinal problems facing the Church.

An impressive group of pastors and laypersons attended the consultation. Moderators for the sessions were Bishop William Cannon, Billy Abraham, Bishop Mack Stokes, John Ed Mathison, David Seamands, and Maxie Dunnam. Addresses were given by Steve Harper of A Foundation for Theological Education (AFTE), Thomas Oden of Drew, Geoffrey Wainwright of Duke, George Hunter of Asbury, and Bill Hinson, pastor of First Church, Houston.

Though Good News had arranged the original conversations and had been involved in logistic support, it was Good News's intention that if anything came out of the consultation, it belonged to somebody else. Good News support, if it came at all, would come from afar. The purpose was to involve moderate and centrist church leaders who shared many of the concerns of Good News, but who did not wish to be identified with Good News.

Out of "Consultation on the Future of the Church" came "An Invitation to the Church." The invitation was issued, asking others to join in "exalting Jesus Christ as we confront the crisis of faith within The United Methodist Church." The final draft came from a committee consisting of Thomas Oden, Billy Abraham, Leicester Longdon, Budd Sprague, Mark Horst, and Paul Stallsworth. Five bishops were willing to sign on to the document: William Cannon, Earl Hunt Jr., Richard Looney, Mack Stokes, and William Morris.

A year later, in April 1995, in response to "Invitation to the Church," some nine hundred persons gathered in Atlanta, Georgia, and adopted a Confessional Statement, affirming Jesus Christ as Son, Savior, and Lord. Out of that meeting, the Confessing Movement was formed. Its first published pamphlet, "What Is the Confessing Movement Within The United Methodist Church?" laid out its goals and strategies:

> The Confessing Movement is a witness by United Methodist lay men and women, clergy, and congregations who pledge unequivocal and confident allegiance to the Lord Jesus Christ according to "the faith

which was once for all delivered to the saints" (Jude 3). . . . This faith
centers on Jesus Christ, fully God and fully man; and on His life, death,
resurrection, ascension, and promised return as attested in Holy
Scripture.[24]

The purpose of the new movement was stated in a simple and straight-
forward way:

The Confessing Movement will contend for the apostolic faith within
the United Methodist Church. The Confessing Movement will seek to
reclaim and reaffirm the Church's ancient ecumenical faith in Wesleyan
terms within United Methodism. The Confessing Movement will work
in humility and reverence to clarify the doctrinal center and boundaries
of classical Christian teaching.[25]

The need for the Confessing Movement had come about because of the
present crisis facing the Church:

Those who treat theology as a matter of personal experimentation have
in recent years gained a new level of audacity. They have used the
umbrellas of pluralism and inclusiveness to support an agenda of theological relativism, which hedges and equivocates on all doctrinal defi-
nitions. This in effect invites both laity and clergy to imagine that
anything goes in United Methodist theology, and that there are no
boundaries whatsoever. Some United Methodists elevate their private
experience to the position of judge and arbiter of Christian faith. Others
exchange the historic faith for political, therapeutic, sexual, or gender-
based ideologies with religious veneers. This abandonment of classical
Christianity is occurring in a church that has nearly lost its immune
system with regard to false teaching—in a church that appears fearful
of, and perhaps unwilling to face, even a minimal level of doctrinal
discipline.[26]

The pamphlet and the organizing statement went on to assert that the
Christian faith was of divine origin, not a human construct, that its doctrine was binding, and that the issue was integrity. It called on the
Council of Bishops to assert their traditional doctrinal teaching authority. And, as over against those who claimed that The United Methodist
Church was not a confessional body or confessional church, it argued that
the Church was a confessing community of faith in principle, if not in
practice, because of constitutionally established doctrinal standards.

That such bold and (perhaps) grandiose statements could even be
made in 1995 was itself a sign as to how far the Church had changed since

nearly thirty years earlier when Good News was first conceived. With the forming of the Confessing Movement, doctrine would now become a matter for serious discussion in the Church.

The forming of the Confessing Movement also offered a clearer picture of the evangelical constituency of the Church. Though there was certainly no conflict between Good News and the Confessing Movement, and though most Good News supporters also immediately gave support to Confessing Movement, the contrast between the two groups, especially in their origins, was noticeable.

The Confessing Movement made its appeal primarily to established and traditional pastors and congregations; Good News originally made its appeal primarily to the populist, primarily rural and small town, and the revivalist background constituency of the Church. The Confessing Movement was organized in a major hotel in a major city; Good News was organized in the basement of a small church in Elgin, Illinois.

The Confessing Movement drew heavily from the Southeast and South Central Jurisdictions; Good News found its strength in the North Central and Northeastern Jurisdiction. The Confessing Movement sought boldly to change the direction of the denomination; Good News, at least at the beginning, sought primarily for understanding and inclusion for evangelicals in the denomination. The Confessing Movement sought to influence by thoughtful theological treatises and public statements; Good News sought to influence by a magazine and by dialogue sessions with boards and agencies and seminaries.

The Confessing Movement never developed a confessional statement like Good News's Junaluska Affirmation. It rather appealed simply to the doctrinal standards of the Church and the historic faith. By the time the Confessing Movement was launched, the *Discipline* had become friendly in its theological statements and no further confessional statement was necessary. The Junaluska Affirmation of Good News came shortly after the 1972 statement of the *Discipline*, which encouraged doctrinal statements under the idea of pluralism.

Even though a number of persons who identified with the Confessing Movement did not identify with Good News because they believed Good News too divisive and abrasive, the Confessing Movement soon became as controversial, if not more so, as Good News. Good News had been dismissed by many as "fundamentalist," "literalist," and a "throwback to the past." Even some friendly evangelicals had believed that The United

Methodist Church had no future with the ideology advanced by Good News.

But now the same charges would be leveled against the Confessing Movement. By the time the Confessing Movement came on the scene in the mid-1990s, the theological scene had shifted. Religious observers both inside and outside of the Church noted it was not evangelicalism (called "fundamentalism" by many) that was dying with no future, but rather the old-style liberalism that still dominated the seminaries, the episcopacy, and the boards and agencies. For one hundred years, by de-emphasizing the supernatural and by politicizing religion, liberalism had sought to make Christianity acceptable to and penetrate and influence the secular culture around it. By the 1990s, it was evident the liberal enterprise was failing badly. Under an entrenched liberal bureaucracy and episcopacy, the Church had been losing members at the rate of 250 every day between 1968 and 1995.

Despite the confident predictions of liberal religious observers and academic leaders during the 1920s, 1930s, 1940s, 1950s, 1960s, and 1970s, fundamentalism never died as it was expected to do. Fundamentalist, evangelical, and charismatic ministries and churches were springing up on every hand, not only in the United States, but also around the world. Evangelical churches and ministries seemed attractive and vital; the mainline institutions seemed dead and irreverent. Renewal was no longer a concern of just Good News. Other movements and ministries were forming: A Foundation for Theological Education, the Institute on Relgion and Democracy, the Mission Society for United Methodists, Aldersgate Renewal Ministries, the Transforming Congregations ministry, LifeWatch (the newsletter of the Taskforce of United Methodists on Abortion and Sexuality), the RENEW network for women, and Bristol House, LTD, to note some of the larger ones.

None of these renewal efforts was received warmly by the institution. Indeed, with each new group, the critical defensiveness on the part of the mediating elite became even more shrill. It seemed not to matter which group was being criticized, the charges always seemed the same: The renewal groups and ministries were accused of representing an uncritical biblicism; of being motivated by fear and controlled by right-wing reactionaries; as being divisive; as being somehow in conflict with the *Discipline*; as being racist, sexist, homophobic, literalistic, exclusivistic; and as wanting to take over the denomination.

An example of this critical reaction appeared in the summer of 1998 in the *Omaha Sunday World-Herald*. After Mark Tooley wrote about the Confessing Movement in a commentary entitled "Traditional Methodists Chafe Under Liberals" that was carried in several papers, a response written by four pastors from the Nebraska Conference appeared in the paper on July 12, 1998. Authored by G. Richard Carter, Loren L. Mollins, Hughes B. Morris Jr., and Lowen V. Kruse, under the title, "Confessing Movement Unofficial Fringe Group," the article laid out a typical institutional reaction to the Confessing Movement.

> [The Confessing Movement is] a fringe group with no official connection with the United Methodist Church. It clearly does not represent our tradition and is declared an opponent of many parts of the official Book of Discipline of our church. It is trying for a take-over.
> "The Confessing Movement can justly claim to speak for most United Methodists" [Tooley quote]. Most United Methodists have never heard of it. They would be confused by presenting Jesus as a new trinity, but when they heard the mean-spirited conclusions they would turn away.
> The Confessing Movement has much to say about Jesus, which is nice. But then it goes to a basic premise that there is no other name but Jesus through which one can have salvation. That kind of proof-texting, ignoring other major passages of scripture which give another witness, would block non-Christians from heaven. Jews, Hindus, Moslems and all who never heard of Jesus are out.
> Further, if we as church members do not agree with that judgment, we are headed for eternal punishment. There are plenty of folks who believe this line of thought, and we respect their right to do so, but this has never been the position of the Methodist tradition. John Wesley rejected it plainly.[27]

Fringe group or not, by 2003, a total of 632,000 individuals, 1,416 churches, and 3,975 clergy had identified themselves as part of the Confessing Movement. The first director of the Confessing Movement was Ira Gallaway, one of the original organizers of the Houston Declaration. Gallaway had been associated with several evangelical renewal efforts including the Mission Society for United Methodists and the Institute of Religion and Democracy.

In 1997, Patricia Miller, a laywoman from Indianapolis, Indiana, and a state senator in Indiana, was hired as executive director for the Confessing Movement. Senator Miller had been active in South Indiana leadership positions before she assumed responsibility with the Confessing Movement. She also became a member of the Executive Committee of the World Methodist Council.

Although the official Church media, the seminaries, the boards and agencies tended either to ignore the Confessing Movement, to dismiss it as another fringe group out to divide the Church, or to express no interest in engaging in conversation, there was at least one serious response to the Confessing Movement. In March 1996, just before the General Conference in Denver, a six-page paper entitled "A Critical Challenge to the Confessing Movement" was circulated to all of the delegates. The signers were well-known seminary presidents and professors, pastors, and agency personnel: Frank Dorsey, Charles Baughman, John B. Cobb Jr., E. Dale Dunlap, Evelyn Fisher, James Lawson, Don Messer, Jeanne Audrey Powers, Tex Sample, David Schoeni, Edward P. Stevenson, and John M. Swomley.

The paper stated that its goal was to engage the Church in critical dialogue. The signers recognized that the issues raised by the Confessing Movement had much to do with the understanding of who United Methodists were. They further asserted that they, the writers, were committed to a conciliar understanding of the Church rather than a "confessionalism" that, according to them, stood as a litmus test of authentic faith.

The Critical Challenge paper took issue with Confessing Movement statements in five areas: Scripture, the early church, Wesley, theology, and ethics.

Scriptural Perspective

The Critical Challenge paper argued that the Confessing Movement did not recognize that Scripture could be interpreted in a number of ways and that the movement did an injustice to emphasize only that Jesus Christ be confessed as Son, Savior, and Lord and reduce references to Christ almost exclusively to his death and resurrection without recognizing the importance of his life and teachings: "It is clear that perhaps half of the New Testament understands obedience to the will of God as expressed in the teachings of Jesus to be the criterion for salvation. . . . Confession without obedience is inadequate."[28]

Early Church Perspective

According to the paper, the Confessing Movement identified the "apostolic faith" with selected creeds and did not recognize the diversity of theological interpretations in the New Testament and the early church:

> [The creeds] are the product of debate framed by Greek and Roman philosophical categories, and come from an overtly patriarchal, classist, and pre-Copernican (pre-scientific) society. They were developed within a church that was unified with an imperial government, and reflected strong political as well as theological influences. The vast majority of believers were excluded from the conversations; no women or "common folk" were even involved in the process.
>
> Giving almost exclusive attention to the creedal expression of the apostolic faith effectively discredits much authentic and faithful theology since that time.[29]

For the paper to put such emphasis on the creeds and the early church implied that God was working not in the world today through new understandings and interpretations. New problems required new theological resources and a willingness to accept new truth.

Wesleyan Perspective

According to the writers of the Critical Challenge paper, John Wesley and Wesleyanism were never a part of the "confessing" tradition. Wesley rather used the "conciliar" approach, appealing to conferencing and discussion to arrive at a faithful understanding of doctrine. The writers argued that though Wesley did refer to "essentials," he did not identify a specific number of what those fundamental doctrines are. Nor did Wesley hold that there was only one definitive interpretation of the "essential" doctrines. Faithfulness to the Wesleyan tradition called for practicing diversity since no one group had a monopoly in regard to the saving revelation of God.

The paper argued that the Confessing Movement was really holding to the doctrine of *sola scriptura* (Scripture only), a view rejected by the present doctrinal statement in the *Discipline*. The writers further argued: Though the Church does have doctrinal standards, identified primarily as the Articles of Religion and the Confession of Faith, the Church does not need a "revisionist" confessing movement to interpret further a limited, acceptable interpretation of what the standards meant. The Wesleyan tradition had never been defined only by right doctrine.

Theological and Christological Perspective

According to the Critical Challenge paper, the Confessing Movement seemed most troubled by feminist theology and by theologies that reflect the experiences of those who were previously silent. Its theology was implicity divisive and exclusive. It threatened the significant theological contribution of the United Methodist heritage that had come to be called the Wesleyan Quadrilateral. It selectively used Scripture and tradition to discredit reason and experience. The Confessing Movement reflected an authoritarian and exclusive Christology:

> Perhaps the most troubling aspect of this christology is its subtle idolatry. In effect, the "confessional statement" deifies apostolic formulations of the meaning of the life, death, and resurrection of Jesus the Christ. It codifies a narrow christology which seemingly takes the place of God. This christology is not about personal or social transformation, but is one used as a weapon against others. This is not life-giving christology but rather is life-denying christocentrism.[30]

Ethical and Social Action Perspective

The paper charged that the Confessing Movement was working from an understanding of salvation that was primarily personal and privatistic. It failed to relate sin to social structures that oppress, leaving the impression that sin related only to personal vices. The Confessing Movement, in denying the claim that the individual was free to decide what is true and what is false, basically denied the place of conscience.

Conclusion

The paper then concluded: The Confessing Movement statement was ultimately divisive because it implied that persons supporting the

Confessing Movement would support the denomination only when it conformed to Confessing Movement terms. Though United Methodists had a right to set limits on their support of the denomination, the Confessing Movement's statement set limits that were extraordinarily narrow and un-Wesleyan. When viewed as a whole, the evidence suggested that the movement was promoting a reformed theology and confessional stance rather than, and at the expense of, Wesleyan conciliarism:

> An alternative vision is that the church is healthier when it is confronted and responds to the challenges of prevailing injustices within the church and society. It is a healthier church when it confronts diversity in scripture out of a recognition that different New Testament writers presented different theological interpretations of Jesus, the place of women, and other social and cultural systems of their day. In short, controversy, in love and with civility, has certain value over dogmatism.[31]

Struggling for Doctrinal Integrity: The Look Ahead

Where does The United Methodist Church go from here? For such renewal movements as Good News and the Confessing Movement, doctrinal integrity and faithfulness to the gospel is at the heart of the problems of United Methodism. Though the paper "A Critical Challenge to the Confessing Movement" was directed primarily to the original Confessing Movement organizing statement, it could well have been addressed to the total program of Good News and the Confessing Movement and the other United Methodist renewal movements. It was (and still is) a thoughtful and thorough (for its length) stating of the doctrinal issues that face the Church from the liberal institutional perspective.

Good News and the Confessing Movement would take issue with a number of the charges expressed in the Critical Challenge paper. At the same time, the fact that the paper was even written was in itself hopeful. There is a more appropriate response to the evangelical presence than just institutional defensiveness.

Thirty years earlier, at the beginning of Good News, neither the Confessing Movement statement nor the Critical Challenge response would have been possible. Much of United Methodist seminary teaching did not even refer to, let alone give any credence to, what is today known as the doctrinal standards. Nor did it deal seriously with Wesley's references to "the essentials." The one understanding that brought Ed Robb and Albert Outler together was their common conviction that theology in The United Methodist Church was in a state of disarray.

In one important aspect, Good News and the Confessing Movement have been successful beyond measure. The Church is again discussing doctrine! The Critical Challenge paper, prepared by some of the best-known self-acknowledged liberals in the denomination, admitted that Wesley did have basic doctrines. The paper did not identify these "doctrines" as love, acceptance, pluralism, experience, or the application of faith to the social situation (as liberals were apt to do in earlier discussions), but recognized the existence and the importance of doctrines of original sin, justification by grace through faith alone, the deity of Christ, the Atonement, the Holy Spirit, and the Trinity. If the Church can agree that there are such things (essential doctrines), then it can get on with the task of how these doctrines or teachings can be understood and applied, and renewal will be in the Church's future.

CHAPTER TWELVE

METHODISM'S POPULIST WING, PART II

The parking lot was full of vans. There were a few SUVs and some sedans, but mostly vans. Vans with car seats. Vans with car seats meant lots of children. This in itself was a sign that this was not a usual United Methodist church.

It was the first Sunday in January of 2003 at Hanfield United Methodist Church in the North Indiana Conference. We were arriving for the fourth worship service of the morning. The foyer was jammed with groups of people talking about the snowstorm the night before, the Purdue ball game, and their daughters' dance classes. There was a coat-rack, but it was hard to get to because children were underfoot and teenagers were in the way. At least one person over sixty (besides us) was there; the father of the pastor was visiting from Florida. He was the only person I saw with a white shirt and tie. Not even the pastor wore a tie.

In the Harvest Room (sanctuary), the chairs were filling. The front of the room was taken up with instruments for the praise team: four guitars, a keyboard, a drum set, three microphones, and a chair for the person who signs for the deaf. There was no "altar," or even a respectable communion table. The communion elements were on a card table. This was not a usual United Methodist church.

Does United Methodism still have a populist wing? This study has suggested that the kind of evangelical Methodism that Charles Keysor and the Good News movement sought to rally—Methodism's "silent minority"—has always played a significant role in the life of Methodism. Its predicted demise never took place. And, as the Church enters the twenty-first century, it can be argued that this form of Christian faith not only is flourishing, but also represents one of the best hopes for the future of United Methodism.

The Good News movement always claimed to be working for church renewal. But what are the signs of renewal? Will renewal have taken place when evangelicals control the Church's boards and agencies, or even when evangelicals have meaningful representation on boards and agencies? Will renewal have taken place when bishops who will hold the Church accountable to its own doctrinal standards are elected? Will renewal have taken place when the seminaries seek to serve the Church rather than to impress the academic world?

Not necessarily. If, as Good News and the Confessing Movement have always claimed, the local church is the primary center of God's activity, then one needs to look at how the local church is doing to discern signs of renewal. Renewal is about not the church as institution, but the church as the faith people of God. Renewal takes place when lives are transformed through Jesus Christ, are gathered into the community of believers, and then reach out to change the world. I was convinced I was seeing renewal that Sunday at Hanfield.

Issues that Hanfield has faced, and still are facing, are issues of change and conservation. What part of Methodist ethos and doctrine (as in "conservative") should be preserved, and what part should be changed (as in "liberal" or "contemporary")? Evangelicalism is sometimes interpreted as a kind of conservatism seeking to retreat to some golden era of the past, fighting against societal change, and preaching a gospel no longer relevant. These charges are not without some truth because evangelicalism encompasses a number of subcultures, some of which can rightfully be labelled conservative, fundamentalist, reactionary, and, in certain situations, racist and homophobic.

But there are forms of evangelicalism that are dynamic, creative, reformist, and adaptable. This evangelicalism is faithful to its own heritage but always willing to adapt that heritage to new situations. John

Wesley argued that he was preaching no new gospel—he had no quarrel with the Articles of Religion of the Church of England—but he was willing to apply the old gospel in new ways. And so he initiated the use of lay preachers, started preaching in the fields and on the street corners, used contemporary tunes for Methodist poems, and organized his followers into societies. At the same time, Wesley's "essential" doctrines were also the essential doctrines of all other evangelical groups.

Wesley's followers in America took the Wesleyan style and message and applied it to the American situation. They adopted the Episcopal form of church government, but the earliest bishops were not like their counterparts in the Anglican Church, whose positions were linked with privilege, respectability, and civility. Earliest Methodist bishops rode horseback across the mountains, slept in frontier cabins, and presented an easily understood salvation message. Populist Methodists initiated the camp meeting, the protracted revival service, the altar call, and the mourner's bench. They offered in their preaching not scholarly discourse, but emotional fervency, homey illustrations, and personal testimony. These believers put the Wesley poems to their own popular tunes and developed the spiritual, the Sunday school song, and the gospel song. They did not suppress raw emotion, which included shouting and fainting and jerking.

Early populist Methodists were reformist, but it was bottom-up reformation. If the denomination took a stand against war, slavery, worldliness, and alcohol, and for women's rights, it was not because the General Conference or the bishops passed resolutions and then sought to rally local churches to follow the learned wisdom of leaders. Denominational resolutions about alcohol and slavery and war and worldliness grew out of the preaching and the convictions of Methodist believers in local situations.

Methodism was a major force in defining evangelicalism in America, not only in the focus on the doctrines of evangelicalism, but also in its style and ethos, a style and ethos that was continually adapting to its cultural situation. In the content of the gospel, though Methodists were not known for systematic theology, their preaching seldom departed from the evangelical themes of sin, the blood of Jesus, the new birth, and holiness of life.

The institutionalism of the present day developed in a different direction and reflects a perspective quite different from those earliest populist Methodists. A portion of Methodism, uneasy with the excesses of early

Methodist piety, sought (and still seeks) respectability and acceptance in the modern world. The constant theme of this kind of Methodism was (and is) that the gospel be "relevant" to the modern mind. But "relevance" in this case appears to be directed toward compromising and adjusting to the belief systems and the style of what is sometimes called "the modern mind." If the modern mind has trouble with an "exclusionary" message that claims Jesus Christ is the only way to salvation, then, according to this form of Methodism, the exclusionary nature of the message should be de-emphasized. If the modern mind is enamored with pluralism, then theology must be pluralistic and even relativistic. If the secular liberal world believes that racial diversity is best modeled in a quota system, then the Church must adopt a quota system. If the modern mind has problems with religious supernaturalism, then the Church must base its message on something other than supernaturalism.

At the same time, establishment institutionalism, though most ready and willing to change or reconstruct the content and core of the message, is discouragingly tradition-bound under the weight of its own operational style. Present-day religious institutionalism operates with a curia of mediating elite, whether in the seminaries, the episcopacy, or the boards and agencies, which assumes its own special wisdom is best for all groups in the denomination. The "elite" know best what Sunday school material should be used in various United Methodist churches and prepares that material according to its own ideology. The "elite" set the mission philosophy and the educational philosophy and social ideology that local churches are to live by. This philosophy and ideology does not grow out of the life and ethos of the people, but from the studied opinion of experts. The "elite" argue that revelation and its understanding are not to be restricted to Scripture and tradition, since God is revealing new truth all the time, and they, the elite, are best qualified to interpret what the new truth is. And those who disagree with these philosophies and ideologies are labeled "divisive" and "disruptive," not loyal to the denomination and "not truly United Methodist."

And the larger world is increasingly unimpressed. It can be argued that the institutionalism of the mediating elite, not populist evangelicalism, is what is in danger of becoming irrelevant. This institutionalism has compromised away the content of the gospel while still tradition-bound in its own structures. This was always Charles Keysor's argument (who believed it even in the late 1960s), and it expresses the sentiments of many of those who have associated themselves with Good News.

At the same time evangelicals can also be culture bound and inhibited by their own traditions. Deadness is not to be identified with any kind of theology. The countryside is strewn with abandoned Methodist churches that were once vital but through the course of time could not relate to the people around them. Like Jesus' parable of the vine and the branches, they were cast forth as a branch and withered since they bore no fruit.

My first acquaintance with Hanfield was through one of its old patriarchs, Milford Hall, in the early 1970s. Milford would come to the Good News evangelical fellowship groups and give testimonies about his own conversion and glorious revivals of the past. Then he would ask prayer for his church, Hanfield, that it might once again see revival. One of Milford's sons was in the ministry; two were in the church. They and their friends would have a lot to do with Hanfield's future.

In 1982, when Tim Helm was appointed pastor, Hanfield claimed a worship attendance of eighty-five. The church was located in Grant County, Indiana, at a country crossroads cluster of sixteen homes called Hanfield. The church "program" had not changed much for the past fifty years. It was typical "old-time" Methodism: a missions emphasis, a Sunday school, Sunday morning and Sunday evening worship, a summer Bible school, potluck dinners, an emphasis on gospel music, frequent altar calls, a Wednesday prayer meeting, and a yearly revival. The church had been blessed—if that word can be used—by a long series of district superintendents who had never tried to make Hanfield something it was not. Its pastors, if not exciting or seminary trained, were dedicated men who fit into the church's style and belief system.

Tim Helm fit Hanfield. A graduate of Asbury College and Seminary, he thrived on the church's revivalist and Holiness tradition, its missions emphasis, and its prayer emphasis. The church's evangelical heritage was not redirected, but invigorated with the pastor's commitment to prayer, his vision to increase the church's missions involvement, and his desire to win new persons to Christ.

Within the first year, conversions were reported, people were responding to altar calls, and the attendance increased to 115. From there it grew to 120 and then to 131. Then, it seemed, the church hit a plateau. Attendance remained constant for two years. Some decisions needed to be made. One of the most important of those decisions was made by the pastor himself. The bishop and cabinet, noting that Hanfield had done well and that the pastor had the qualities many churches were seeking, believed that the time had come for Tim Helm to be advanced to a "new opportunity," to a situation where there would be more money and more potential. Hanfield, after all, had probably grown as much as it could. It was poorly located and in an area with limited growth possibilities. The pastor prayed—and turned down all of the potential new appointments. He believed God had a plan for Hanfield and he was to be part of that plan.

Meanwhile the church was experiencing tensions even from its modest growth. Children of previously unchurched families were not behaving well in church. Facilities were crowded, and there was no room to expand. The church was landlocked by cornfields, and the owner of the cornfields was not interested in selling any land. The parking lot needed to be expanded. When it was proposed that the parking lot be paved, the longtime members pointed out there were no paved parking lots within six miles of the church, the parking lot had always served them well, and they were perfectly happy with the parking lot as it was.

These issues were made a matter of prayer. Did God have a plan for Hanfield? If the plan was to reach new people for Christ, did it also involve taking risks and stepping out by faith? The matter was presented to the congregation. A vote was taken to trust God for the winning of new souls and for growth. The parking lot was paved. Could the church add new staff? Staff was added. Could the fellowship hall be divided to create a new nursery for small children? This seemed a lot to ask. To give up the fellowship hall was to give up the fellowship dinners and the sense of church community associated with the dinners. But maybe small children were more important than fellowship dinners. The hall was divided.

Could the church go to two services? Decisions that might seem logical to outsiders seemed much more difficult to those who found blessing in being together in one worship service. It was a matter of prayer. The church began planning for two services.

Then the church took some ideas from the conference New Generation Program, one of the components of which was telemarketing. Could the church dial up one thousand homes in the surrounding area, including the city of Marion (the nearest city), to invite people to a country church nine miles away that would be starting a second worship service? The idea seemed preposterous. Who would want to come, and who could find the church even if they did want to come? It was a matter of prayer. The church used the conference office to dial up nine hundred homes. A number came. Some were converted, and the new converts had new sets of friends to invite to the church. From 1987 to 1991, the attendance increased from 132 to 196.

Now the church faced the biggest problem of all. What had seemed unthinkable was now expressed: Could the church relocate in order to build? The church building had been erected in 1969. The labor and the prayers and the financial commitment of all of the old families were in that building. To expand, yes, but to relocate? That seemed far too radical. But it became a matter of prayer. Some of the prayers were directed toward the owner of the cornfields. Could her heart be softened to sell the church some land so that the church could expand on its same location?

There was turmoil. How was God directing? The answer came in a challenge from United Methodist missionary John Enright in Zaire. John Enright had a vision of a campground in Nyembo in Congo, based on the same idea as the North Indiana campgrounds at Epworth Forest. The campground needed a chapel. Could Hanfield help? And now a new thought: Might it be that God was directing Hanfield to build, but neither in the cornfields nor in a relocated spot, but in Zaire? It became a matter of prayer. Everything in Indiana went on hold while they raised the money and a team traveled to Nyembo to build the chapel. It was a two-year project.

At the end of two years, the church was ready to think again about its own building. The church made a decision that seemed unthinkable before: They would relocate, four miles away, on a state highway. But how could it be built? Young families with children and new converts tended not to be tithers. The church took a leap of faith.

At the same time, the matter of worship style had come up. After a church-growth conference sponsored by the annual conference, the pastor, and then a few with him, became convinced that if the church were to reach the gen-Xers, the kind of music and the style of worship would need to change. Hanfield had experimented with "contemporary" music and with worship teams, but something more was needed. A decision was made to commit the church to praise and worship music.

The key to making this work was to find a music and worship leader. But who? And how could the church afford this in the midst of relocating and building? In Colorado, a young couple named Matt and Amy Morrison had recently graduated from college with music degrees but had been unable to secure teaching positions. At a United Methodist church service one morning, the pastor preached on the theme "God Is Calling You." The young couple suddenly wondered if they had been looking for employment in the wrong places. Was God calling them to Christian service? As gen-Xers, they did a natural thing and sought to determine

God's will by searching for opportunities on the Internet. Almost imme-diately they noted on the United Methodist website an opening for some-one to develop a new music program at a place called Hanfield in far-off Indiana. It appeared to be a church attuned to gen-X culture and the technological world.

They misread what Hanfield was. In many ways, Hanfield was still operating like the little country church it had been for the last one hun-dred years. The church had a notice on the website because a conference staff person worshiping at Hanfield, Dave Mullins, had put it there. Otherwise, the church had only one computer and did not even have a fax machine. The church was strongly evangelical; Matt and Amy had no background in evangelicalism. Furthermore, the young couple were trained in classical music and had limited knowledge about what praise and worship music was. Yet with one visit to Hanfield, they believed this was where God wanted them to be. They had discovered evangelical faith. By this time it was 1997, and the worship attendance was at three hundred.

The move to the new building came with overwhelming sadness inter-mingled with joy. Hanfield, as many people remembered it, was no more. The congregation was in a new, strange place. Yet the people were the same. Now there were new pressures, especially financial pressures. One hundred and twenty giving units pledged $900,000. The church still needed to sell the previous building, a fairly new building in good condi-tion. But who wanted a building in Hanfield, at a crossroads that could not be found? The Free Will Baptist church nearby needed the building but had not expressed interest because it had no money.

Time for more prayer. Had the church not committed itself first to mis-sions? Had not God blessed them in order that they might be a blessing to others? The church sensed another unusual leading: Hanfield would sell its building to a sister congregation, the Free Will Baptists, for $1.

Meanwhile, the church continued its unique emphasis on missions. Despite its financial pressures, it continued to tithe for missions. In addi-tion, it developed its own cross-cultural missionary program by bringing to its congregation at three-month intervals an overseas missionary or national to serve on the Hanfield staff and present the gospel in a new context.

I was aware of most of these developments the Sunday I worshiped at Hanfield in January 2003. After thirty minutes of music, the pastor, Tim Helm, asked the congregation to open their Bibles to Acts 15. The sermon was how the church was to deal with conflict. One could hear the rustling of pages turning as all throughout the congregation Bibles were opened.

I recalled an incident forty-five years earlier, in seminary. The professor was arguing that many churches were being hampered by an outmoded "biblicism." They had no future unless they would adopt the findings of the historical-critical method of understanding the Bible. A student pastor asked how to accomplish this since the people he was serving were, in his words, "literalists" who insisted on bringing Bibles to church and talked about "getting back to the Bible." The professor asked if these were young people or old people. "Old people mostly" was the reply. "Well," the professor responded, "be patient. One more generation and those people and that attitude will be gone."

The generation the professor referred to had gone, and the generation following that, but in many churches the Bibles have not disappeared. And the Bibles are being carried not by old people, but by a new generation: by teenagers, college students, and young adults. The sermon on resolving conflict was in one sense a sermon about the events of Hanfield.

I thought of Milford Hall, the old patriarch who prayed for revival at Hanfield thirty years earlier. Milford would not have recognized the new Hanfield. The trappings of its old Methodist Protestant, revivalist past were gone. The 1969 building Milford had worked so hard to get built was no longer the center of worship. Gospel music was in the background. Sunday evening services had been replaced with new programs. The Wednesday night prayer meeting was gone. Even the old-style revival meetings were gone. The church had no room for the fellowship dinners. Still, the Bible message being proclaimed was the same Bible message Milford remembered. Milford Hall's prayers had been answered, but in a way Milford would not have expected. The 2002 worship attendance had been tabulated. The weekly average was 960.

Is Hanfield an anomaly? Is its growth and vitality an exception in an otherwise disintegrating denomination?

Less than ten miles from Hanfield, on the other side of Marion to the west, is another open country United Methodist church. Mt. Olive was also a church steeped in revivalism. It was located on a country crossroads, but without even a cluster of houses to mark the location.

In 1991, the attendance at Mt. Olive was 131. The church had a series of evangelical pastors and for an open country church was strong and viable. When another Asbury graduate, Doug Barton, was appointed to the church in 1991, the church began to grow. It signed up for the conference New Generation Program. A farmer who had been reluctant to sell the adjoining cornfields had a change of heart and donated some land. Church facilities were expanded. A new Family Life Center was built. A worship style designed to reach gen-Xers was adopted. By the end of 2002, in three different kinds of worship services, the country church was reaching about 450 in attendance.

Less than twenty-five miles west from Mt. Olive on a county road is another small cluster of ten or so houses called McGrawsville. If possible, the church was even more obscurely located than Hanfield or Mt. Olive. The largest town in the school district had less than one thousand people. The county the church is located in was declining in population.

In 1980, the church was on a circuit and reported an average attendance of seventy-three. The newly appointed pastor, Harvey King, was a course-of-study pastor nearing retirement. McGrawsville, with its one hundred members, was the largest church he had ever served. To an outsider, all of this together did not seem like a formula that would lead to renewal. What McGrawsville had in its favor was a group of dedicated, strongly evangelical laypeople who believed that God could bring revival.

Harvey King was blessed and energized by the laypeople he had inherited in his new church. When he retired five years later, the attendance had increased to 114. The church was very aggressive about the kind of pastor they wanted, and an Oral Roberts University graduate was appointed. In two years, the attendance increased to 165. That pastor was replaced by another Oral Roberts graduate and that pastor by Greg Hiatt, an Asbury graduate.

McGrawsville did not need to relocate to grow. Families were willing to drive fifteen and twenty miles to worship with a congregation with a strong children's program and a missions program, and where people were giving testimony to the new birth in Jesus Christ. As in the case of Mt. Olive, the cornfields surrounding the church were made available, and a whole new church campus developed. In 2002, the attendance average was 550. The missions budget exceeded $75,000.

Forty miles farther west in the small town of Dayton, Indiana, population 250, is the Dayton United Methodist Church. The Dayton church had always been known as an evangelical congregation. In the late 1980s, the church was so adamant about its need for an evangelical pastor the cabinet considered it an uncooperative church with a questionable future. The bishop and his cabinet gave it a chance with John Walls, a transfer to the conference from The Free Methodist Church. One of the first decisions made by the new pastor with some committed laypersons was to undergird the church with prayer, and to that end, a prayer group was organized to meet at 7:00 A.M. five times a week. The Sunday worship attendance sparked from 126 to 158 to 235 to 273 in three years. At the end of 2002, the attendance was averaging 590. The early morning prayer group still meets.

Across the state from Dayton, in the city of Muncie, at Union Chapel Ministries, 1,700 worshipers gather each weekend in worship. The 1,700 does not include the 500 teenagers who gather for praise and worship each Sunday evening. In 1981, Union Chapel was part of a two-point circuit in rural Delaware County with a worship attendance of 85. It too was a church steeped in the revival tradition, and when the new pastor, Greg Parris, an Asbury seminary graduate, came that year, three women, Opal, Gladys, and Flossie, shared that they had been praying regularly for revival. A revival was held—an old-fashioned revival with singing, preaching, and altar calls—and a number of people were converted. For the next ten years, attendance figures read: 85, 103, 138, 193, 320, 415, 545, 609, 768, 874. When the small country church could no longer hold the crowds, the congregation moved to a school. Four years later, they bought the buildings of a Ford dealership and relocated to the outskirts of Muncie, Indiana.

Along the way, the church became identified with the charismatic movement. It took on a college ministry and a ministry to youth. It also committed itself to the poor and the problems of the inner city. When the city of Muncie had to close three community centers, Union Chapel offered to operate two of them. The church developed its own outreach and missions ministry. In 2001, it paid out $500,000 to support that ministry.

Far to the north in the conference in Granger, Indiana, a suburb of South Bend, pastor Mark Beeson was assigned to a new church start in 1986. This church did not start with a base of believers with a Methodist revivalist past, but was founded on the model of Willow Creek Community Church in the Chicago Area. It would be an attempt to apply the methods and approach of the evangelical church-growth movement to a Methodist doctrinal base. The Methodist emphases on sin, atonement, salvation, and the new birth resonated with the worshipers, many of whom had to overcome their prejudices against United Methodism.

By the beginning of 2003, the average worship attendance had reached 3,584, the largest church in attendance in the whole North Central Jurisdiction and one of the five largest churches in the denomination. Of that number, 828 were children who had been separated into a separate worshiping-learning environment.

Unfortunately, the institutional church has been slow to pick up on the dynamics that make churches such as Hanfield, Mt. Olive, McGrawsville, Dayton, Union Chapel, and Granger so vital. If nothing else, along with the growing influence of renewal groups such as Good News, the Confessing Movement, the Mission Society for United Methodists, and UMAction, they represent to many people the growing "conservative" trend in society, a trend that for many United Methodist leaders is not necessarily to be encouraged.

This study has sought not only to trace the history of Methodist evangelicals, but also to understand that history as connected to a larger movement in Methodism that has been labeled populist evangelicalism. That populist evangelicalism, of which Good News is a part, has not died (as was predicted) nor has it been replaced. Rather, it is alive and well and represents one of the best hopes for renewal in The United Methodist Church. This is illustrated by the churches in the North Indiana Conference that are experiencing renewal.

Perhaps one other commentary on these developments is worth noting. Rodney Stark and Roger Finke have been studying American religious developments for a number of years. Their two best-known studies are *The Churching of America, 1776–1990: Winners and Losers in Our Religious Economy*,[1] and *Acts of Faith: Explaining the Human Side of Religion*.[2]

Stark and Finke have traced many of the same developments observed in this study, but from the perspective of another discipline (sociology). Basing their analysis in the book *Acts of Faith* on insights from Ernst Troeltsch and then H. Richard Niebuhr (*The Social Sources of Denominationalism*), Stark and Finke have noted the difference between what they call "sect" and "church" (which correspond roughly to what has been called in this study "populist evangelicalism" and "establishment institutionalism"). Religious groups known as "sects" have a "high-tension" faith, at odds with the culture around them. They have strict standards and well-defined boundaries. Much of the church growth in America, according to Stark and Finke, has come from groups showing these sect-type characteristics. Almost inevitably, however, as these groups become successful, they make their peace with the world; move toward education, wealth, secularization, and sophistication; and seek to become adaptable and acceptable to the larger culture. Along the way they exhibit more and more church-type characteristics and a "low-tension" kind of faith. And in every case, a "low-tension" kind of faith is a weakened and declining kind of faith. Though Stark and Finke test their observations on such diverse groups as Baptists, Mormons, and Roman Catholics, they are especially intrigued with Methodists.

Stark and Finke note that from 1776 to 1850, the percentage of Methodist church adherents grew from 2.5 percent of American adherents to 34.2 percent.[3] During that time, Methodists operated essentially without colleges or seminaries, with minimal church structure, and with a heavy reliance on circuit-riding preachers and lay pastors. They represented "high-tension" religion. There was a price to be paid for being Methodist. There were moral, behavioral, and doctrinal expectations.

As Methodists coveted the status and prestige of Presbyterians, Episcopalians, and Congregationalists, they began to develop the characteristics not of a sect, but of a church. They added colleges and seminaries, built prestigious church buildings, and added "professional ecclesiastics." Theological liberalism (an attempt to make the faith acceptable to the modern world), a "low-tension" characteristic, was added to the mix after 1900.

In 1890, Methodists could still claim 84 of every 1,000 American adherents to religion. But with the exodus of many of the Holiness people, who epitomized most clearly the various sect-type characteristics in the denomination, and with the increasing movement toward liberalism, Methodism began its steady decline. Even though Methodist membership was continuing to increase through the mid-nineteenth century, it was increasing at a slowing rate, and the Methodist share of the total population was actually shrinking. Finally, in the mid-nineteenth century, Methodism began to lose membership and attendance, despite the increasing population of the country. In terms of "market share" (a favorite phrase of Stark and Finke), Methodism, along with other mainline denominations, was in dramatic decline. By 1990, the Methodist market share had been reduced to only 36 out of every 1,000 American adherents to religion. In other words, the Methodist share of the American religious scene had been reduced by more than one-half, from 8.4 percent to 3.6 percent in the 100 years between 1890 and 1990.[4]

If this analysis is correct, the prognosis for "low-tension" forms of religion can only be further decline. It should be noted that a somewhat similar point was made by H. Richard Niebuhr:

> Denominationalism in the Christian church is such an unacknowledged hypocrisy. It is a compromise, made far too lightly, between Christianity and the world. Yet it often regards itself as a Christian achievement and glorifies its martyrs as bearers of the cross. It represents the accommodation of Christianity to the caste-system of human society.[5]

Niebuhr, in his book *The Social Sources of Denominationalism*, does not use the word "populism" (as in this study); but in his analysis of denominations and sects in America, he speaks of the tensions between urban and rural religion, Modernism and Fundamentalism,[6] and frontier and established society. Even in the 1920s, his prognosis for the future of the churches was pessimistic.

Is there any possibility for "church-type" forms of religion ever to reverse their decline? According to Stark and Finke, it is improbable; but if there were a reverse, it would come through a movement from church-to-sect, that is, from religion that was "low tension" to a religion that is "high tension."

It is at this point that Good News enters the scene in the Stark-Finke analysis. A movement from church-to-sect in United Methodism is most unlikely from within the official structures of the denomination. From the Good News perspective, there seems to be no recognition on the part of either the bishops or the boards and agencies that the policies and the ideology and the leadership style of the past fifty years have been a major factor in the denomination's disintegration and decline. Every effort to bring about constructive change in agencies such as, say, the Women's Division, has been resisted, even as those agencies slide further and further into irrelevance. The future of The United Methodist Church, if it is to be determined by the state of its present leadership, is dismal. Pluralism, "tolerance," and institutional loyalty are not the paths to renewal.

Stark and Finke, of course, do not comment specifically on the present internal affairs of United Methodism. They are more interested in the bigger picture of how and why religious bodies thrive and decline. In their analysis, they conclude that a movement from church-to-sect, and from a religion that moves from "low tension" to "high tension," would most likely come from outside of the official structures as a movement along-side official structures. It would be a new "Holy Club," not unlike the Holy Club the Wesleys established at Oxford.

Stark and Finke suggest that, within United Methodism, the Good News movement, as well as the Confessing Movement, possibly offer that kind of church-to-sect, "low tension" to "high tension" possibility. These movements have attempted "to increase tension with the dominant culture by reestablishing clear boundaries."[7] The question is whether these groups have had any effect on the denomination.

Stark and Finke sought to answer the question by studying churches pastored by persons involved in Good News and the Confessing Movement. They chose North Indiana to make their study and compared the ministry of the pastors associated with the North Indiana Evangelical Fellowship with other pastors in the conference. Using 1995 statistics, they discovered that of 568 ministers in the conference, 21 percent (121) were on the Evangelical Fellowship mailing list. That number increased to 31 percent among "full connection" pastors.

Their conclusions? First, pastors in the Evangelical Fellowship were younger than other pastors. Sixty-two percent of the Evangelical Fellowship pastors entered the conference after 1980. This was to be compared with 43 percent of the pastors not on the list who had entered the ministry after 1980.

In terms of churches served, the study revealed that in the years 1993 to 1995, churches served by pastors on the North Indiana Evangelical mailing list increased an average of 4.5 percent in attendance, while churches served by pastors not on the list decreased by 1.3 percent. Of those pastors on the mailing list who came into full connection after 1980, the increase in attendance was 7.9 percent.

In terms of church finance, churches served by pastors on the Evangelical Fellowship mailing list increased during the same period by 21.6 percent, compared with the 6.2 percent increase of those churches with pastors not on the list. Of those pastors affiliated with the North Indiana Evangelical Fellowship who came into full connection after 1980, expenditures increased 41.4 percent.

Mention of the Evangelical Fellowship in North Indiana serves as an introduction to one more piece of the Good News story, that of conference renewal groups associated originally with Good News and later also with the Confessing Movement. If, as this study has suggested, Good News is best understood as a populist, grassroots, bottom-up form of

Methodism, displaying, in Stark and Finke terms, "high-tension" faith, then the question can be asked how this has been demonstrated practically.

The North Indiana Conference group will be used as an example since that is the one I helped start and have worked with.

In early January 1971, I was with a number of pastors from North Indiana who attended the Congress on Evangelism held in New Orleans. A rather raucous group of us were at a restaurant one evening when I noticed a single figure over on the side eating alone. It was Charles Keysor. I had had correspondence with Keysor (and, in fact, was one of the original responders to his article "Silent Minority"), but we had never met. I can remember my first reaction: I wanted to meet him, but he and the group he represented were so controversial that I was reluctant to meet him in front of my fellow pastors. I did meet him when our table scattered, and Chuck Keysor and I made arrangements to have breakfast together the next day.

I discovered the next morning how much Chuck Keysor and I had in common. We had graduated from the same seminary; we had read many of the same books; we agreed that the most serious problem of the Church was the official Sunday school curriculum. Charles Keysor was informed (in a way other Methodists I knew were not) about the growing renaissance of evangelical thinking and influence. He could discuss with intelligence *Christianity Today*, Youth for Christ, and dispensationalism. More important, Charles Keysor had a vision for Methodism. He really believed that evangelicals working together could bring renewal to the Church. He convinced me that I should take the lead in starting a Good News group in North Indiana.

I shared the idea with my district superintendent, Evan Bergwall. What about gathering evangelicals in the conference together for a group that could study together and fellowship together? Bergwall was encouraging but advised that the bishop and cabinet be always informed of what we were doing. And so a group of five pastors put together a mailing list of persons, lay and clergy, that we considered might be interested in an evangelical group. In our first meeting in spring of 1971, about forty persons showed up.

There was an instant sense of unity. The conference was experiencing stress that in some instances verged on trauma. The Methodist-EUB merger in Indiana sought to re-form five conferences into two. Despite all of the talks about unity and common purposes and a "new day," there was a lot of mistrust and maneuvering based on former conference traditions and loyalties. The old traditions of the various conferences were not easily giving way to new traditions, and in a number of instances, more good was lost than gained. The merged conference was already in serious decline in membership and attendance (and would remain so for the next fifteen years).

The sense of oneness of the evangelical group crossed all former conference and denominational lines. We got acquainted, told our stories, and prayed and worshiped together. We also talked about the kind of group we wanted to be. We had already observed that across the denomination there was no one model of what an evangelical, or Good News, group might look like. Of those already formed, some were primarily clergy, some primarily lay. Some were prayer and fellowship groups, others were activist groups (with some conservative agenda). Some were angry-sounding, some were not. Some were initiating evangelical programming—primarily in the areas of camping and youth—and others were not. Some were closely aligned with Good News, others were not.

All of the conference groups that had formed or were forming were the consequence of the work of Charles Keysor, the magazine, and the fledgling Good News board. But the interest of the institutional Church was not in evangelical renewal. That interest was rather in a radical social and theological agenda—the Secular City, Death of God, Feminism, Black Power, Vietnam, Marxism, and liberation movements of all varieties. The late 1960s and early 1970s were times of great turmoil. In this climate, Good News was viewed by many as a last-gasp sort of fundamentalism. Others expressed a conviction that the evangelical presence was needed, but even these were continually urging caution. The sin to be avoided at all costs was not unfaithfulness or heresy, but "divisiveness."

The result of this climate in the church was that some of the evangelical groups forming found it expedient to claim some distance from Good News.[8] My vision for the North Indiana group was that it would be a study and discussion group that would deal with theological and social issues of the day. It would not be just a front for Good News.

Those who responded to the invitation to come together had other needs and interests. Whether a front for Good News or not, what many craved was evangelical fellowship. The phrase "spiritually starved" was heard not infrequently. The group wanted encouragement. It wanted a place where evangelical concerns could be openly discussed. Persons wanted to sing choruses and gospel songs and to pray and talk about evangelical programs that worked. They wanted a "safe place" where people could be themselves and not have to put up a veneer of institutional correctness.

And so the earliest every-other-month meetings became praise and testimony meetings. They were basically Methodist class meetings where we spoke about how it was with our souls. We took the name the North Indiana Evangelical Fellowship. And, whether we desired it or not, the group became a "Good News" group. The *Good News* magazine immediately listed us along with fifty or so other groups known as Good News renewal groups.

The group attracted a number of dedicated laypeople—it was here we first became acquainted with such churches as Hanfield, Dayton, and McGrawsville—many in Lay Witness Mission work. It was early in the charismatic movement and a number of persons interested in the Holy Spirit were involved in the meetings. The pastors who came tended to be young pastors and Course of Study pastors. No established or large-church pastors identified with the group. I remember the remark of one pastor who said, "I admire what you are doing, and only wish I had had the courage to do something like this years ago." But even then he did not join with us.

One of the first efforts to reach out beyond the group was to offer to sponsor a (7:00 A.M.) prayer and praise service during each of the mornings at annual conference (this effort would become a regular part of the conference program). Because of an expressed concern about the camping program, several of the group volunteered to be camp directors. Some of the group took the leadership of the Bible Conference, an (approved) evangelical alternate conference senior high camp, with emphasis on preaching and Bible study. The group offered a Labor Day weekend (Sunday afternoon and Monday) at Oakwood Park, one of the conference camp grounds. It was called a mini-convocation and was patterned after the regular Good News convocations, with preaching, workshops, and programs for children and youth. For nearly twenty-five years, this group brought in the best-known names associated with evangelicalism within The United Methodist Church and attracted up to three hundred in attendance. Ed Robb, Paul Morrell, Robert Coleman, Dennis Kinlaw, Thomas Carruth, and Virgil Maybray were among the speakers who came for the two-day event. Later the group began sponsoring the Evangelical Fellowship annual conference banquet, which became one of the best-attended conference banquets.

The "political" efforts of the group were minimal, but the group did circulate Good News petitions to General Conference. In 1979, the group made its first effort to affect the election of delegates to General Conference. In 1983, the group prepared a position paper on issues facing the Church. The paper was sent to potential delegates to the General Conference, asking if they could support the evangelical position on the issues. The reaction was not positive, not because of the positions taken, but because of the existence of the paper itself. The old arguments were trotted out about "labeling" and being "divisive." Those who objected to a position paper argued that persons should be elected to General Conference based on not what they believed, but their activity in the conference and their institutional loyalty. Still, others responded positively to the idea that a delegate did represent the conference, and therefore beliefs and convictions ought to be made public.

Did the North Indiana Evangelical Fellowship have any effect in the life of the annual conference? No official conference priorities were directly changed because of the North Indiana Evangelical Fellowship. As far as is known, no new programs were initiated or old programs closed down because of the group. If there was positive effect, it was in the immeasurable area of changed attitudes and spirit. Angry people became less angry. A number of pastors and churches felt free to pursue an evangelical ministry, believing they would be supported, not hampered, by the conference. Others simply felt better about being United Methodist.

In the mid-1980s, the annual conference made some decisions that would affect churches like Hanfield and Mt. Olive. In a period of eighteen years, from 1968 until 1985, the North Indiana Annual Conference had lost fully one-third of its entire membership. Worship attendance had declined by 22 percent. If was obvious that something needed to be done. Churches were disheartened; the conference seemed to be disintegrating. A decision was made to secure the services of Carl George of Fuller Seminary as a church-growth consultant. Out of those consultations, the conference committed itself to some new goals: to start new churches, to profile pastors in a different way to determine better how they could be deployed, and to revamp the old style of conference staffing. Instead of assigning staff to resource boards and agencies, staff would be deployed to resource local churches. A new position was created, Director of Local Church Ministries, and then two more positions, associate Directors of Local Church Ministries.[9] The job descriptions read that 80 percent of the directors' time was to be spent in the local church. These were changes strongly supported by the evangelicals in the conference.

The conference then adopted a new program that grew out of the consultations with Carl George and the experiences the directors were having in local churches. One hundred and fifty churches signed up to be part of the New Generation Program, which involved training and a commitment in several areas: ministry to children (primarily establishment of Kids' Clubs); invitation, emphasizing teleministry (phone calls); an emphasis on nurturing of newcomers; and effective worship, emphasizing contemporary worship. For many churches, the conference had suddenly become friendly. It was giving instead of taking.

The argument can be made that when the North Indiana Evangelical Fellowship became less active in the mid- and late-1990s, it was not because of failure but because of success. For whatever reason, the climate of the annual conference had become more evangelical-affirming. Prayer groups and the sharing of testimonies were becoming a part of district activities. The conference began encouraging the very kinds of programs that the Evangelical Fellowship had advocated: Walk to Emmaus, Alpha, John Maxwell, covenant groups, Disciple Bible Study, and church growth seminars. The camping program had renewed its commitment to evangelism and discipleship. In 1995, the annual conference approved a resolution, "To Affirm a Confessional Statement of the Confessing Movement Within The United Methodist Church."

The experience of the North Indiana Evangelical Fellowship is not necessarily typical in the denomination. Every conference evangelical group has its own story. Some are stories of success, others of ineffectiveness. Some groups faced open hostility (and still do).

Are there signs of renewal in The United Methodist Church? One would be hard-pressed to be hopeful if the only knowledge of the Church were through contact with its Council on Bishops, its boards and agencies, and some of its seminaries. But the essence of the Church is not in the Council of Bishops or the boards and agencies or the seminaries. The essence of the Church is in the faith of its people, gathered together in local churches for worship, service, and prayer. In this faith, in many local churches, vitality is found. That is the hope for United Methodism.

NOTES

1. Methodism's Populist Wing, Part I

1. Peter Cartwright, *Autobiography of Peter Cartwright* (Nashville: Abingdon Press, 1956), 64.

2. Richard Wheatley, "The Revised Methodist Hymnal," *The Methodist Quarterly Review* (July 1879): 527.

3. James Fry, "The Early Camp-Meeting Song Writers," *Methodist Quarterly Review* (July 1859): 407.

4. There was little difference between "white spirituals" and "Negro spirituals" in the earliest camp meetings. Camp meeting hymnals such as *The Revivalist* (Joseph Hillman Publisher, 1868), which gathered many of the earliest camp meeting tunes and texts, did not distinguish between the two.

5. The similarity between official Church responses to slavery in the 1840s and homosexuality in the 2000s is uncanny.

6. Ellen Jane Lorenz Porter, writing on the history of The Evangelical United Brethren Church hymnody ("The Hymnody of The Evangelical United Brethren Church," *The Journal of Theology* [1987]: 74) argues that EUBs (and Methodist Protestants) never had the music problems of the Methodists, because EUBs never made the distinctions of "official" and "unofficial" the way Methodists did. The EUB reluctance to label "official" or "approved" carried over into areas of education, evangelism, and support of institutions as well. For this reason, most of the discussion about populist Methodism deals primarily with The Methodist Episcopal Church and not with the Evangelical Church, United Brethren Church, and The Methodist Protestant Church.

7. Jonathan Weaver, "The Outlook," *Telescope* (25 February 1885), quoted in *Biography of Jonathan Weaver, D.D.*, by H. A. Thompson (Dayton: United Brethren Publishing House, 1901), 285.

8. James W. Lee, Naphtali Luccock, and James Main Dixon, *The Illustrated*

History of Methodism (St. Louis and New York: The Methodist Magazine Publishing Co., 1900), 628.

9. Quoted in John Leland Peters, *Christian Perfection and American Methodism* (Nashville: Abingdon Press, 1956), 139.

10. Quoted in Vinson Synan, *The Holiness-Pentecostal Movement in the United States* (Grand Rapids: Eerdmans Publishing Company 1971), 50.

11. Peters, *Christian Perfection and American Methodism*, 141-43.

12. Ibid., 143.

13. Lee, Luccock, and Dixon, *Illustrated History*, 718-41.

14. Nathan O. Hatch and John H. Wigger, eds., *Methodism and the Shaping of American Culture* (Nashville: Kingswood Books, 2001), 16.

15. For all of the efforts of the denomination in the last half of the twentieth century to strengthen the black church and to eradicate racism, the percentage of African Americans as a part of the denomination decreased from the 9 percent to 4 percent (at the beginning of the twenty-first century).

2. Methodism's Silent Minority

1. Editorial, *The Christian Century*, 24 June 1926: "It is henceforth to be a disappearing quantity in American religious life, while our churches go on to larger issues" (p. 799).

2. The last seminary among the mainline denominations to "fall" was Princeton in 1929, when Gresham Machen and other orthodox professors were purged.

3. For a commentary on these developments from that time, see Riley Case, "Neo-Evangelicalism: New Life on the Right," *Christian Advocate* (26 April 1962): 7-8.

4. Charles Keysor, editorial, *Good News*, 1, no. 1 (Spring 1967): 2.

5. Spurgeon Dunnam, editorial, *Texas Methodist* (6 September 1968). It should be obvious that a statement like this would not be made by an institutionally kept or "official" press.

6. These particular letters are from the July-September 1969 issue of *Good News* (pp. 2, 5).

7. One early question facing the Good News board had to do with the sharing of the mailing list that had been assembled from ground zero. It was determined that it would not be shared or sold to anyone unless there was a clear indication that such a group was not politically motivated but shared a common Good News goal of spiritual and theological renewal within The United Methodist Church.

8. And a most interesting character in the history of early renewal efforts. In a fifty-five-year ministry, from 1874 to 1929, Munhall had conducted more than 500 revival campaigns, in which more than 200,000 persons were reported to have been "scripturally converted." He was a six-time delegate to General Conference from the Eastern Pennsylvania Conference. Information about Munhall and other Methodist reforming evangelicals can be found in Howard Glen Spann, "Evangelicalism in Modern American Methodism: Theological Conservatives in the 'Great Deep' of the Church, 1900–1980" (Ph.D. diss., Johns Hopkins University, 1994), 148.

9. Walker, a recent Perkins graduate, was one of the first persons to respond to Chuck Keysor's article "Methodism's Silent Minority." He was on the original board and prepared to make a long-time commitment to Good News. Walker served as chair of the board and for many years edited *Catalyst*, the Good News resource for seminary students. Forty years later, he and Dale Bittinger were the only persons still on the Good News board who were there from the beginning.

10. An incident that had much to do with Asbury temporarily losing its accreditation with the Association of Theological Schools. In retrospect, Asbury's loss was a gain for the evangelical cause overall. Thompson was one of the few evangelicals to be associated with a United Methodist seminary in the 1960s. He was held in high respect in part because of his ability to link together evangelical faith and social action. When he spoke at the first convocation, he argued that racists should leave the Church. He authored several articles in *Christian Advocate,* supportive of the evangelical cause. Unfortunately, his witness was cut short because of an untimely death in 1972.

11. Lundy became the first and only bishop or former bishop ever to identify openly and personally with a Good News–sponsored project.

12. Oral Roberts had to cancel later and was replaced by Akbar Abdul-Haqq of the Billy Graham Association.

13. Letter from C. Edwin Murphy (13 March 1970). There are copies of these and other letters in the Good News archives at Asbury Theological Seminary in Wilmore, Kentucky.

14. Charles Keysor, "Coming Out of Exile," (13 March 1970) *Good News* (July-September 1970): 22.

15. Most of these were probably graduates of Asbury.

16. Twenty-one percent were undecided, which is an indication that many grassroots United Methodists were simply unaware of those issues that captured the attention, the devotion, and the time and efforts of institutional leadership.

17. Charles Keysor, editorial, *Good News* (April-June 1972): 16-17.

18. "Good News for Methodists," *Christianity Today* (25 September 1970): 23.

19. It is of great irony that an agency responsible for public relations in the denomination should also posture itself as independent and objective. Official church communications have always been controlled by the institution from the earliest days of the *Methodist Quarterly Review*. Its editors have come up through the institutional ranks, and it reports its news through the colored glasses of the institutional well-being. It is hard to imagine official United Methodist publications, for example, doing investigative and critical reporting on episcopal or institutional appropriateness.

20. Spurgeon Dunnam, "Constructive Divisiveness," *Texas Methodist* (24 September 1970); reprinted in *Good News* (October-December 1970): 108. Dunnam was one observer who understood from the beginning that the greatest tension in the Church was not the evangelicals versus the social activists, but evangelicals versus status quo institutionalists, on the one hand, and social activists versus status quo institutionalists, on the other hand. Or to put it another way: It was not the right wing against the left wing, but both wings against the dead middle.

21. Claude H. Thompson, "Reflections on Dallas," *Christian Advocate* (26 November 1970): 13.

22. When Good News board member Spann asked Keysor to West Texas to lead a revival in 1968, Keysor admitted it was the first time he had ever even attended a Methodist revival. He also at that time had his first taste of fried okra.

23. There is no record from any conference that any graduate from a liberal seminary needed to attend a conservative seminary for "balance."

24. Charles Keysor, "Answer to an Ex-Fundamentalist," *Christian Advocate* (14 October 1971): 13. Tabor's article appeared in the May 13, 1971, issue.

25. Marcius E. Taber, "An Ex-Fundamentalist Looks at the 'Silent Minority,'" *Christian Advocate* (13 May 1971): 12.

26. Charles Keysor, "Methodism's Silent Minority," *Christian Advocate* (14 July 1966).

27. Ibid.

3. Cyanide in the Church School

1. Charles Keysor, "Cyanide in the Church School," *Good News* (January-March 1970): 32.

2. This comment is based on personal recollection. There was no reaction "officially" in print, but friends of Good News and potential friends reported that the criticism leveled against Good News over this article was extensive. This was at a time when support of the church school curriculum material was a matter of loyalty.

3. *Teacher I and II* (Spring 1969); quoted in Charles Keysor, "Cyanide Revisited," *Good News* (July-September 1970): 19.

4. It also served several other purposes. It was a wake-up call for a number of evangelicals who up to this time simply did not believe that anything objectionable ever appeared in official material.

5. It must be noted, however, that Chuck Keysor discovered a number of "crises." Within the few issues of the magazine, there was a faith crisis, a missions crisis, a doctrinal crisis, and a spiritual crisis.

6. *The Book of Discipline of The Methodist Church* (Nashville: The Methodist Publishing House, 1968), par. 1134.

7. Henry Bullock, speech to the Conference on Educational Ministries, Chicago, Illinois, 1969.

8. Addie Grace Wardle, *History of the Sunday School Movement in the Methodist Episcopal Church* (New York: The Methodist Book Concern, 1918), 91.

9. E. B. Chappell, *Recent Development of Religious Education in the Methodist Episcopal Church, South* (Nashville: Cokesbury Press, 1935, 1969), 76.

10. Ibid., 11-12.

11. Ibid., 22-23.

12. Ibid., 23.

13. Ibid., 11.

14. As with almost all of the issues in the Church, there was an underlying and unstated conflict between the early Methodist democratic vision that all believers, especially Spirit-filled Christians, are competent to give Christian leadership and guidance, and the view developing with institutional Methodism that only specially trained leaders—a mediating elite—should give such leadership.

15. Chappell, *Recent Development*, 11-12.

16. William Henry Burns, *Crisis in Methodism*, 2nd ed. (Chicago: Christian Witness Co., 1909), 19.

17. L. W. Munhall, *Breakers! Methodism Adrift* (Chicago: Christian Witness Co., 1913).

18. Ibid., 100-101.

19. Harold Paul Sloan, *The Child and the Church* (Red Bank, N.J.: Standard Publishing Company, 1916).

20. Pelagianism is the ancient heresy that claims that each person is capable of exercising his or her free will in such a way that he or she goes through life without ever having committed a sin.

21. Chappell, *Recent Development*, 62.

22. John Q. Schisler, *Christian Education in Local Methodist Churches* (Nashville: Abindgon Press, 1969), 76.

23. Ethel L. Smither, *The Use of the Bible with Children* (New York: Abingdon-Cokesbury Press, 1937).

24. Ibid., 23.

25. Ibid., 28.

26. Ibid., 31.

27. Ibid., 64.

28. Ibid., 81.

29. Ibid., 126-27.

30. Ibid., 121.

31. *The Book of Discipline of The Methodist Church* (Nashville: The Methodist Publishing House, 1952), par. 233.3.5.

32. There are several examples of evangelical teachers selecting only the Bible for study without any other interpretative materials and being told this would be impossible because it was "not approved."

33. These quotas were based on gender, race, age, and former denominational loyalties. The "inclusive" church never did "include" persons with different theological views. Evangelicals were particularly excluded.

34. See "Toward a New Day in Ministry to Youth," *The Church School* (October 1967): 13.

35. The *Discipline* defined youth as those between the ages of twelve and eighteen. Many of the so-called youth were actually college students.

36. This information was shared at the consultation for conference and youth coordinators held in Nashville, Tennessee, on September 28–October 1, 1976.

37. Martin R. Chambers, "Non-Approved Church School Lesson Material Can Be Subversive," *The Church School* (September 1964): 32.

38. Ibid.

39. Ibid., 30-31.

40. I remember making this point to a former EUB staff member in the 1970s. I asked: "How could you so easily give up the good you already had for this?" He thought for a while and then answered: "We are United Methodist now."

41. Frank Stanger, president of Asbury Seminary, Bill Wilson, a psychiatrist from North Carolina, and Charles Britt, a pastor from Texas, were unapologetically evangelical.

42. The idea, in retrospect, was wildly impractical. It would not have worked to have it edited and written by liberals, and it is hard to imagine the Curriculum and Program Committee turning the editing and writing to untested evangelicals.

43. By the same token, the committee would never admit that black United Methodists might be better served with materials that reflected African American culture and experience. In 1984, the General Conference authorized $400,000 to be used for the development of black curriculum. It never happened.

44. Several persons, even outside the evangelical community, have commented

that Keysor's essay on confirmation that appears in the teacher's edition of *We Believe* was one of the best statements on the meaning and theology of confirmation available at that time.

45. One suggestion was to include in the confirmation offerings the *Abingdon Catechism*, which predated modernism and was still available, though it was never advertised and never included in catalogs, through Cokesbury.

46. I wrote the materials for the confirmation class that I was teaching in my church at the time, a lesson a week. The youth were most helpful in offering feedback.

47. The official church materials have been revised several times since, with each revision being more balanced theologically and more acceptable to evangelicals. For a review of all these from a Good News perspective, see "Whither Confirmation," *Good News* (November-December 1994): 24-27.

48. At the end of seventeen years, the materials had sold nearly a half million units and had garnered about 20 percent of the market.

49. It has always been the contention of Good News that the true centrists in American Protestantism are evangelicals in mainline denominations. They understand both extreme liberalism and extreme fundamentalism and could (and should) be able to bridge the gaps between the two.

50. This was especially true of David C. Cook and Scripture Press. These two publishing houses had a fairly significant number of United Methodist churches as customers. They advertised regularly at the Good News convocations and made regular contacts with Chuck Keysor, who knew the publishing world and had once been an editor at David C. Cook.

51. One last gasp effort at enforcing uniformity was a letter in May 1980 from Bishop Joel D. McDavid and the cabinet of the Florida Conference to all pastors. The letter said in part: "As the Cabinet and the Bishop of the Florida Conference, we would urge all of you to make strong effort to see that only United Methodist literature is used in the Sunday school and other educational work of the local church. This literature is prepared by our church under the balanced direction of a curriculum committee, and it is supportive of Methodist theology and polity. It is the only material written from this full perspective, and is of the highest quality."

52. It is difficult to design a study that would prove this statistically, but almost every evangelical United Methodist pastor has a portfolio of stories of families, often including their own children, who abandoned the United Methodist ship for other churches or ministries. Frequently, the Sunday school was a contributing factor. Numbers of families who stayed loyal to the denomination credit Good News and the hope for renewal as influencing their decision.

4. Doctrine Gone Astray

1. One of the best-known quotes from John Wesley on this matter is from *Plain Account* (1738): "Orthodoxy, or right opinions, is, at best, but a very slender part of religion, if it can be allowed to be any part of it at all."

2. The best example of this is hymn 339 in *The United Methodist Hymnal* (Nashville: The United Methodist Publishing House, 1995), "Come, Sinners to the Gospel Feast." Wesley hymns and Methodist gospel hymns frequently use the word

"come" as an invitation to sinners. The hymns of Isaac Watts and other Calvinists tended to use "come" in reference to believers ("Come, ye that love the Lord").

3. "On the Death of the Rev. Mr. George Whitefield," *The Standard Sermons of John Wesley* 53 (London: Epworth Press, 1956), 522.

4. Colin W. Williams in *John Wesley's Theology Today* (New York: Abingdon Press, 1960) lists these: the deity of Christ, the Atonement, justification by faith alone, the work of the Holy Spirit, and the Trinity (pp. 16-17).

5. Sermons II, 223.

6. Sermons I, 159.

7. This is from the 1848 Methodist Episcopal hymnal. All Methodist hymnals since Wesley have followed a somewhat similar order. United Brethren and Evangelical Association hymnals were also based on this order. Other Wesleyan bodies, such as the Church of the Nazarene, have also used this scheme.

8. *The Standard Catechism* (Nashville: Abingdon Press, 1929). The 1929 catechism is almost identical to earlier catechisms. While Cokesbury catalogs did not advertise the existence of the catechisms, this version was available through the 1980s.

9. Charles Wesley, "O For a Thousand Tongues to Sing," *The United Methodist Hymnal* (Nashville: The United Methodist Publishing House, 1989), 57.

10. William Cowper, "There Is a Fountain Filled with Blood," *The United Methodist Hymnal*, 622.

11. Matthew Simpson, *A Hundred Years of Methodism* (New York: Phillips & Hunt, 1876), 150.

12. This is discussed in chapter 1.

13. These and others are documented by Howard Glen Spann, *Evangelicalism in Modern American Methodism: Theological Conservatives in the "Great Deep" of the Church, 1900–1980* (dissertation, Johns Hopkins University, 1994), 50-63.

14. Episcopal address of the General Conference of The Methodist Episcopal Church, South (1906).

15. Ibid.

16. Wilbur Fisk Tillett, *A Statement of the Faith of World-wide Methodism* (Nashville: Publishing House of The Methodist Episcopal Church, South, 1906). Methodism had not at this point given up on creeds. It is just that some wanted a new one to reflect present realities. Evidently, nothing ever came of the action or the commission that supposedly would write the new creed.

17. Ibid., 61.

18. These originally appeared in the *Christian Advocate* and later were made into a book with the same title, *Fundamental Doctrines of Methodism*, compiled by H. H. Smith.

19. Francis J. McConnell, *The Essentials of Methodism* (New York: The Methodist Book Concern, 1916).

20. Ibid.

21. Ibid.

22. "What Is Disturbing the Methodists," *Christian Century* (20 May 1926): 637-40.

23. George Herbert Betts, *The Beliefs of 700 Ministers and Their Meaning for Religious Education* (Nashville: Abingdon Press, 1929). The study was one of the Abingdon Religious Education Monographs with John W. Langdale, general editor, and George Herbert Betts, editor.

24. Ibid., 22

25. Ibid., 43.

26. Ibid., 57.

27. Quoted in G. W. Ridout, *The Present Crisis in Methodism and How to Meet It* (Louisville: Pentecostal Publishing Company, n.d.), 29.

28. See Francis John McConnell, *Borden Parker Bowne* (New York: Abingdon Press, 1929), 228-39.

29. Borden Parker Bowne, quoted in Ridout, *Present Crisis in Methodism*, 30.

30. In its dispensational form, it not only added a premillennial pretribulational eschatology, but also posited as a corollary the view of an apostate church.

31. Truly spoken. However, it evidently did not occur to *Christian Century* that both could be wrong (Editorial, *The Christian Century* [24 June 1924]).

32. See chapter 7.

33. On at least four different occasions in the 1960s, *Youth Leader* magazine carried articles condemning "unofficial" organizations such as Youth for Christ and Young Life.

34. Roy L. Smith, *Why I Am a Methodist* (New York: Thomas Nelson & Sons, 1955).

35. Ibid., 85-92.

5. Missions Without Salvation

1. Philip Hinerman, "Missions Without Salvation," *Good News* (January-March 1972): 40.

2. My seminary professor was Don Holter, later Bishop Holter. I checked my old classnotes to confirm this.

3. William Ernest Hocking, *Re-Thinking Missions: A Laymen's Inquiry After One Hundred Years* (New York: Harper and Brothers Publishers, 1932), 21.

4. Creighton Lacy, *"Adam, Where Art Thou": An Interpretative Report of the Interfield Consultation Held at Epworth-by-the-Sea* (Board of Missions of The Methodist Church, 1956), 57.

5. In 1984, the General Conference assigned the Board of Church and Society the task of providing guidelines for economic boycotts. While the board was debating a proposed grape boycott, the Board of Global Ministries on its own declared a boycott with minimal prior study or discussion.

6. This was taking place when the rest of the Church was still dominated by white, male liberals, and when women were still not accepted as clergy. The Board of Missions was one place women had influence.

7. Reported in *United Methodist Reporter* (6 November 1981).

8. David Seamands, "Missions Without Salvation, Part II," *Good News* (April-June 1972): 25.

9. *The Book of Discipline of The United Methodist Church* (Nashville: The United Methodist Publishing House, 1972), par. 803.2.

10. This was a typical reaction of the institutional liberals of the time that expressed itself not only in talks with the Board of Global Ministries, but also in conversations with curriculum editors and with the seminaries. It was an unwillingness to admit that Good News types or other evangelicals had any more right to the word than they, who had long given up on doctrines of original sin, the

blood atonement, and salvation only in Christ. It was basically a discounting of the evangelical position by obfuscation.

11. Eugene Smith, quoted in Bill Buchanan, "What Is 'Evangelical Missionary'?" *United Methodist Reporter* 2, no. 17 (12 April 1974): 1.

12. Ibid.

13. From my personal notes taken at the pastor's school.

14. Quoted in *The Faith That Compels Us*, by H. T. Maclin (Norcross, Ga.: The Mission Society for United Methodists, 1997), 31.

15. Dow Kirkpatrick, quoted in "Two Sundays in May: Castro and Wesley," *The United Methodist Reporter* (22 July 1977).

16. Ibid.

17. Sergio Arce, quoted in "Seminary Head Says Marxism Most Important," *The United Methodist Reporter* (9 September 1977).

6. Seeking to Offer Balance

1. David Jessup, "Preliminary Inquiry Regarding Financial Contributions to Outside Political Groups by Boards and Agencies of The United Methodist Church, 1977–1979" (7 April 1980), 1.

2. Besides their involvement in the forming of the Institute of Religion and Democracy, the Shells headed the legislative efforts of Good News at General Conference in 1980, 1984, 1988, and 1992. Don Shell was invaluable when Good News made the change from the old ways of accounting to a computer system.

3. United Methodist Communications, "The Use of Money in Mission—An Opportunity for Understanding" (17 October 1980), 5. All of the grants in question were directly related to a particular political or economic system (that of the far left). The "white paper," or inter-office correspondence, was arguing that criticism of grants and ideology tied to political and economic systems must be discounted because they are obviously the servant of a particular political or economic system.

4. Ibid.

5. The cover letter by Bishop Nichols was much less strident than the paper itself. Nichols argued that the allegations of Jessup needed careful response (his letter was written before the white paper was composed) and that every board and agency "must be responsive to inquiries and criticisms." Several months before this controversy, Nichols, in a personal meeting with the Good News board, had encouraged Good News in its efforts (see chapter 9).

6. David Jessup, *Response to Newscope* (December 1980), 1-2.

7. Richard John Neuhaus, "Christianity and Democracy: A Statement of the Institute on Religion and Democracy" (Washington, D.C.: The Institute on Religion and Democracy, 1981), 12-14.

8. Circuit Riders was a politically conservative organization of mostly Methodist laity who criticized what they considered were the socialist leanings of Methodists Federated for Social Action (which had a semiofficial relationship with the Church at that time) during the early 1950s.

9. Roy Howard Beck, *On Thin Ice: A Religion Reporter's Memoir* (Wilmore, Ky.: Bristol Books, 1988), 80-81.

10. "Warring Over Where Donations Go," *Time* (28 March 1983): 58.

11. Betty Thompson, "If You See It in the Digest, Virginia, Is It So?" *Response* (September 1982).

12. The actual IRD board was never that large. It has fluctuated between twelve and eighteen members.

13. *The United Methodist Reporter* (1 April 1983).

14. Joshua Muravchik, "Pliant Protestants," *The New Republic* (13 June 1983): 18. Muravchik had been a writer for *The New York Times Magazine, Commentary,* and other magazines.

15. It was "secret" because the issue of whether or not to launch such an investigation was never discussed by the Board of Church and Society, but only by a select number of staff. The elected board was not pleased that such a study involving the use of church apportionment money to investigate a church-related group should be conducted without their approval.

16. "I Am Not Making These Charges," *Christianity and Crisis* 43, no. 4 (21 March 1983): 75.

17. *Newscope* 8, no. 12 (24 February 1984).

18. Ira Gallaway, *Drifted Astray* (Nashville: Abingdon Press, 1983).

19. Ole Borgen, "One Mission—One Missional Purpose" (address given at Good News Convocation, Anderson, Ind., 1983).

20. A statement easily contradicted. Numbers of bishops were asking for missionaries as the Mission Society for United Methodists discovered when they were able finally to make missionaries available.

21. Richard G. Hutcheson Jr., "Crisis in Overseas Mission: Shall We Leave It to the Independents?" *Christian Century* (18 March 1981): 290.

22. This is reported and discussed in *The Faith That Compels Us* by H. T. Maclin (Norcross, Ga.: The Mission Society for United Methodists, 1997), 47-53.

23. Ibid., 47. Maclin spoke personally with seven bishops in the Southeastern Jurisdiction who shared their personal concerns. However, none spoke out publicly or was known to have raised a voice in the Council of Bishops.

24. Billings was in contact with the AFL-CIO officials, charging (at least as publicly quoted): "The heavy barrage of 'attacks' has gone beyond the bounds of the right of an individual to criticize." Her response (as explained in a personal letter) was that she was only seeking to "define the relationships of Jessup, organized labor, and the Women's Division commitment to labor." However explained, it was interpreted as an effort to intimidate, if not as an outright demand for firing.

25. Wade Crawford Barclay, *History of Methodist Missions,* vol. 3 (New York: The Board of Missions of The Methodist Church, 1957), 141.

26. Petition 0329, 1984 General Conference. This was a meaningless gesture since the board believed it was already doing these things. In years to come, the efforts to discount the work of the society would refer to the action of the General Conference, which recognized only one official society. There is no evidence that any effort was made to hold the board accountable to the General Conference's wishes concerning evangelism and Wesleyan theology.

27. A number of persons would see this as one of the low points in the history of the Council of Bishops, to use the power of the hierarchy to seek to ostracize and invalidate the preaching of the gospel by faithful United Methodists.

28. For a discussion of this, see *United Methodist Reporter* (27 September 1985).

29. Raymond and Rhea Whitehead, China: Search for Community (New York: Friendship Press, 1978)

30. Quoted in "A Brief History of the Women's Renewal Movement Within the UMC," comp. Faye Short (July 2002).

31. Between 1967 (including figures from both Methodist and EUB women's groups) and 2001, membership in United Methodist Women declined by 54 percent.

32. John Stumbo moved to Helen Rhea's hometown, Fort Valley, Georgia, became involved in politics, won a race for mayor on a reformist and inclusive platform, and brought healing in a racially troubled community.

7. Vital Piety and the Mind

1. Russell T. Hitt, "Capital of Evangelicalism," *Christian Life* (April 1952): 16-18.

2. *The Book of Discipline of The Methodist Episcopal Church* (New York: W. Ross, 1784).

3. Some of this is discussed in *The Churching of America 1776–1990,* by Roger Finke and Rodney Stark (New Brunswick, N.J.: Rutgers University Press, 1992), 76 ff.

4. Peter Cartwright, *Autobiography of Peter Cartwright* (New York: Abingdon Press, 1956), 64.

5. This figure is arrived at by using the "religious preference" tables of the 1860 census. "Methodist" in this accounting includes all Methodist denominations, north, south, white, and black, as well as United Brethren and the Evangelical Association.

6. Presbyterians had founded Hanover College and Wabash College and controlled the board at Indiana University.

7. Allen Wiley, *Life and Times of Rev. Allen Wiley, A.M* (Cincinnati: L. Swormste, 1853), 68.

8. Quoted in George R. Crooks, *The Life of Bishop Matthew Simpson* (New York: Harper & Brothers, 1891), 504-5.

9. Ibid., 514.

10. Myron F. Wicke, *A Brief History of the University Senate of the Methodist Church* (Nashville: Board of Education, the Methodist Church, 1956), 10.

11. Ibid.

12. Ibid., 12.

13. Ibid., 9. According to Wicke: "No other single institution reappears as frequently in Senate minutes as this Indiana college" (p. 9).

14. This was never officially so recorded. This information comes from personal conversation with some of the persons involved.

15. Quoted from James Tunstead Burtchaell, *The Dying of the Light: The Disengagement of Colleges and Universities from Their Christian Churches* (Grand Rapids: Eerdmans Publishing Company, 1988), 267.

16. O. E. Brown, "Modernism: A Calm Survey, *Methodist Quarterly Review* 74, no. 3 (July 1925): 396-97.

17. C. G. Thompson, "Theological Seminaries: An Evaluation," *Methodist Quarterly Review* 74, no. 3 (July 1925): 415.

18. Finke and Stark, *Churching of America*, 206.

19. See Howard Glen Spann, *Evangelicalism in Modern American Methodism: Theological Conservatives in the "Great Deep" of the Church, 1900–1980* (dissertation, Johns Hopkins University, 1994), 216.

20. *The Book of Discipline of The Methodist Episcopal Church* (Nashville: The Publishing House of The Methodist Episcopal Church, 1924), para. 458.5.1.

21. Ibid., para. 503.4

22. William Henry Bernhardt, *The Influence of Borden Parker Bowne Upon Theological Thought in the Methodist Episcopal Church* (dissertation submitted to the Graduate Faculty in Candidacy for the Degree of Doctor of Philosophy, University of Chicago, 1926).

23. Ibid., 122; see also pp. 9 and 11.

24. Spann, *Evangelicalism in Modern American Methodism*, 201.

25. Some of the accounts record, "with jeering." Some observers refer to the Sloan effort as the last gasp of "fundamentalism" in The Methodist Episcopal Church. The Methodist League for Faith and Life, which some have compared with an early form of the Good News movement, soon disbanded. It should be clarified that Sloan and other leaders of the League saw themselves not as fundamentalists, but as traditional Methodists.

26. Quoted in Frederick A. Norwood, *From Dawn to Midday at Garrett* (Evanston: Garrett-Evangelical Theological Seminary, 1978), 165.

27. Louis Cassels, "Approving Those Agnostic to Basic Christian Doctrine for Ministry a Seminary Headache," *Paterson News* (17 June 1967): 14.

28. From a Religious News Service release, quoted in *Christianity Today* (15 January 1971): 21.

29. Charles Keysor, editorial, *Good News* 1, no. 1 (Spring 1967): 2.

30. According to the seminary catalogs of the period, forty to fifty graduates of these two schools were enrolled at Garrett. The seminary would regularly visit the schools for recruitment purposes. By 1965, the seminary was not recruiting from evangelical schools, which the person in charge of recruitment admitted to this writer as a conscious choice.

31. *The Book of Discipline of The United Methodist Church* (Nashville: The United Methodist Publishing House, 1972).

32. Some of this "contending" was done by way of correspondence between Good News leaders and seminary presidents or deans. Some was done by renewal groups who asked for an audience to express concerns. East and West Ohio renewal groups met on at least four different occasions with persons from METHESCO (the United Methodist seminary in Delaware, Ohio) to express these concerns.

33. William Stringfellow, "Myths, Endless Genealogies, the Promotion of Speculations and the Vain Discussion Thereof," *Sojourners* (August 1977): 13.

34. Waits eventually became the most open of any of the presidents or deans toward Good News concerns (as far as the 1970s were concerned). Possibly because of the presence of Claude Thompson and persons such as Bill Cannon, Candler had attracted a number of evangelical and charismatic students. Waits expressed interest in bringing an evangelical on the faculty to function in the role that Claude Thompson had filled. Candler also was offering a course on contemporary evangelical theology.

35. Good News's Task Force on Seminary Life, "A Report on the Visitation Program to United Methodist Seminaries" (1975), 1.

36. Some of the comments were sad: "I am not able to say anything. I am already being marginalized."

37. Remark made in my presence.

38. Adon Taft, "Seminary Avoids Pitfalls," *Miami Herald* (3 November 1979).

39. Good News seemed much better informed about the actual numbers of students attending non-United Methodist seminaries than the General Board of Higher Education and Ministry, which either did not have means or the desire to track this statistic.

40. A number of people wanted to see Asbury denied approval. Asbury's high view of Scripture troubled a number of persons who believed this led to literalism and narrowness of spirit. Asbury had won accreditation in 1946 only to lose it in 1951 after an incident involving Claude Thompson, who, under pressure, left Asbury to teach at Candler (and became the strongest friend Good News had in the seminaries in the early years). Asbury regained accreditation in 1960, but the experience was still fresh in many persons' minds. Although a number of conferences welcomed Asbury graduates, still others found reasons to refuse graduates or required them to attend a year at a United Methodist seminary. Asbury was already enrolling more United Methodist candidates than any of the official seminaries. In the end, Asbury had enough friends (political clout) and was knowledgeable enough in the ways of the Church to pass the first review. These comments are made on the basis of personal conversations with Dr. Frank Stanger, president of Asbury Seminary at the time.

41. Remark made in my presence.

42. When United Methodist seminaries offered such things as goddess worship, witchcraft workshops, and open advocacy for the homosexual lifestyle, they customarily defended their actions on the basis of "freedom of academic inquiry."

43. Roy Howard Beck, "Some Seminary Deans Shocked by Rejection," *The United Methodist Reporter* (July 1981).

44. Quoted in Crooks, *Life of Bishop Simpson*, 504-5.

45. Robert G. Bottoms, North Indiana Conference, 2001.

46. Ibid.

8. Reclaiming the Wesleyan Heritage

1. Ed Robb, "The Crisis of Theological Education in the United Methodist Church" (address delivered to Good News Convocation, Lake Junaluska, N.C., 1975), 33-34. The entire address can be found in the Fall 1975 issue of *Good News*.

2. Ibid., 36.

3. Albert C. Outler, *Evangelism in the Wesleyan Spirit* (Nashville: Tidings, 1971), 34-35.

4. Albert C. Outler, *United Methodist Reporter* (8 August 1975).

5. Albert C. Outler, "A Fund for 'Evangelical Scholars,'" *The Christian Century* (6-13 February 1980): 138-40.

6. This report comes by way of a personal interview with Ed Robb.

7. This story is well told by Bob Parrott in the biography *Albert C. Outler: The Gifted Dilettante* ([Anderson, Ind.: Bristol Books, 1999]: 286-92). It is significant that the book was published by Bristol, originally the publishing arm of Good News.

8. "A Message to the Methodist Church from the Council of Bishops," *Motive* (December 1958): 12.

9. Article I.

10. "Our Theological Task," from *The Book of Discipline of The United Methodist Church* (Nashville: The United Methodist Publishing House, 1972), 69-70.

11. The note was sent April 10, 1972, less than a month before the General Conference. It is not that Good News could have had the slightest influence anyway. Good News was not a factor in any way at the 1972 General Conference.

12. Letter from Albert Outler to Charles Keysor (29 August 1972).

13. Letter from Charles Keysor to Albert Outler (15 September 1972).

14. "Methodist Malaise," *Time* (8 May 1972). The article starts out with this observation: "The United Methodist Church is a case of a great American success story that is going bad." The official United Methodist press, of course, made none of these observations, serving (as was its custom) the institution.

15. It must be noted that this crisis of conscience only affected a few. The greater number of evangelicals, like the rest of the Church, were either clueless about the implications of the statement or else believed that it did not affect the day-to-day life of the Church.

16. "Our Theological Task," *Discipline*, 81.

17. Charles Keysor and C. Philip Hinerman, letter to the Good News board of directors (17 July 1972).

18. Charles Keysor, "Where Do We Go From Here," *Good News* (Summer 1972).

19. Ibid.

20. News release dated August 19, 1974, from United Methodist Communications.

21. Stanger had the most to risk by being involved in the project. He still needed to protect the image of the seminary and its tenuous approval with the University Senate, and association with Good News could well tarnish him and the seminary with charges of negativism and divisiveness. On the other hand, the whole evangelical community would be diminished if there was no evangelical response to the doctrinal statement, or if the statement would be done poorly. It helped that Lawrence Souder, a friend and former parishioner of Stanger, was a member of the committee.

22. Albert Outler would later observe that of "all the groups in the church," only Good News took the 1972 statement with enough seriousness actually to attempt to "clarify the premises on which they operate."

23. Letter from Albert Outler to Paul Morrell (31 March 1975).

24. While there was no written response to Outler on this point, it might well have been pointed out that Wesley's *Standard Sermons* and the earliest Methodist hymnals were arranged precisely around these theological themes.

25. Roger Burgess, "Has Good News Become Bad News?" *Interpreter* (September 1975).

26. Chester E. Custer, *The United Methodist Primer*, rev. ed. (Nashville: Discipleship Resources, 1986).

27. Ibid., 51.

28. Ibid., 60.

9. Good News As Political Caucus

1. Quoted in *Hoosier United Methodist* (April 1983): 16 (italics added).

2. Kenneth A. Briggs, "In Established Churches the Faithful Are Restless," *The New York Times* (11 September 1977).

3. George Vecsey, "Good News Evangelicals Worry Leaders of the Methodist Church," *The New York Times* (10 April 1979).

4. In a letter sent to MFSA supports in April 1979, George McClain reported that 15,000 copies of the reprint would soon be gone.

5. "Apostles of Reaction," *The Social Questions Bulletin* 68, no. 6; vol. 69, no. 1 (November-December 1978; January-February 1979): 19-20.

6. Ibid., 21.

7. Like many critics, including some official United Methodist agencies, MFSA put quotes around "Good News" to disassociate the name with any suggestion that it was connected with the real Good News (or gospel) of the New Testament.

8. "Apostles of Reaction," Part II, 3.

9. Circuit Riders was a politically motivated group of primarily laypersons that was organized to counteract the liberal, socialist-leaning ideology of MFSA in the early 1950s (the McCarthy era).

10. "Apostles of Reaction," Part II, 3.

11. Ignacio Castuera, *United Methodist Reporter* (10 November 1978).

12. "'Good News' Blasted for 'Parochialism,'" *United Methodist Reporter* (13 October 1978). McIntyre was critical of a *Good News* article that linked Marxist thought with communism and atheism. According to McIntyre, such "poor logic" ignored fifteen years of serious Marxist-Christian dialogue. McIntyre went on to argue that "no serious theology will be done in the next twenty years that does not include serious dialogue with Marxist sociological categories." He also spoke of the worldwide decline of capitalism.

13. We are making a distinction here between "conservatives" and "evangelicals." Many evangelicals are conservative in politics, but a number are not. Likewise, although a number of conservatives in politics and social matters are evangelical in theology and ethos, many are not.

14. It was for this very reason that the magazine was presented as a "forum." Keysor believed that in a free and open discussion of ideas others would be convinced of the truth of the evangelical perspective.

15. In light of this, the criticism that Good News was divisive was ill-founded. It is true that Good News was highly critical of a number of things in Methodism but this in large part was because it saw the denomination disintegrating and no one seemed to be caring. People associated with Good News often discussed how much longer they could "stay" (in the same way that evangelicals had used that language since the 1890s), but there never was even discussion, let alone an attempt, to form a new denomination.

16. In this respect, Good News could hardly be labeled "conservative." There was an institutional conservatism that resisted new evangelical expressions, but this did not characterize Good News. Even Asbury College and Seminary resisted charismatic expression for a number of years. Charismatic expression was a part of Good News meetings and gatherings up until the time that Renewal Services Fellowship was formed.

17. *Good News* vol. 1, no. 3 (Fall 1967).

18. Raymond H. Wilson, news release (2 May 1968).

19. Charles Keysor, "Editor's Thoughts About General Conference" (Summer 1972).

20. See for example, Charles Brewster, "The Evangelical Comeback—A Hope and a Danger" (January 1971): 13-17.

21. Charles Keysor, confidential report to Good News board of directors (1968).

22. Ibid.

23. Charles Keysor, *Good News* (October-December 1970): 80.

24. Charles Keysor, confidential report to Good News board of directors (1971).

25. Dick Johnson, "General Conference—Year of the Caucus," *Engage* 4, no. 6 (March 1972): 55-58.

26. Helen Rhea Coppedge and Robert W. Sprinkle, letter to the North Georgia Delegates to the 1972 General Conference (1972).

27. Operating on a shoestring budget the attendees met in homes of church members and held their meetings at a youth hostel.

28. Most of the memos and "confidential" reports can be found in the Good News archives located at the Good News office in Wilmore, Kentucky.

29. Good News minutes (23 April 1974), 3.

30. There were a few exceptions. The Curriculum Resources Committee, for example, placed several evangelicals on the committee as at-large members, and sought to employ a few evangelicals as writers.

31. Charles Keysor, "The Gathering Storm," *Good News* (Spring 1974): 22.

32. "United Methodism: On a Collision Course?" *The Michigan Christian Advocate* (19 September 1974).

33. Sharon Mielke, "Caucus Assumes Lower Profile," *The United Methodist Reporter* (5 May 1976).

34. Ed Plowman, "United Methodists: The View from Portland," *Christianity Today* (18 June 1976).

35. The idea that Good News was basically "southern-based," at least at this time in its existence, is a curious misperception. Despite the fact that Good News had an Asbury (and thus Kentucky) connection, Good News was slow to pick up support from the Southeast Jurisdiction. Bob Sprinkle and Helen Rhea Coppedge were the first real supporters from Georgia. That the Southeastern Jurisdiction was slow to respond to Good News was a matter of discussion on several occasions in Good News circles. The common interpretation was that the Southeast was more naturally evangelical to begin with, but was also more institutional in many ways. The Southeastern Jurisdiction, for example, was the heaviest supporter of official United Methodist Sunday school material,

36. "Methodism's Spirit of '76: Don't Rock the Church," *The Christian Century* (26 May 1976): 508.

37. James M. Johnston, "Carter Is Religious Newsmaker of '76," *Milwaukee Sentinel* (1 January 1977).

38. Perhaps more than any other group Good News has been aware of the loss from United Methodism of some of the strongest laypersons and most promising ministers. Robert Sprinkle was always interested in urban ministry and left to be pastor of Circle Church in Chicago, an interracial and evangelical work that had been pastored by David Mains.

39. Adon Taft, "Methodists Refuse to Bar Homosexuals from Ministry," *Miami Herald* (23 April 1980).

10. Growing Evangelical Presence

1. The investigation was done on behalf of Good News by staff person Diane Knippers. If Diane Knippers (who later would become president of Institute of Religion and Democracy) was known for her cynicism over church politics, she had good reason.

2. Charles Keysor, *Good News* (March-April 1981): 70.

3. Defined as persons who answered affirmatively in polls to three questions: "Would you say you have been born again or have had a born-again experience . . . when you committed yourself to Jesus Christ?" "Do you believe the Bible is the actual word of God and is to be taken literally, word for word?" "Have you encouraged other people to believe in Christ?"

4. Two years later, Keysor was sufficiently troubled by the direction of the church that he finally transferred his credentials to the Covenant Church, a denomination which he felt was evangelical without being fundamentalist, but still allowed a great deal of freedom of conscience, which Keysor always sought. He pastored a church in Florida before his death from the prostate cancer in October 1985.

5. Personal letter dated November 24, 1980. Ed Robb papers, archives, Asbury Theological Seminary.

6. While Nichols was cautious about any personal criticism of the Board of Global Ministries, there was a feeling that his strong words of encouragement to Good News grew in part out of his frustrations as chair of the World Division.

7. There is reason to believe that Spurgeon Dunnam, editor of the *Reporter*, chose to do the feature on Good News at that particular time because of Keysor's leaving. It was an opportunity for reflection about the role of Good News in The United Methodist Church.

8. Ray Nichols, quoted in Roy Howard Beck, "'Good News' Has Not Been All 'Bad News' for UMC," *United Methodist Reporter* 9, no. 8 (30 January 1981).

9. James Heidinger, *Good News* (May-June 1981).

10. In the late 1990s, retired pastor and longtime board member John Grenfell gave considerable time traveling around the country to be an advocate for those evangelicals who were being abused by the system. By the end of 2002 he had become involved in more than 20 different situations.

11. Jean Caffey Lyles, "Curing What Ails the General Conference," *Quarterly Review* (Winter 1983).

12. Hymns sung in chapel, for example, often became political statements, with students changing, or not changing, language according to their own preferences, leading, as more than one observer put it, to a babble of sounds.

13. In January 2002, Seamands received the Ed Robb award from Good News for service rendered on the part of evangelical renewal. It was noted that Seamands was a delegate to General Conference on six occasions and made four different minority reports in that period that were approved by the General Conference.

14. Good News by this time was accustomed to the reasoning of the institutional mind-set. This reasoning would sound something like: (1) It is not helpful to label some persons as "evangelicals," implying that others in the church are not;

(2) and, even if it were, Good News, as an unofficial group, should not be "repre-sented," because it would imply that other evangelicals not associated with Good News would not be represented. The institution would pick the "evangelicals," who might or might not be associated with Good News. It should be added, how-ever, that Good News was consulted in the picking of the Hymnal Revision Committee and one person, Riley Case, though not made an official member of the committee, was made a "consultant."

15. *Interpreter* magazine (May-June 1985) carried a news story and an invitation to the Church for suggestions and input. The committee did receive a number of responses.

16. In the district where I served as district superintendent, one-third of the churches used as a primary hymnal something other than the official hymnal. There were reports from other areas where the percentage was as high as two-thirds.

17. It became one of the most successful hymnals ever published. By the year 2002, 4.5 million hymnals had been sold.

18. James Heidinger, "United Methodism Moves Toward Center," *Good News* (May-June 1988).

19. James Heidinger, "A New United Methodism in the Making?" *Good News* (November-December 1988).

20. Letter from William Cannon to James Heidinger (1988).

21. James Heidinger, Report of Editor/Executive Secretary of the Good News Board of Directors (7-8 July 1990).

22. Figures were taken from the *General Minutes of the Annual Conferences*, 1991 and 1995.

23. According to statistics issued by the Research Office, National Program Division of GBGM (copyright 1989), the area in which the California-Nevada Conference is located grew by a population of 1,869,713, or 18.1 percent from 1980 to 1988. When Gerald Kennedy was bishop of that area, church membership increased from the years 1953 to 1964 from 143,000 to 270,000. By 1994 the mem-bership was 113,193.

24. Social Principles, para. 71C.

25. A number of liberal activists opposed efforts to call attention to the plight of persecuted Christians because they believed that somehow these efforts were part of some larger conservative political agenda. See Robert McClean, "Stealth Attacks on the Churches," *Christian Social Action* (September 1997): 28-31.

26. *Circuit Rider* (September-October 2000): 33.

27. Tom Oden, "Mainstreaming the Mainline: Methodist Evangelicals Pull a Once 'Incurably Liberal' Denomination Back Toward the Orthodox Center," *Christianity Today* (7 August 2000): 59-61.

28. Harry C. Kiely, "The Conservative Shift in The United Methodist Church," *Christian Social Action* (November-December 2000): 14.

29. Ibid.

30. Ibid., 15.

31. Ibid.

32. Ibid., 16.

11. The Struggle for Doctrinal Integrity

1. Bud Herron, *United Methodist Reporter* (23 July 1976): 1.

2. These comments are based on personal observations at the sublegislative committee meetings and knowledge of what many of the petitions were about.

3. Good News was considered a self-selected group and thus, so it was argued, could not represent all evangelicals. Furthermore, some in the Church were still arguing that all in the Church were "evangelical," and it was inappropriate to include a special interest group that seemed not to have the larger interests of the Church at heart. One bishop argued, "If we included someone from Good News we would have to include persons from the gay caucuses."

4. *The Book of Discipline of the United Methodist Church* (Nashville: The United Methodist Publishing House, 1972), 41.

5. Ibid.

6. Ibid.

7. Ibid.

8. Ibid.

9. Ibid.

10. This was illustrated in a personal conversation with a major staff person from the Board of Global Ministries. When I asked why the board literature never seemed to speak of the biblical truth of the Atonement, that Christ died for our sins, the response was, "The General Conference has not spoken on that yet."

11. Richard John Neuhaus, "A New Methodism Afoot?" *The Religion & Society Report* 5, no. 4 (April 1988): 2.

12. Donald Messer, "Current Statement Is Better Than Radical Surgery Being Proposed," *The United Methodist Reporter* (1988).

13. The meeting was intended for orientation and information rather than a debate on the issues.

14. From personal notes taken at the meeting for delegates.

15. The letter can be found in the Ed Robb papers in the archives of Asbury Theological Seminary.

16. Letter from Albert Outler to Bishop Earl Hunt.

17. James M. Wall, *Christian Century* (18-25 May 1988): 491.

18. Ibid., 492.

19. James Heidinger, *Good News* (July-August 1988): 100.

20. Once her name was associated with Good News, Faye Short discovered it would not be possible for her to continue as a district or conference United Methodist Women officer.

21. Paper written by Evangelical Council for United Methodist Women/Renew (March 1994).

22. Ibid.

23. Catherine Keller, "Hereticizing 'Wisdom,'" The *United Methodist Relay* (April 1994). Dr. Keller was a professor at Drew Theological Seminary.

24. The Confessing Movement, "What Is the Confessing Movement Within The United Methodist Church?" (1995).

25. Ibid.

26. Ibid.

27. G. Richard Carter, Loren L. Mollins, Hughes B. Morris Jr., and Lowen V. Kruse, "Confessing Movement Unofficial Fringe Group," *Omaha Sunday World-Herald* (12 July 1998).

28. "A Critical Challenge to the Confessing Movement" (March 1996).

29. Ibid., 2.

30. Ibid., 4.

31. Ibid., 6.

12. Methodism's Populist Wing, Part II

1. Roger Finke and Rodney Stark, *The Churching of America, 1776–1990: Winners and Losers in Our Religious Economy* (New Brunswick, N.J.: Rutgers University Press, 1992).

2. Rodney Stark and Roger Finke, *Acts of Faith: Explaining the Human Side of Religion* (University of California Press, 2000).

3. Ibid., 145-47.

4. Stark and Finke, *Acts of Faith,* 265. At the same time, the Southern Baptists, a "high-tension" religion, had increased their share of adherents to 1,000 Americans from 33 in 1890 to 61 in 1990. The Church of God in Christ went from 0 per 1,000 American adherents in 1890 to 22 in 1990.

5 H. Richard Niebuhr, *The Social Sources of Denominationalism* (New York: Living Age Books, 1929), 6. While Niebuhr's phrase "denominationalism" corresponds roughly to what Stark and Finke have called "low-tension" faith and what this study has called "establishment institutionalism," it must be noted that Niebuhr was mostly interested in social and economic classes in his discussion of "sect" and "denominationalism." His main point was that creative religious vitality almost always comes from the poor and disinherited peoples of the world who arise as "sects" but who, after a generation or two, become middle class, compromise with the world, and become denominations. Stark and Finke have broadened the idea considerably and argue that though it is true that the poor and disenfranchised are often attracted to a faith that costs ("high tension"), religious vitality is not linked wholly to class and economic considerations, and vitality does not necessarily fade after a generation.

6. Ibid., 84.

7. Stark and Finke, *Acts of Faith,* 267.

8. As I review my own correspondence of this period addressed to our bishop and to several district superintendents, I am presently dismayed that I was reflecting this same kind of caution.

9. Two persons who were key figures in these decisions, Michael Coyner and John Hopkins, later were elected to the episcopacy.

INDEX